BOLD
PURPOSE

BOLD
PURPOSE

*Exchanging counterfeit happiness
for the real meaning of life*

DAN B.
ALLENDER

and

TREMPER
LONGMAN III

Tyndale House Publishers, Inc.
WHEATON, ILLINOIS

Visit Tyndale's exciting Web site at www.tyndale.com

Designed by Timothy R. Botts

Edited by Lynn Vanderzalm

Library of Congress Cataloging-in-Publication Data

Allender, Dan B.
  Bold purpose / Dan Allender and Tremper Longman.
     p. cm.
  Includes bibliographical references.
  ISBN 0-8423-5351-8 (hardcover : alk. paper)
    1. Bible. O.T. Ecclesiastes—Criticism, interpretation, etc.
2. Christian life—Biblical teaching. I. Longman, Tremper. II. Title.
BS1475.2.A55 1998   98-19883
223′.806—dc21

Printed in the United States of America

04 03 02 01 00 99 98
8   7   6   5   4   3   2   1

To our oldest children
Anna and Tremper
You have taught us to hope against hope.

ACKNOWLEDGMENTS

If it takes a village to raise a child, then a book takes no less than a family, friends, business associates, and countless supporters to see it come to fruition. We hold many people dear in the launching of this child.

Tyndale has been a safe harbor in which to work out our ideas and the unusual form—both fiction and nonfiction—that we thought best encapsulates the compelling richness of Ecclesiastes. Lynn Vanderzalm, our editor, has again been a generous, patient, and visionary champion of our labor. In the many periods of revision and change, her voice has called us to find meaning in frustration.

Working with my best friend on a project that touches the core issues of life has prompted many discussions that find their way into this book and others that await a time when we are mature enough to say well the things we have vocalized to each other. Our greatest gift from God is our families, but our friendship, which began when we were thirteen, is a mysterious, living testament to God's surprising goodness.

Our families are the ground of our existence and the meeting place for God to work and woo us to himself. None have invested their lives more richly or winsomely in our labor than our wives. Becky and Alice are unquestionably godly women who love us and enjoy us.

We owe thanks to many people who heard our ideas for this book and gave us good guidance and suggestions, but we would especially like to thank Dan McGlinchey, who took the time to read through the whole manuscript and give us his helpful advice. We also thank Nate Taylor, a young man whose creativity promises wonderful things for his future.

Finally, all gratitude goes to our God, who has not only purchased us through his Son's death but has also honored us to be co-laborers with him of the message of life in Christ. We are grateful men and are honored to be invited into your life to consider with you the glory of God.

CONTENTS

1

The Awakening

T HE ALARM clattered. It was an old Timex, rounded like the sun with a gold rim that ran around the laminated face. Each time it went off, it shook the nightstand next to Noah's bed. Its early morning clamor awakened him to what some might view as the bright beginnings of a new day.

For Noah, the alarm ended the best part of the day. He would have to wait nearly sixteen hours before he could crawl back into the warm, womblike comfort of his down-covered bed. He had opposed his wife's purchase of the Austrian comforter; it seemed ridiculous to pay several hundred dollars for a huge white blanket, but after the first week of sleeping under it, he realized it was the second-best purchase of their married life. The best was the large king-size bed that allowed him the privilege of sleeping with his wife when he wanted to but also having the space he craved.

Noah loved bed. All day long he dreamed about the delicious moment when work was done and he could retire to bed. *Retire.* The word had the sound of noble elegance. Retire for the day. Work was behind him, and the sweet darkness of sleep would shroud the day in billowy forgetfulness.

Noah reached over to the nightstand, grabbed the clock by the neck, and strangled out its last sound. He rose, and before his feet hit the floor, he was already thinking about the day. He had the Pearson Furniture proposal to make.

Pearson Furniture, a conglomerate that sold upscale furniture for reasonable prices to baby boomers, was an odd company. The chief counsel of the firm had a midlength ponytail. The CEO wore jeans. And yet they had positioned themselves as one of the up-and-coming companies for the next century.

Noah Adamson was a stockbroker with the Chicago office of Brothers Consolidated, a firm that traded in "shorts." Short sales represent the dark side of the stock market. Most investors buy a stock that looks as if it will increase in market value. "Shorters" buy the rights to shares but hope that the stock is overvalued and will fall so they can purchase the stock well under the value that it currently holds.

In a few hours Noah would announce to the decision makers of Brothers Consolidated his advice to sell the Pearson stock. This would not be welcome news. Essentially Noah would be telling his bosses that they had made a huge, huge mistake.

Noah did not think about that unpleasant task any longer than it took him to walk to the bathroom. He thought about the Bible study he had agreed to go to tonight. As he looked at his sleeping wife, Joan, he felt deep anger and resentment toward her. *Why do we have to go to one of these groups? I'm a Christian. I go to church. I support a conservative agenda. So why do I have to go to another bare-your-soul-and-feel-deeply-until-someone-tells-you-how-to-live Bible study group?*

He went to the group partly because he felt Joan needed the social contact. She found few outlets in life other than driving their twin sons to school and caring for the normal details of an upper-middle-class Chicago life. The Bible study was her break from routine, her one serious opportunity for contact with other adults. Noah also figured it was her one way to exact a pound of spiritual flesh for his apparent lack of involvement in the things of God.

The group was beginning a new study about the book of Ecclesiastes. Noah had read a few sections of the book a few years back, and it had troubled him. *Eat, drink, and be merry. Everything is meaningless. Everything is merely a chasing after wind.* There was a dull, gruff, gnawing ache in him as he thought of looking into the eyes of the troubling book. He loved the slogan Why ask why? And his memory of the book of Ecclesiastes was fused with the feeling of irritation that it did not have a clearer and more hopeful message. Why ask why?

Then Noah remembered the real reason he was dreading the Bible study. It was not just the troubling book, but it was also the thought of listening to Jack, the great-guide-of-all-knowledge-in-the-Bible leader. He feared that Jack would make this difficult book into a model of order and logic, practicality and boredom. Noah didn't know what irritated him more: chaos and confusion or pabulum and boredom. He could not figure out which was worse: despair or Jack. But he knew he would read a few chapters of the book before going to the study—he simply could not bear the thought that Jack would know more about the book than he did. At least he would be familiar with the first two chapters.

As Noah brushed his teeth, he looked into the mirror and envisioned the people who would be at the Bible study. Jack was by profession a trial lawyer and by avocation a prophet of right religion and good living. Noah liked Jack, though he was afraid of his penetrating mind. Jack could be a normal man who talked sports and was up on the market, but in the Bible study he lost his worldly focus and took on the air of a champion for God.

Jack's wife, Marcia, was an enigma. She was gentle, but she had the mental swiftness of a cheetah and the spark of a poet. Jack and Marcia were an odd combination of bravado and depth. Noah liked Marcia, but he did not want her to influence his wife. Joan was a quiet woman, and Noah was happy for her to remain unassuming. They had a good marriage: dull, normal, and under his control. Marcia had a strange pull on Joan, and Noah was not pleased.

Noah thought about where each person would sit in Jack's living room. Normally Jack and Marcia sat on the floor near their fireplace. Jack often had his arm around Marcia, and they looked like older models for a

J. Crew catalog. Mimi and Jessie, both thirtyish single women, would sit on the couch adjacent to the fireplace. The two women were as different as yin and yang. Mimi was usually dressed in black; Jessie favored the strangest combinations of calico, jeans, and country schlock. Mimi had never been married; Jessie was recently divorced from an abusive alcoholic after ten tumultuous years. She had one child, a school-age girl named Erin. Noah liked both women, but he didn't like to spend any time with them.

For that reason he didn't really know either of them. Most of what he knew about Jessie came from Joan. Joan had spent a little time with Jessie. Both Noah and Joan were a bit uncomfortable with Mimi. The pastor of their church had asked if Mimi could join the group, and everyone, except Marcia, seemed rattled by her. Mimi hid neither her past nor her pain. She seemed like an open wound, and Noah did not like messes.

Rounding out the group were Mark and Suzi, a newlywed couple who had recently joined the group. Mark worked as a general handyman, and Suzi was a hairstylist.

Noah looked at the mirror and saw his graying temples and frothy mouth. He rinsed his mouth, spit, and washed the toothpaste out of his brush. He was not looking forward to this Bible study. Thankfully it was many hours away and would be followed by the best part of the day: sleep.

As he splashed on some aftershave lotion, Noah looked into the eyes of a man who was about to cause big trouble for his superiors. His agenda was to topple his nearest rival in the firm. His enemy, Jonathan, was a man who had been with the firm years before Noah came on board. Jonathan was debonair, confident, and shrewd. He earned his high-six-figure income on connections and an Old World facade.

Noah had risen through the ranks of his peers because of his penetrating guesswork in picking stocks that were likely to fall. He did his research and investigated each company's portfolio, but his real ability was in reading people. He studied people. And his unique gift was tracking the company's culture. He viewed each company like a family, getting to know each family's myths, secrets, and weak spots. Each corporate family is based on the CEO's personality and vision. Noah knew that if he got to know the background, bias, and beliefs of the people at the helm, then it would not be hard for him to predict when the company would overextend itself and tumble into the abyss.

Noah was a shark. He loved to travel alone in the dark recesses of the Internet, scavenging everything written about the corporation and its owner. He often went back to the stories written about the CEO in high school and college to discover the points of formative failure, tragedy, and loss. Noah's work made him feel like an adventurer, a spy who knew how to make the computer spin and the soul reveal what he needed to know to win.

And win he did. Noah was seldom wrong. He was seldom questioned. He loved his work.

2

Abundant Life in a Meaningless World

"I HAVE COME that they may have life, and have it to the full." We all love that verse from John 10:10 (NIV). When we first became Christians, the promise of abundant life sustained us. But for many people, the abundant life seems to have evaporated.

Abundant life in the nineties seems like little more than a brief break to catch the evening news before returning to the nonstop bustle of shuffling the kids to another lesson or meeting, checking the answering machine, reading E-mail, and doing the necessary things to keep a household running.

We are all trying to make life work. We go to our jobs. We labor. We play. We worship, and we rest. But the real energy of most days is spent in getting done whatever we need to do to stay a few steps ahead of the whirling, crowding chaos. Kids need to practice their spelling. The car needs more oil. A batch of mail needs to be opened—and we all know it holds bills that require a return to the constant whir of work, wondering how it will all pan out in the end.

For most busy, stressed, and overcommitted adults the only break is periodically plopping in front of the television for the escape that comes as we see other characters live out their lives rather than think about our own. Some of us resort to watching the news so that we feel connected to our world without having to think about our own small corner of the globe. Escape is our form of rest in a world that seems to be bumping along like a bus that has lost its driver.

Then again, we are people of faith—believers who trust the Bible to be true and the comfort of Christ to be real. What do we who know truth have to do with those lost on the bus that is careening down the road?

We suffer setbacks. We have children who listen not to the melodies of our fine hymns but to the angst of contemporary poets. We struggle with illness and failure and wonder how to connect the Bible to the daily intrusions of uncertainty and the small but unsettling losses of the day.

We long for a meaningful life, but many of us have exchanged meaning, purpose, and abundance for overcommitment, pressure, and hectic schedules. It is time to reflect and regroup.

What are we chasing after? What are we looking for? As Christians we say we are looking for God, but when we stop to reflect on our lives, we wonder if we are more caught up in the pursuits of our culture. We wonder if we are looking for God in all the wrong places.

Few of us are doing things that are clearly and fundamentally wrong. We are responsible people who work hard, love our kids, interact with our friends, pursue wisdom and a deeper walk with Christ, enjoy a few moments of laughter, and try to keep our bodies healthy. We are trying to live balanced lives, but life itself continues to unsettle all our efforts to keep plugging ahead.

It is easy to do what is right without really considering why, but we often find that we lose our joy in righteous living. The abundant life seems like a lost memory or, worse, a false promise that has never materialized.

In some ways we believe we are living life to the full. Life is full of activity, full of achievements, full of relational contacts. To some degree the chasing satisfies us. After all, it is a nineties kind of thing. But we feel only a veneer of satisfaction. When we look deeper, we see that we have lost our passion, our spark. If we dare to look truth full in the face, we have to admit that we have lost a sense of meaning or purpose. The promise of the abundant life seems empty.

This book issues an invitation to return to the sense of purpose and meaning that many of us had in our early Christian lives. It is an invitation to rediscover the abundant life.

How will that happen? We must be willing to be honest with ourselves, admitting that much of our current frenzy is chasing after the wind, or, if we are brutally honest, chasing after false gods.

No real change comes from merely doing things differently. Real change comes when our hearts pursue the narrow way that at first seems more difficult than the problems we face. This new course of life sets the possibility for new decisions and behavior.

But many voices in our day prefer to tell us what to do. We read, listen to tapes, and hear sermons about how to get a better handle on the simmering uncertainty that surrounds us. These voices, often solidly biblical, offer steps that promise a better world, an improved marriage, more obedient and culturally unaffected children, and success in our work without losing our families.

We know we should do these things, but the steps often become a new law, a new standard, a new set of expectations. Rather than merely feeling overwhelmed by the chaos, we also feel guilty for not doing better at managing it.

MUCH of this book will follow the lives of eight people as they confront the chaos of their lives and learn from their Bible study of Ecclesiastes. The fiction chapters are intended to help you reflect on your life and the lives of your friends and family members. Interspersed among the fiction chapters are chapters that comment on the fiction and explore the question of meaning and the major subthemes of Ecclesiastes. As was the case in our earlier book, *Intimate Allies,* Dan does the primary writing on the fiction chapters and Tremper does the primary writing for the nonfiction chapters.

The book of Ecclesiastes is a dialogue between two wise men. One is likely a skeptic; the other is a person of faith. The man of faith listens to the skeptic's cry but does not dispute his claims. Instead, he uses the skeptic's honest reflections on the grime of life to disturb and then to point to one single basis of hope and meaning.

The skeptic assaults all efforts to make life work and sends several strong messages:

- Control will always slip out of our grasp.
- Relationships will always disappoint.
- Work will leave us frustrated.
- Pleasure is always fleeting.
- Wisdom is never an adequate guide.
- Spirituality usually gives in to legalism.
- Life ends in decay and death.

NO WONDER Ecclesiastes is not a book that most Christians enjoy reading. Yet it is this disturbing message that allows us to see through the fog of our hectic lives and see to the final conclusion of the book: *We find bold purpose when we fear God.*

THE FEAR of God is a rich Old Testament concept that is intended for us as contemporary Christian readers as well. It is the climactic thought of the book of Ecclesiastes (12:13) and signals the desired attitude that we are to have toward God. On the one hand, the fear of God is not the terror that sends us running in horror, and on the other hand, it is not simply a quiet respect. It is an acknowledgment that we live in relationship to the God who created us, indeed, who created the entire universe. It is a widemouthed awe that is not at odds with love but teaches us that God is vastly superior to us and must be placed first in our lives. And here is the practical implication of the fear of God as it plays a role in our lives: To fear God is to put him first, above all things. It is the fear of God that enables us to find meaning in the paradoxes—that in losing control, relationships, work, pleasure, wisdom, spirituality, and life itself, we find not only meaning but also God himself. The end result of understanding the book of Ecclesiastes is knowing that the skeptic's statements are not the answer. The ultimate answer lies in the paradoxes:

- Control leads to surrender to God's will.
- Relationships lead to trust in God's love.
- Work leads to laboring for God's kingdom.
- Pleasure leads to a hunger for God's coming.
- Wisdom leads to a humble curiosity to know God.

- Spirituality leads to embracing God's wild heart.
- Life leads to a joyous celebration of death and resurrection.

THE BOOK of Ecclesiastes invites us to look into our struggles in order to get a glimpse of God. The major voice in Ecclesiastes is a disturbing one, but it is also a very contemporary one. It echoes many voices in our culture and in our lives. If we allow ourselves to be disturbed, we will find a more essential and solid hope than the promise of merely making life work.

PART ONE

Chasing after
POWER

3

The Strategy

NOAH pulled into the Brothers Consolidated staff parking lot and noticed someone getting out of a car that had just parked in his spot. Noah felt his temples pounding. No one parked in his spot.

Noah was a senior analyst; the interloper was a new kid who had recently joined the firm as a researcher. Noah fumed and then pulled into a spot quite far from the entrance. He considered his options: announce in furious terms his displeasure and demand the kid move his car; wait until he could denounce the upstart publicly in jocular terms that humiliated the kid while painting himself as the patient but not-to-be-trifled-with older executive; call a tow truck and leave the kid stranded at the end of a grueling, underpaid day. Noah never considered

ignoring the offense as a small irritation, but soon the pleasure of under-
mining Jonathan, his account rival, took his mind away from his plans
for the kid.

What a day this could be—the day he had been waiting for. Soon after
joining the firm, Noah had realized that he couldn't make it to the top as
long as Jonathan had the boss's ear for all final decisions. He knew he
had to topple Jonathan.

Today senior staff members were going to review their portfolios and
reassess all their past decisions. It was a crucial day, and the Pearson Furniture account was Noah's ace in the hole. The stock had dropped a few
points on the Nasdaq. It appeared to be sliding downward, but Noah
knew it was just a minor blip in Pearson's progress. Pearson Furniture
had recently bid to place some of their products in a national chain of
business stores and had been turned down. Ostensibly, they had been
turned down because their line was not well developed and their offering
incomplete. Secretly, Noah believed they were turned down because
Pearson Furniture was so good and so innovative that they would soon
take over the business market.

Brothers Consolidated would see the rejection of Pearson as a sign of a
good stock to buy as it slid. Noah's firm wanted the stock to fail, and
Jonathan would argue with suave confidence that his decision to select
Pearson as a loser had been confirmed.

But Jonathan knew nothing about the personalities behind Pearson
Furniture. He knew, as did everyone else in the business world, that the
CEO, Scott Fitch, was an upstart, a renegade, and an unconventional
player. But Jonathan didn't know anything about Fitch's past, his personality, or his passion.

Noah did.

Noah had followed Fitch's life. He had learned from senior staff people
at Pearson Furniture that Fitch was a strange man. Noah had a tape of a
talk Fitch had given to his staff. During the speech Fitch had wept when
he talked about a Pearson truck driver whose son had died of cancer.
Fitch talked about his amazement at the man's heart to suffer for his son.
Fitch was a hard-driving entrepreneur, but rather than talk to the staff
about corporate policy or profits, he shared what the truck driver had
taught him about life. Fitch ended his speech by describing the kind of
husband, father, and friend he wanted to be. He reflected on what a cor-

porate structure would be like if it were driven by humane passion rather than merely on business principles.

Noah was haunted by Pearson's CEO. Noah found Fitch's jeans culture repugnant and his tears maudlin, but he was drawn by both Fitch's head for success and his heart for love.

Noah's instincts told him that Fitch would use the rejection by the national chain to spur on his troops into setting up a national business furniture wing under the Pearson name. They would go beyond providing furniture for families to opening up more and more markets for business clients. Noah knew the stock was soon going to rise. He could not wait for the meeting to begin.

Noah sat next to his boss, Lee, who was the senior vice president of research and analysis. Noah's tactic was to support Jonathan's counsel until the Pearson Furniture discussion began. When Lee brought up the Pearson portfolio, Noah constrained himself to avoid appearing excited. Jonathan took the lead with enthusiasm. He saw this stock as a major card in advancing the third quarter's sluggish sales. He used the exact phrases Noah had predicted he would, and it appeared to be a foregone conclusion that Pearson would be a major stock the firm would highlight as a great buy for its clients.

Lee was about to move to another stock: "Any more discussion on Pearson? It appears we have a winner here, and due to Jonathan's careful tracking, we may make this a great quarter."

Noah shifted in his chair and warmly said: "Could I offer a minority view? I don't doubt Jonathan has done his homework, but let me ask him to give us his analysis of what Pearson Furniture has done with a few of its other setbacks."

Jonathan smiled wanly and turned to the boss with a mildly distasteful look and shrugged his shoulders.

Noah moved quickly. "Jonathan, are you aware of how Fitch handled the lawsuit that almost ruined his first start-up business? Or how he spent Christmas Day a few years ago loading trucks when they were behind on delivering their products after the storm tore through their distribution center?"

Jonathan didn't even know the CEO's name or about the first business. He had never researched the CEO's life or leadership style. But Jonathan did know how to handle questions.

He looked at Noah and began to deliver his response with rhythmic disdain. "No, Noah, I'm also not familiar with his psychological profile or his high school grades, but I understand he is short and therefore may have a Napoleon complex." The room roared with laughter. Round one went to Jonathan.

Noah smiled. He wanted to be made the fool. He was not interested in winning this fight. He merely wanted to position himself as the one dissenting voice that warned against betting the ranch on Pearson Furniture's falling in value. When the stock soared, he wanted to be remembered as the voice that could have saved the firm a massive amount of money and that avoided the wrath of countless investors who would scream bloody murder.

Noah laughed and said, "I never thought to look at his high school grades, but I will. Until then, I do think that Fitch's track record in college ought to tell us something. He flunked out of three colleges and finally made it through after seven years. He then started four businesses that were eventually sold to his competitors because he beat the socks off each one of them in their key markets. The man is a wizard, and he thrives on adversity. I'm sure you're also aware there is no one better at pitching investment bankers. He has the uncanny ability to live with ambiguity until others bolt, and then he calmly walks into the bank and takes the largest share of the prize. Let me play prophet. I think Fitch will . . ."

Noah laid out a scenario of what he thought Pearson Furniture might do in the next six months. Noah ended with the simple statement, "If we want to make any profit, I think we should sell what we have now and then cover our losses by buying this stock to grow."

The room was silent. Jonathan was furious—and shaken. Sweat gathered on his forehead. Lee was somber. He looked at Jonathan and said, "Respond."

Jonathan's words were not confident or smooth, but he did offer a different scenario that made up for his lack of detailed analysis with a recitation of past successes.

The decision on the Pearson account eventually swung back to Jonathan's side, but Noah was not concerned. The doubt he wished to create had been left on the table as clearly as the perspiration that slid down Jonathan's cheeks.

It was a good, good day. When Noah walked by the kid who had taken his parking spot earlier in the morning, Noah smiled and remarked warmly on the kid's natty tie.

The Bible Study

It had been such a good day that Noah was unprepared for his wife's remark that they would dine out since they were going to the Bible study. He had utterly forgotten about the evening plans to read Ecclesiastes. But he knew it was pointless to protest. This time he couldn't even use the guise of the I-have-suffered-the-slings-and-arrows-of-outrageous-fortune exhaustion to excuse himself from going. He had come home way too happy to pull off that one. The kids were at a neighbor's house for the evening. Noah was stuck.

As Noah and Joan ate a quick dinner at a restaurant near their house, Joan began to talk about the book of Ecclesiastes. "I just don't understand why God allowed Solomon to do all the things that he did. I mean, how could he have had that many wives?" Noah wondered the same thing, but for very different reasons. His mind flitted to the power of having a harem and picking a woman to be intimate with as casually as if he were picking out a pair of shoes. He felt his breath quicken. But the thought of trying to resolve conflict with a thousand women took his breath away. He was glad that the Bible allowed only one wife.

While driving to the apartment of the couple who were hosting the Bible study that night, Noah began to ponder questions similar to the ones Joan had raised. How did Solomon justify having so many wives and concubines? What did God think about Solomon's lifestyle? Why is there no apparent condemnation of his sin?

They drove into the apartment complex and parked as close as they could to building 204, where Mark and Suzi lived. Joan and Noah had not been to Mark and Suzi's apartment before, so it took them a bit of time to find it. Noah hated the first few minutes of walking into any gathering. It was not that he was unfriendly or that he lacked social confidence. He just hated the small talk, the jockeying for position, meeting the expectations. If people around Noah saw him as the expert, then he adjusted himself to be the Wise One and stayed aloof from those who saw themselves as "normal." Or if people saw him as a plain Joe, a nameless face in the crowd, then he endured the loneliness of insignificance and tried to ignore why he felt like a failure. In either case, he felt as if he could never win.

Suzi answered the door and giggled, "Hi, are you here for the Bible

study? Of course you are, Noah." Noah was always mildly irked by Suzi.
She seemed so vacuous, so spacey.

Noah and Joan walked into the dark apartment, a throwback to the
seventies—orange-and-brown shag carpet, even a Lava lamp that was a
replica of Elvis Presley. An Elvis Presley Lava lamp. Noah did not know
whether to laugh or vomit. His reaction was not religious as much as it
was aesthetic. He hated having no control over what assaulted his senses.
His nausea passed, and after far too long a time of forced conviviality, the
Bible study began.

Jack, the lawyer and leader of the group, convened the gathering.
"Folks, why don't you grab one more of those fine brownies and your
drinks, and let's get this ship out of the harbor." Jack had attended Anna-
polis for two years, and many of his conversations were tinged with the
salt of his nautical days.

Jack began by introducing the new topic of the group's study. "As you
know, we are launching into a new study tonight. I hope you will be as
excited about studying Ecclesiastes as I have been in preparing for our
time together."

Noah grimaced. Another expectation for him to be passionate. Wasn't
it enough that he had come to the study?

Jack continued, "With your permission, rather than go chapter by
chapter through this great book, I thought we would go theme by theme
and see if we can cut to the chase by getting back to the one simple
thought of the book. I hope that you all were able to read the book in
preparation for tonight. What is the one word that kept sticking in your
mind as you worked your way through it?"

Noah felt a tinge of guilt at having read only two chapters, but then he
felt a bit of righteous indignation that such a demand had been put on a
busy person like himself.

Fortunately Mimi broke the silence. "Meaningless. The book kept talking about life being meaningless."

Jack nodded. "Right, and didn't that strike you as strange? After all, as
Christians we know that God has given us abundant life now. But here is
a wise man who seems depressed about the state of the world and his
relationship with God. To be honest, I really didn't know how to take the
book, so I started looking at some commentaries and reading the whole
book a few times. Fortunately, it's not too long.

"At first I was a little disappointed with the commentaries. They disagreed in their perspectives on the book, but they all pointed to the last few verses of the book—especially the last two verses—as providing the important teaching. Here, let me read those two verses to you: 'Here is my final conclusion: Fear God and obey his commands, for this is the duty of every person. God will judge us for everything we do, including every secret thing, whether good or bad.'

"Now, this seemed more 'biblical' to me than 'meaningless, meaningless, everything is meaningless,' and I tried to understand the connection between the two. I went back to the commentaries and saw that the book really has two speakers: One is known as the Teacher; the other is known simply as the wise man. The wise man is the one who fears God and who concludes the book with a final perspective.

"And if you look closely, you will see that when the Teacher talks about 'life under the sun'—that's his phrase to talk about life apart from God, life from the purely human perspective—is meaningless, he is speaking in the first person. You know, 'I saw this,' 'I did this.' But at the end of the book, the speaker is talking about the Teacher: 'The Teacher was like this,' 'the Teacher did this.' Those are some of the clues that two different 'voices' speak in the book.

"Now some people think that the two 'voices' are really the same person, and that was my thought. I pretty much believed that the Teacher was Solomon. I thought the book was written after he faced the foolishness of his youth, when he turned against God and started worshiping the gods of his foreign wives.

"I know this is a little tedious, but I think it is important."

Noah blushed and hoped that Jack had not seen his yawn.

Jack pressed on, "I just have a little more. Some new commentaries, though, suggest that we are really dealing with two different speakers, neither of whom is Solomon. The one in the main part of the book is a jaundiced, skeptical, old teacher, who, on the basis of his observations of life, asks some very tough questions about relationship with God. He is the Teacher.

"The second is another wise man who wants his son, mentioned in the twelfth verse of chapter 12, to face the irregularities, apparent contradictions, and unpredictability of life. The interesting thing is that the second wise man actually affirms many of the Teacher's observations. In fact—and this is mind boggling—the second wise man does not reject any of the conclusions the Teacher reaches. It's as if the second teacher is saying, 'Everything you say about life is true. But you see only part of the picture. Your perspective is merely "under the sun." You need also to see what life looks like from "above the sun," from God's perspective.' But don't reject the mad wisdom gained by looking under the sun.

"This is a bit more radical than I prefer to admit. It almost seems as if the last voice, the voice of the godly wise man, ought to have critiqued the Teacher's radical statements. That is, he does not dispute the idea that life 'under the sun,' which may mean 'apart from God,' is meaningless. Instead, the second voice affirms the statements and then uses them to draw us to a brutally honest vision of life. But he then turns his son's attention to what is really important: fearing God.

"Whichever view of these two voices is correct, the point is that we need to read this book carefully to see what the author is really saying about God, the world, and ourselves. I really think this could be a meaningful Bible study. But we need to be aware that Ecclesiastes is not a book evangelicals are comfortable with, at least in the way that most of us think. We need to keep that in mind as we get into the rhythm of this study.

"Let me quickly list the topics this strange book covers. We are going to focus on control, relationships, work, pleasure, wisdom, spirituality, and life and death. We will take a stab at covering each topic, but given that life is messier than an outline, we will see what we cover as we go.

"Tonight we will look at the issue of how desperately we work to control our lives. I don't know about you, but life seems to get out of hand sometimes, and it drives me crazy when it does. Next week we will look at the topic of relationships, then work. That's an area where life can often get out of control, so you can see how these topics kind of overlap. The book asks some searing questions, and while we may find them disturbing questions, I think they will help us gain a new perspective on our lives.

"The Teacher's basic question is this: Is life worth living? That's a fair question. And I assume that as we discuss this book and how its themes play themselves out in our personal lives, we will come to a better understanding of who we are and why God put us where he did. Let's try not to get bogged down in the depressing aspects of the book. Instead, let's work *through* the Teacher's cynicism, recognizing that his perspectives represent those of most of the people around us."

NOAH was looking at Marcia's legs. He had ceased to listen to Jack when he had said the book was difficult to understand. Marcia had shifted in her seat, and her well-cut, tan legs stretched out like an invitation to slip into a blue green pool rather than sit in the hot sun of Jack's patter. Marcia was neither young nor stunningly attractive, but her short, brown hair and her frighteningly green eyes gave her a captivating, feline appearance. She was gentle and gracious, but Noah had noticed she held her own in discussions and did so with quick wit and intensity.

Noah looked at his wife, Joan. She smiled and appeared attentive, but he assumed she had no idea what Jack was talking about. The contrast between the two women was painful. He loved Joan, but he was intrigued by Marcia. Joan was nearly ten years younger than Marcia and in many ways far more attractive, but it was not pure beauty that aroused Noah. It was the mystery, the aroma of the unknown, untasted potential that drew his eyes to Marcia.

As Jack finished up his introduction to Ecclesiastes, he turned to Noah. "Is there anything on your mind, Noah? You seem particularly lost today in your own world."

Noah smiled. "No, Jack. Sorry if I wasn't paying attention. I may have been wandering back to the slavish lusts of the day's business." The group laughed. They loved Noah's quirky remarks that answered without ever really revealing his thoughts. Joan blushed. But Noah merely smiled and looked back into Marcia's eyes. For a moment, she caught his gaze and then turned awkwardly toward Jack. It was the first time he had seen her lose composure.

Noah looked at Jack and noticed a slight rise in Jack's chest, a tightening of his hands, and a pinkish cast creep across his left cheek. Noah swore Jack was angry, but Jack smiled and said, "Well, Noah, I suspect a whole lot more is going on in that sharp mind of yours than you are going to tell us." Noah looked at the Bible on his lap. He felt no pressure to respond to Jack's comment. Noah felt on top of things, in control. His day had been full of sport, success, and desire. He was eager for sleep. Sweet sleep.

RELIEVED when the Bible study was over, Noah walked to the parking lot slightly ahead of Joan. When he reached the space where he had parked the car, he found only a note held in place by a large stone.

The car was gone.

The note said: "Your car was parked in an unauthorized spot. Your car can be retrieved at the 285 Garage off of Wadsworth and 285. The car will be released for $100.00. We take cash only."

4

"I Ought to Be Able to Control My World"

WE ALL operate out of a faulty assumption that sounds something like this: "If only I could control my world, life would be manageable, and it would have meaning and purpose." Related to that assumption is an equally faulty one: "I ought to be able to control my world." Before you dismiss that statement too readily, think about your life. How much energy do you spend trying to manage your family life, your job, life at church, and relationships?

Do any of the following scenarios sound familiar to you?

"TYPICAL. I have only fifteen minutes before work starts and a half-hour ride ahead of me. When will I ever get it together? Oh, no. The gas gauge is on empty. I should have gotten gas last night, but that church meeting went so late. I had better call the secretary to tell my first appointment to wait for me. She also better cancel my lunch meeting because I have to finish the report for Carl by three to catch the last half of my son's football game. I may have to leave the game a little early to get a brief workout, but if I leave, it might disappoint my son. I'll stay and try to slip out to the fitness center tonight, perhaps drop off the dry cleaning on the way. I will probably get everything done today if nothing unexpected turns up. Of course, I can't remember the last day nothing unexpected turned up."

- *"The grandkids again tonight! Why does my daughter think I have nothing better to do? Don't get me wrong, I love the kids. But I also have a life of my own with things to do and people to see. I will have to stay up late to do the laundry. And then it will be hard to fall asleep. How can I tell my daughter I am just too busy to take care of the kids four nights a week? I know she is struggling to stay on top of things as well."*

- *"I knew I shouldn't have taken that extra course! Between work and my children, it was just too much. Since Ralph left, I just haven't had a minute to myself. Maybe that's good, not to have too much time to think. But I need just one evening or even an hour to let my mind vegetate and not do laundry, dusting, or preparation for the next day. Will it ever end?"*

MAYBE you aren't married or don't yet have children. Maybe you now have an "empty nest." But few people today escape the fast-paced race we call life. We rush from place to place, our eyes on the clock. We try to keep our lives under control, but in our clearer moments, we realize that achieving our goal of control over life is as possible as catching the wind. . . .

The Advantages of a Disciplined Life

We all want control over the chaos of our lives. We don't like unwelcome surprises, and we plan and work hard to keep them at bay. We think ahead about the consequences of our actions, and we are not pleased when someone—a child, a friend, a stranger—disrupts whatever order we can find in our lives.

We want more power because we think that if we have more power, we will have more control. Power and control are potential avenues of meaning in life. That is, we gain joy and a feeling of significance by gaining control through power. The opposite, being pushed around by forces and people outside of ourselves, means that our lives are ruled by chance and are therefore without meaning.

We often try to gain control through rules. Consider all the rules that govern our lives. While these rules may seem reasonable, they can easily become demands that take away the depth, vitality, and thrill of life.

It's not that our rules and routines are wrong, but they often end up controlling us rather than helping us control our lives. We have our daily lists of "things we need to do" to keep life in control. We need to do the laundry, prepare food, wash the dishes, drive our children to school, and keep our bodies in shape. At work, we have sales to make, forms to fill out, patients to see, classes to teach.

We need to do these things to keep our lives running, but chasing after control in this way robs life of passion. In the midst of pursuing the things we *ought* to do, we often lose our passion to do the things we enjoy doing.

Noah is a good example. Noah believes he is a Christian, but he really is a stock analyst; his job is his source of meaning. His passion is the hunt for information to make a deal that will not fail. He loves the chase and the smell of battle. When he is not at war in his work, he loves to sleep. Sleep is his one escape. In sleep nothing is required of him, and life works, at least to a degree. Sleep for Noah is a re-entry into Eden.

Noah goes to a regular Bible study, not because he wants to learn about the Bible, but because he wants to please his wife and do what's "right." He has taken on many of the values of religious people because it is easier to be on the side of the majority rather than to suffer the judgment of those with whom he might differ. But Noah seems happy. He doesn't have to think in areas that trouble him; instead, he is free to dabble in faith, know he has heaven ahead, and then focus his considerable talents on the real task: making war at work.

Noah avoids what makes him feel uncomfortable. He gives himself deeply to what provides him a relative amount of power and control over his life. Consequently, he avoids his wife and relationships in general. He chases after knowledge in his field. He spends considerable time prowling the Internet and reading reports in his area of expertise. Like many men, Noah has found one area in which he excels, and that area takes the vast majority of his waking thought and energy.

Noah is a man committed to controlling his world—and the Bible does not contradict his desire. It is merely opposed to the way he seeks to achieve it.

We live with the myth that we ought to be able to control our lives. So we work harder and plan more efficiently. Is that a bad thing?

Is Control Bad?

No. Control is not necessarily a bad thing. Indeed, the Bible encourages us to exert control in several areas.

The book of Proverbs, for example, encourages us to plan for the future. Planning involves using our mental power in order to control the future. Planning is never precise and is always full of risks, but if we don't plan, we are irresponsible. "Plans go wrong for lack of advice; many counselors bring success" (Prov. 15:22). And when we submit those plans to the Lord, he will bless them. "Commit your work to the Lord, and then your plans will succeed" (Prov. 16:3). God wants us to plan. He wants us to think of the consequences of our actions. Generally speaking, no one can have a significant measure of success without foresight and the ability to affect the shape of the future.

The Bible tells us to discipline and control not only our own lives but also the lives of the people under our care. Proverbs reminds us, "Discipline your children, and they will give you happiness and peace of mind" (Prov. 29:17).

Even more important, control is a way of bringing order out of chaos. We know from Genesis that as a result of the Fall, our world is wired for chaos. To cope with that chaos, we need wisdom. The Old Testament wisdom literature speaks to us about "navigating life" in the chaos.

Biblical wisdom is built on the premise that there is an underlying order to creation. God created the world; it is not the product of chance. Certain causes produce certain effects. If I go up to my wife and hug her, it will produce one desirable effect. But if I speak harshly to her, it will produce a different and negative one. Different words and different actions will produce different effects.

To some extent, then, we can control how people respond. For example, when we encounter a fool, we need to know what kind of fool he is. Is he one who will get worse if we take his arguments seriously and respond to his points? Or will he be one who thinks he is right if we do not answer him? Once we determine these things, then we can give the right (apt) reply, and: "Timely advice is as lovely as golden apples in a silver basket" (Prov. 25:11).

Our desire for control seems supported by the way of wisdom presented in the Bible. If that is the case, then the next logical step is to master wisdom, to learn the principles embedded in books like Proverbs, and then simply to apply them to the right situations. The book of Proverbs, after all, appears to be a list of insightful statements about how we ought to live life, a kind of divine self-help book that will take us through all the struggles of life, the turmoil of relationships.

BUT when our control is an expression of our need to run our own lives because we don't trust God, then control is a bad thing. Abraham is an example.

Abraham: Grasping for Control

God gives Abraham a series of promises that will shape his future (Gen. 12:1-3). These promises included the fact that he would be the father of a huge nation that would be God's special people.

However, for that promise to come true, Abraham needed a son who would begin the process leading to a special people who would bless the whole world.

Abraham waited, but nothing happened. He began to doubt whether God would follow through with his promise. Abraham did not doubt God's existence, but he thought that he needed to take steps to bring the promise to fulfillment.

So Abraham took control. First, he adopted Eliezer, his household servant, to be his heir (Gen. 15:2). This was in keeping with the societal norms of his day. If a man and a woman had no natural heir, they could adopt their head servant to carry on the family line.

God appeared to Abraham, according to Genesis 15, and patiently assured him that the delay was not a sign that God wanted him to take steps to assure a progeny. Indeed, God reaffirmed his promise to Abraham in dramatic fashion by taking on the appearance of a flaming torch in a smoking pot and passing through the halves of slaughtered animals. This ritual was a way of saying, "If I don't keep my promise, may I become like these animals." Of course, God cannot die, but he condescended to a human ritual to place Abraham's mind at ease.

And perhaps that worked for a while, but Abraham again began to worry. God still had not acted. Sarah was not pregnant, and they were getting older. Once again, Abraham turned to a human convention to grasp at the promise and bring control into his life. He took on a concubine, an acceptable practice in his society for a couple who could not produce an heir.

Again showing his great love for Abraham and his enormous patience, God assured Abraham that he would provide an heir who would be the result of his union with Sarah. Abraham didn't trust God. The more Abraham grasped for control, the more trouble he brought on himself. The family conflicts that resulted from his efforts are well known. Sarah felt insecure in her relationship with Abraham as she saw Hagar and her young son, Ishmael. Indeed, once we take into consideration that Ishmael is the father of the Arab nations and that Isaac is the father of the modern Jewish nation, we can see the level of chaos that resulted from Abraham's frenetic exertions.

Life Is Untamable

We are no different from Abraham. When we face a problem or an obstacle, we take control and try to change it. Maureen and Kevin are two examples of people who tried to do that in their lives.

Maureen, a fortyish woman, had been feeling quite unattractive. She had gained some weight and hadn't taken care of her appearance. She noticed that her husband, Bill, had not shown sexual interest in her lately. She looked into the mirror and could hardly blame him.

But life had been busy. She had three kids, a part-time job, and an active social life. In the midst of the hecticness of life, she had neglected her body.

She knew what to do, and she just did it. In one morning, she made appointments with her hairstylist, went to a tanning salon, and started her new daily workout. She told her family that they would have to take care of themselves in the morning. Their clothes would be washed and ready, but they needed to get their own breakfasts and lunches. Maureen told them it would be good for them to learn responsibility.

Within two weeks Maureen noticed the difference in her appearance. She looked and felt much better. She was proud of herself for having seen the problem, identified a solution, and done what she had to do to make it happen.

But she was surprised that Bill was not aroused to new levels of involvement with her. One evening as she was getting the clothes ready for the next day, she asked him, "You seem a little put off with me lately. What's wrong?"

Bill responded, "Maybe I am being a bit selfish, but your early-morning workouts are putting a big strain on me. You're getting a workout while I'm scrambling to help the kids fix their breakfast, pack their lunches, and get to school on time. I've been late for work twice this week, and my boss is not at all pleased."

Perhaps Bill shouldn't have been helping the kids so much. Perhaps he should have let them go hungry a few times to show them they needed to make their lunches. Perhaps there were other things Maureen and Bill could have done to get around these specific problems, but the point is this: We have only so much energy and so much time. When we try to "fix" one area of our life, another one will likely get out of whack. It is simply impossible to control all aspects of our lives at one time.

Quite simply, life is untamable. But that does not keep us from trying, some more than others. Take Kevin, for instance. Kevin knows he is a controlling person, but he feels helpless to stop himself, even though he sees that his need to control can cause lots of damage. Perhaps it was his dominating father or his Navy training, but the thought of not keeping things in control scares Kevin to death.

Kevin doesn't think that others notice the fear in his eyes. He is a large, physically imposing figure with a loud voice and a quick temper. His wife, two daughters, and son know not to cross his will. He has power over them, but he does not control their feelings toward him. He wants their affection, but he wants power over their lives even more. What would happen to them if he let them do what they wanted? He shudders just to think about it.

Exhausted from his day, Kevin collapses into bed after the late-night news. But like clockwork, he awakens every morning at two o'clock and begins to worry about the next day. Sure, he eventually falls back to sleep, but he dreams the rest of the night about the tensions that will face him the next day—bills that need to be paid, a boss that can't be controlled, and the possibility that his wife or one of his kids could get beyond his control and into some kind of trouble.

Kevin's life looks good on the outside, but it is not so good on the inside. It is a cross he is willing to bear for the sake of his wife, kids, and his own sanity.

But here is the problem: All the energy that we exert to be in control eventually assures that there will be even more chaos. The more we try to make sure that there are no surprises and no emergencies, the more likely we are going to get more chaos.

DAN and I struggle with the area of control as we write this book. Several months ago we spent a day in Denver to plot out our writing schedule. Indeed, not only did we plan our schedule for writing this book, but we also put together a writing schedule for the next ten years.

As I left Dan's house to return to my home in Philadelphia, my sights were clear on what I had to do in order to accomplish the task of writing this book. Primed to get to work, I looked forward to the task with great excitement. I felt "empowered" and in control of my work and my life.

Little did I know that I would soon feel very out of control.

5

Restoring Power through Surrender

I GOT HOME from the airport, had a relaxing time with my family, and headed to bed, anticipating the next day's work. At three o'clock the phone rang, and even though I should have been alarmed because the call was coming in the middle of the night, I was too dulled with fatigue to be nervous as I answered the phone. It was my wife's stepmother. She sobbed, "Tremper, Bill just died!" It took a moment to register, but then I realized that my father-in-law had just passed away.

One phone call changed our lives for the next weeks. My writing schedule, my attempt at controlling my life, was seriously disrupted.

You have probably had similar experiences. Your well-laid plans and your attempts at controlling your life are disrupted by illness, financial upset, other people's decisions, and a host of other events that remind us that we can't control our lives. But that doesn't keep us from exerting enormous energy to create either a moment of control or at least the illusion of having life in order.

Think of Noah. He knew his business, and even though he didn't win the skirmish at work, he believed he would win the war. He prepared and plotted victory.

While we can achieve a significant level of control, we realize that keeping all the plates spinning is no more possible than grasping the wind. We must bow to the seasons of order and disorder God establishes in our lives.

The Teacher Questions God's Order

The book of Ecclesiastes contains a long speech by someone who simply calls himself the Teacher. He speaks in most of the book of Ecclesiastes (1:12–12:8). His words are framed by the words of another wise man, who assesses the Teacher's thought for his son—and for us, his readers (Eccles. 1:1-11 and 12:9-14). The Teacher sees life from a perspective that is "under the sun," that is, a solely human perspective (Eccles. 1:9, 14; 2:17; 5:18). In contrast, life "above the sun" is life seen from God's eternal, all-knowing perspective.

While the Teacher's comments about life will often shock and disturb us, if we are honest we will have to admit that his perspective often mirrors our own. Far too often we are frustrated with life because we are convinced that God is not in control and that he is leaving it all up to us.

The Teacher believed that God has created the opportune moment for everything. In one of the Bible's most moving passages about control and order, the Teacher shares this perspective:

There is a time for everything,
a season for every activity under heaven.
A time to be born and a time to die.
A time to plant and a time to harvest.
A time to kill and a time to heal.
A time to tear down and a time to rebuild.
A time to cry and a time to laugh.
A time to grieve and a time to dance.
A time to scatter stones and a time to gather stones.

A time to embrace and a time to turn away.
A time to search and a time to lose.
A time to keep and a time to throw away.
A time to tear and a time to mend.
A time to be quiet and a time to speak up.
A time to love and a time to hate.
A time for war and a time for peace.
Ecclesiastes 3:1-8

WE find comfort in those words, don't we? They remind us that everything has its proper place.

But here's the rub, according to the Teacher. Sure, God made the proper time for everything. He created everything for its proper place, and this is beautiful, but we can't know these times! We simply can never be absolutely certain that our words or our actions are right for the situation.

Immediately following the poem about time, the Teacher asks some disturbing questions: "What do people really get for all their hard work? I have thought about this in connection with the various kinds of work God has given people to do. God has made everything beautiful for its own time. He has planted eternity in the human heart, but even so, people cannot see the whole scope of God's work from beginning to end" (Eccles. 3:9-11).

God has created a world with order, and we yearn to experience that order. The Teacher tells us that this knowledge is beyond us all, and as a result we are frustrated to the core. "In my search for wisdom, I tried to observe everything that goes on all across the earth. I discovered that there is ceaseless activity, day and night. This reminded me that no one can discover everything God has created in our world, no matter how hard they work at it. Not even the wisest people know everything, even if they say they do" (Eccles. 8:16-17).

The Teacher touches the raw nerve of reality: The world is rigged for frustration. There is a right way to do things, but we will never know for sure what that is. There is a way to make life work, but we will never do it right. It seems almost as if God asks our hungry souls what they want to eat, then prepares it and places it behind an impenetrable glass wall.

In the New Testament the apostle Paul expresses the same truth: "For the creation was subjected to frustration, not by its own choice, but by

the will of the one who subjected it, in hope that the creation itself will
be liberated from its bondage to decay and brought into the glorious freedom of the children of God" (Rom. 8:20-21, NIV). God has "subjected"
the earth to futility. The word Paul uses for *frustration* is the Greek word
that is used in the Septuagint (the ancient Greek translation of the Old
Testament) for the word *meaningless,* the word used most often in Ecclesiastes. In some English versions, this word is translated "vanity" or
"futility." Paul's indirect allusion to Ecclesiastes in the Romans 8 passage
reflects his awareness that God has made sure nothing in life will work in
a way that allows humankind to think they are back home in Eden.

NOAH felt that he ruled his own life. He had a few moments when he felt
the sting of inner uncertainty. On the one hand, he hated to be the
expert: it meant accepting the pressure to perform flawlessly. On the
other hand, he hated to be a "mere mortal," a regular guy; that usually
meant living without praise or respect. But for the most part, Noah
ignored an internal agitation that might signal a lack of control.

But even if we spend lots of energy wresting control from chaos, God
will not let us win what would block us from himself. He actively orchestrates life so that we are continually presented with minor and major dis-
ruptions. Noah was irritated with a junior member of the firm taking his
parking spot. He handled it with a measure of civility, but he did so partly
to gain even greater control over the employee. Within hours, God set the
trap. Noah's car was towed, showing again that life is not tamable. God
rigged the world so that Noah's false sense of security would be exposed
and his presumption of being able to control even that aspect of his life
was upended.

Unfortunately, Christians often ignore God's purposeful disruption,
either assuming it is Satan's assault or just the way life is. Christians too
quickly mask their frustration with the statement, "Well, I may not know
what is going on, but at least God does!" We assume that God will take
care of those who pursue him. We find ourselves attracted to the saying
that God "does not let the righteous go hungry" (Prov. 10:3, NIV) rather
than the sad observation of the Teacher:

> *I have observed something else in this world of ours. The fastest runner
> doesn't always win the race, and the strongest warrior doesn't always win
> the battle. The wise are often poor, and the skillful are not necessarily*

wealthy. And those who are educated don't always lead successful lives. It is all decided by chance, by being at the right place at the right time.

People can never predict when hard times might come. Like fish in a net or birds in a snare, people are often caught by sudden tragedy. Ecclesiastes 9:11-12

THE Teacher does not even find comfort in the idea of an afterlife where God puts everything right. As he looks into the future, he cries out:

This, too, I carefully explored: Even though the actions of godly and wise people are in God's hands, no one knows whether or not God will show them favor in this life. The same destiny ultimately awaits everyone, whether they are righteous or wicked, good or bad, ceremonially clean or unclean, religious or irreligious. Good people receive the same treatment as sinners, and people who take oaths are treated like people who don't. Ecclesiastes 9:1-2

GOD is in control, and we must roll with the punches: "Notice the way God does things; then fall into line. Don't fight the ways of God, for who can straighten out what he has made crooked? Enjoy prosperity while you can. But when hard times strike, realize that both come from God. That way you will realize that nothing is certain in this life" (Eccles. 7:13-14).

No wonder the Teacher concluded that life was like "chasing the wind." Even though we try hard, we will still feel as if we are groping in the darkness with no ultimate success.

People of the nineties spend a lot of physical, emotional, and spiritual energy trying to control their schedules, jobs, and relationships. We think that the solution to our lack of control is to find new systems, new rules, new methods, new "laws" for doing things. We think that if only we have the right systems, we can control the chaos. Our experience and the Teacher's observations deny this. We need to turn from frenetically chasing control to something better. Under the sun, we chase control, but we discover that it is as difficult to grasp as the wind. However, we can choose to move from an under-the-sun perspective to an above-the-sun one.

Let's take some time to explain this terminology, which will play such an important role in this book. We have already observed that the Teacher uses the phrase *under the sun* to describe life and perspective here on earth, apart from God. The Teacher himself never uses the opposite phrase. We are coining it to explain the opposite perspective. In other words, while the Teacher kept his search for meaning and truth utterly earthbound, we want to look at life from God's perspective as he reveals it to us in his Word. How do we move from an under-the-sun perspective to an above-the-sun viewpoint? The answer is found in the final few verses of the book of Ecclesiastes, the words spoken by the second wise man to his son: by fearing God and obeying his commands (Eccles. 12:13). The man says to his son—and to us—put God first in your life. If you want to find meaning and purpose in life, look at reality from God's perspective, not your own limited view.

As we move from a perspective that is "under the sun" to one that is "above the sun," we will find ourselves moving from a grasping at power to a surrender to dependence.

Redemption through Dependency

Our usual strategy for dealing with the mess of life is to seek control over it. We try to gain power in the world in order to have an effective platform to manage our existence.

Power makes us think of politicians and bankers, and most of us don't have that kind of clout. But power comes in gradations. We may experience the struggle for power in the family as we try to keep our kids in line or our parents from interfering. We may seek power in our community by doing volunteer work at the hospital or by running for a local office. We may seek power in our work by climbing up the corporate ladder, trying to become the boss so we can tell others what to do rather than have others tell us what to do.

Power—whether it is the power of status, abilities, career, position—ought to make us feel more in control. But we have seen that it doesn't. We can never tame life. As the Teacher woefully observes, "What is twisted cannot be straightened; what is lacking cannot be counted" (Eccles. 1:15, NIV).

The enigma is that it is God who has done the twisting and produced the lack: "Notice the way God does things; then fall into line. Don't fight the ways of God, for who can straighten out what he has made crooked?" (Eccles. 7:13).

So power does not bring control, and when we realize that, we are disappointed. We begin to feel that life has no meaning. We lose our vitality. The result is that we often give up any meaningful attempts at control. We live halfhearted, passionless lives. Events rule us, rather than the reverse.

Are these the only two options? Do we have to choose between a lifestyle of desperate grasping for control or a listless surrender to the mess?

Abraham: Receiving the Blessing

Let's return to Abraham for a moment. We have already seen him struggle with doubt in his relationship with God. We have seen him grasp at the promises that were at the center of his life.

But something happened to Abraham along the way, something that moved him from the struggle of earthly existence (under the sun) to a fear of God (above the sun). The change didn't happen overnight. It was undoubtedly affected by Isaac's long awaited birth, but more likely it was the result of observing God's grace overcoming obstacles throughout Abraham's life.

Genesis 22 tells the story of the "sacrifice" of Isaac. It is a story hard to fathom, but after the promised heir was born, God asked Abraham to do the unthinkable, take this son and sacrifice him on Mount Moriah.

We don't know what Abraham thought; he might have been angry, confused, and afraid, But we do see his actions: obedience. He takes Isaac to the mountain and surely would have followed through on God's instructions if God had not intervened and provided a substitute.

Abraham had moved from an attitude of anxious chasing to one of divine dependence. He no longer tried to live life according to his own strength; recognizing his weakness, Abraham grew dependent on God. He found meaning and peace not by chasing after power but by surrendering and trusting God.

Notice that the book of Ecclesiastes has the same message. The Teacher fretted about the lack of control over his life. He could not learn from the past; he did not know how to act in the present; he was frightfully ignorant of the future. He was paralyzed with fear.

The second unnamed wise man at the end, though, had the proper antidote for his son: Don't fear your ignorance and lack of control; rather, "fear God" (Eccles. 12:13). Submit your weakness and worries to the One who is truly in control, your heavenly Father.

Paul: Strength in Weakness

In the New Testament we hear bits of the apostle Paul's story, a story that began with a grasping for control over life. If there ever was a type A personality in the Bible, it was Paul. Hear what he says about his life before meeting Christ: "Yet I could have confidence in myself if anyone could. If others have reason for confidence in their own efforts, I have even more! For I was circumcised when I was eight days old, having been born into a pure-blooded Jewish family that is a branch of the tribe of Benjamin. So I am a real Jew if there ever was one! What's more, I was a member of the Pharisees, who demand the strictest obedience to the Jewish law. And zealous? Yes, in fact, I harshly persecuted the church. And I obeyed the Jewish law so carefully that I was never accused of any fault" (Phil. 3:4-6).

Paul tried to find power and control in his own strength (under the sun), but he never found it there. He found true power in his weakness, which he saw when the power of God confronted him on the Damascus Road (Acts 9). As Paul recognized his own limitations and surrendered to God, he found strength. And it was a strength that propelled him to the far corners of the known world of his time. It was a power that pro-pelled him into controversies and situations that not only threatened his life but also, according to tradition, cost him his life. Through Paul's weakness, God exerted his strength powerfully. If we had to pinpoint one early follower of Jesus whom God used to cause his church to grow like a spreading flame, it would be Paul.

Hear what Paul says as he explains an affliction ("a thorn in my flesh") with which he struggled: "Three different times I begged the Lord to take it away. Each time he said, 'My gracious favor is all you need. My power works best in your weakness.' So now I am glad to boast about my weak-nesses, so that the power of Christ may work through me. Since I know it is all for Christ's good, I am quite content with my weaknesses and with insults, hardships, persecutions, and calamities. For when I am weak, then I am strong" (2 Cor. 12:8-10).

How was Paul's weakness converted into such tremendous spiritual energy? Through Christ. And the amazing thing is that Christ not only supplied the divine power, but he also set the example of strength through submission at the apex of his earthly ministry.

Christ: Power through Submission in the Garden

We often lose sight of Christ's agony as he faced the cross. We often think of Christ as facing his death with courage from the very start. But just before his arrest, he described the state of his soul as "crushed with grief to the point of death" (Matt. 26:38). The Gospel of Luke describes

Christ's mental state as "in such agony of spirit that his sweat fell to the ground like great drops of blood" (Luke 22:44).

Christ asked fervently for the cup of suffering to be taken away from him. He really didn't want to go to the cross. But, while Christ was tempted, he never rebelled against his Father's will. Rather, he submitted to him by saying, "If it is not possible for this cup to be taken away unless I drink it, may your will be done" (Matt. 26:42, NIV).

God's will took Jesus to the cross, a place of torture, shame, and death. But it was the only way to the Resurrection, an event of glory, victory, and life.

Jesus is the One who shows us the paradoxical route to meaning in a chaotic and hostile world. He shows us the only source of power and control. Strength is found in our weakness; control is found in our dependency; power is found in our surrender.

Psalm 131: A Prayer of Submission and Contentment

Our society wants to tell us that the only way to a truly fulfilled life is through grasping for power. It shouts at us: Take control of your life! Don't let people push you around! Be your own person! Know your own worth, and don't let anyone put you down!

However, the book of Ecclesiastes asserts that it is impossible to control our lives. Life simply cannot be tamed. The examples of Abraham, Paul, and Christ show a better way: power through submission. We are not strong and in control; we are weak. But God is strong. It makes sense, then, to turn to God in order to find meaning.

Psalm 131 is the prayer of a man whom most would call strong. David was king of Israel, a man who possessed great wealth and commanded huge armies. We know that David struggled with submission. At times we can observe him railing against God and trying to grasp what he wanted (Bathsheba, for instance) through his own efforts. At other times, he waited patiently for God's strength to overcome his weakness. In any case, David left us a prayer that can serve us in our own efforts to overcome the temptations of power and control. It is a prayer that points us in the direction of the only road to peace:

Lord, my heart is not proud;
my eyes are not haughty.
I don't concern myself with matters too great

or awesome for me.
But I have stilled and quieted myself,
just as a small child is quiet with its mother.
Yes, like a small child is my soul within me.
O Israel, put your hope in the Lord—
now and always.
Psalm 131:1-3

THE paradox of the gospel is this: Strength is found in weakness; control is found in dependency; power is found in surrender. Noah, like all of us, fights hard to avoid the paradox of the gospel. He believes, but he prefers a life that is not caught up in the struggles of Christ in the Garden or Paul with his thorn in the flesh. God uses the frustrations of this life and the hurt of relationships to compel us to look beyond what we can control to the God who controls all things in order to woo us to himself. As we move from control to surrender, we move from chasing the wind under the sun to embracing God above it.

Controlling Life: Above the Sun

From above the sun, we conclude that life under the sun was not intended to run smoothly. The road of life is bumpy and filled with obstacles—for everyone. This is the legacy of the Fall (Gen. 3). No one can tame life.

However, it is precisely in the twists and turns that we actually meet God. We find ourselves compelled to surrender to his wisdom not when we feel strong and in control but when life careens off its expected course and we know we can't do anything about it. It is at these moments that we discover we have no control over our world. However, what we control is the search for God in the midst of seeming chaos.

When we are alert to God's working in our life, we can see how intrusions that overwhelm us, even those that are apparently evil, are his way of moving us toward something good. Surrender in this context is not an act of cowardice but an expectation that Romans 8:28 is true, that "God causes everything to work together for the good of those who love God and are called according to his purpose for them."

In his book *Peace, Love, and Healing,* Dr. Bernie Siegel tells a charming but poignant story that illustrates this paradox:

This gentleman has a farm. He loves the old-fashioned way of doing things, so he doesn't have any mechanical equipment and plows his fields with a horse. One day as he was plowing his field the horse dropped dead. Everyone in the village said, "Gee, what an awful thing to happen."

He just responded, "We'll see."

He was so at peace and so calm that we all got together and, because we admired his attitude so much, gave him a new horse as a gift. Then everyone's reaction was, "What a lucky man."

And he said, "We'll see."

A few days later the horse, being strange to his farm, jumped a fence and ran off, and everyone said, "Oh, poor fellow."

He said, "We'll see."

A week later the horse returned with a dozen wild horses following it.

Everyone said, "What a lucky man."

And he said, "We'll see."

The next day his son went out riding because now they had more than one horse, but the boy fell off the horse and broke his leg.

Everyone said, "Oh, poor boy."

But my friend said, "We'll see."

The next day the army came to town taking all the young men for service, but they left his son because of his broken leg. Everyone said, "What a lucky kid."

And my friend said, "We'll see."[1]

HOWEVER, to feel the force of the story, we must tweak it a bit. On one level we could read the story with the understanding that the farmer's "we'll see" means "I hope so"; he is uncertain, but he hopes for the best. That is an under-the-sun perspective. But we can also read the story from an above-the-sun perspective. The farmer's "we'll see" can mean "we'll see God in this"; we are uncertain about the outcome, but we are certain that we will see God at work in the twists, turns, and bumps in the road.

If we adjust our eyes to see God in the midst of the apparent chaos, we will affirm that, although life is not tamable, it is purposeful. Such surrender to God's control and power doesn't mean that we spend less energy, but it does mean that we spend less nervous energy. We can live with a confidence that does not presume on our ability to rope life in but rather grounds itself in the strength and power of the One who made us.

➤ *How Do We Chase after Power?*

1. Over what parts of your life do you feel that you have control? Where do you wish you had more?
2. What do you have to sacrifice to keep order in your life? Time? relationships? leisure?
3. What emotions do you experience when you feel that something is beyond your power?
4. Does the "power of God" have any practical value in your daily life? Describe where you see his power and how it affects your power.
5. How do you and/or your family plan your day, your month, your life?
6. What does it mean to you to surrender your life to God? What does that surrender mean for your planning?
7. Does the realization that life is ultimately untamable cause you to panic?
8. What verses from Scripture give you hope in the midst of panic or helplessness?

PART TWO

Chasing after
RELATIONSHIPS

6

The Ride Home

NOAH was furious about the car. Somehow deep down he should have known the day had been too good to last. He had been trained by a mother whose perky smile had always infuriated him. She was always chipper, one of those early-morning fanatics. She looked so much on the bright side of things that she was blinded to the dark. Noah had made an oath when he was young to major on the negative and provide a cosmic balance to her blithe optimism.

Noah couldn't figure out how he had let down his guard. He should have remembered that apartment complexes are notorious for small-minded people who look to pounce on those who take their parking spots.

To Noah's great embarrassment, he not only had to accept Jack's offer to drive them to the garage, but he also had to borrow one hundred dollars in cash from Jack to pay for the towing.

As Noah and Joan sat in the backseat of Jack's car, Joan chirped away at how nice it was to be with them while apologizing profusely for imposing on them. Noah looked at Marcia's eyes when she turned to talk—they sparkled even in the dark. Her voice suffused the car with a warm, calm reassurance. Noah sat back in his seat when he realized he was staring at her. Normally, he was a model of discretion, a conservative man, a paragon of moral values. But the contrast between Marcia and Joan made his chest tighten in frustration. He didn't want Joan to be engaging and reflective—he liked her to be dull and predictable, but in the presence of Marcia he felt drawn to a desire for passion that he allowed himself to feel only in his work.

Jack interrupted the silence. "Well, Noah, you seemed rather preoccupied tonight. Care to give us an idea what continent you were traveling?" Noah could tell from the tone in Jack's voice that he could not evade the question with a witty, indirect answer.

"Jack, I hate to admit I was lost in the day. We had a huge meeting about a major stock offering, and I was pitted against most of the senior jocks. It was a fairly important Alamo for me if I am going to get the ear of the CEO. I lost the battle, but I think if my instincts are accurate, I may have won the war." Noah loved the repartee with Jack and always anticipated how Jack would move on several fronts at once. But tonight he was tired, furious about the car, irritated at his wife, and far too intrigued by Marcia. He felt weaker than he had ever felt before while jousting with Jack.

Jack stopped at a traffic light and looked at Noah in the rearview mirror. "Noah, how long have I known you?" Before Noah could answer, Jack said: "About three years and two months if I recall accurately." Noah hated the way Jack was both detailed and rarely wrong. "So for over three years I have never heard you gloat or tout a stock, a trade, or a business deal. You are a master of understatement; you ride the thin edge of minimizing all your activities and deals. I suspect you are thinking thoughts you'd prefer to keep to yourself."

Noah was glad the darkness concealed his flushed face. He felt exposed, and for a brief, terrible moment, he thought that he had been caught in his indiscreet thoughts about Marcia and his contemptible attitude toward Joan.

He quickly regained composure and chortled, "Jack, my friend, I know you are an attorney, but sometimes I think you are a frustrated psychiatrist."

"I may be, but what I really would like to be when I grow up is a theologian. Then again, I like to fight over minutiae and actually make some money in the process as well."

Both men laughed, and the momentary tension in the car relaxed as the play of shadow and light crossed their faces.

Jack started up the conversation again. "Noah, I simply don't know you well. For someone I have been around for many years, I find you one of the most impenetrable people I know, or better said, *don't* know. But it would certainly be wrong of me to pry. And also likely pointless, true?"

Noah felt weak and sick. He didn't know how to respond, so he put up a thin shield. "Well, Jack, I don't really know. I guess, like most of us, I know myself the least. But I don't think I'm that difficult to know. Or maybe I am."

Noah was anxious to end the evening and lose himself in sleep. Everyone was a bit surprised when Joan leaned forward and began to talk to Jack and Marcia. "He does that to me a lot, too. He doesn't really answer questions, at least not directly. And I end up making jokes, as you did, Jack. Or I just stare out the window and figure it is my fault for not being bright enough to ask the right questions. Well, Jack, at least with you we know that it's not a matter of not being bright enough to ask the right questions. Maybe Noah is just too smart for all of us."

The silence that followed hung like a shroud. It seemed that no one even wanted to breathe, let alone respond to Joan. The car jerked as Jack pressed on the gas in response to an impatient honk behind him. The light had turned green.

Noah turned to look at his wife, and his eyes flitted between a narrowing fury and a widening disbelief; he had never heard Joan so accurately describe his reluctance to talk about himself. Joan did not look at Noah. She looked forward, staring into the distance, again speaking to no one in particular. "I think Noah is happy to be alone. He is proud to be impenetrable."

If a person could fall off a car seat, Noah would have dropped to the floor. He had never heard his wife use a word like *impenetrable*. He felt true fear. His heart began to beat fast, and he knew that if he spoke, he would reveal his panic. But if he did not break into her monologue, she might say things that were best left to the pleasant vacuum that he thought made up his wife's inner world. He was spared the opportunity when Marcia leaned back to look at Joan. Her face was perplexed but calm. "Joan, what do you think makes Noah hide?"

Joan spoke softly and with almost reverent kindness. "Noah is a jealous man. Not to say he is not a very good man. But he wants what others have. Not their material things. He wants their personal qualities. For example, he likes Jack a great deal. But he would never admit he feels intimidated by Jack's intelligence and competence. I just don't get it. Once Noah feels envious, he admires the person but won't get closer. And if he isn't jealous of a person, then he won't even bother to get to know the person. So, either way, he stays aloof. I know he looks at me as a ditz, and I know I sort of am, but I think he is actually a very confused man."

The car filled with a bright flash when it passed under the sign that announced their arrival at the towing service. In the brief exposure, all the faces in the car were stunned, except Joan's.

Jack drove through the entryway and into a parking place. Joan sat back; a small smile crossed her face. Jack turned and said, "I know you're both tired, but I think this affords us the opportunity to go a bit further than we have in some of our other conversations about what the book of Ecclesiastes has to say to your marriage and our friendship. Noah, I hope you will not turn against Joan. Her honesty has been refreshing."

Noah was caught in the backseat. He could not explode at Joan in that setting. He felt trapped, afraid, and furious. He also felt oddly amazed at his wife. He had no idea she had seen into his heart. "Well, Jack, I guess we can say this has been more of a study about life than I thought it would be when we started the Bible study tonight. And no, I will not make my wife pay when we drive home, though I don't know if I have much to say now."

Jack and Marcia opened their doors and moved the backs of their seats to let Noah and Joan climb out. Jack reached back and grabbed Noah's hand, drawing him out in a strong, swift move. Jack's grip and strength easily made Noah feel like a child in his grasp. Jack smiled, and they shook hands. Marcia and Joan hugged for the first time.

The next few minutes were a blur of passing bills to a huge man with long, greasy hair. When Noah and Joan reached their car, Joan was quiet and Noah was quick. They got into the car as if they were both entering different worlds. Noah was already calculating how many minutes it would take to get home, check the phone machine, finish his E-mails, and then get to bed.

Joan was afraid; she felt lost. She had said more than she intended to say. She had never meant to offer any of those thoughts to anyone, ever. As soon as they got in the car, Noah turned to her and said, "Cute. I did not appreciate your little pop-psychological analysis of me. I don't want that to occur ever again. Ever. Do you understand?"

Joan could not look at him. She said, "I'm sorry, Noah. I didn't mean to hurt you. I got carried away. I guess I was thinking they were friends, and I was thinking during the study how often I just keep our lives under control by not rocking the boat or asking anything of you or anyone else."

Noah snapped, "Well, let's see if we can get you back to the old Joan. You know better than to carry on about our lives in front of anyone." Joan could feel the heaviness of her heart. It felt as if she were wearing a leaden backpack underwater. She began to sink. Noah looked straight out the window.

Joan wanted to escape. Noah's anger triggered an experience she didn't want to remember. In her mind she saw a nine-year-old girl standing at the car door, waiting for her furious father to finish fumbling with the keys to let her in the car.

They had just walked out of her second piano recital, and it had not been a pleasant experience. When it had been Joan's turn to perform, she had walked up to the platform, sat on the piano bench, and placed her hands on the keys. She had waited a moment and began to play.

But what she was playing was not the piece she had learned. She kept hearing another piece playing in the back of her mind. Halfway through the piece the volume in her head increased drastically, and she fell silent. She was stunned by the vibrancy, and the rush that filled her chest made her feel as if she couldn't breathe. She stopped playing. She stared at her hands. They would not play. Suddenly she was aware of the countless faces and the gasp that rose from the horrified audience.

She could not remember the rest of the piece. She took her hands off the keys and then quickly put them back into position. She began the piece again. Her concentration was intense.

But all that she could hear in her mind this time was her father's rising fury. His lungs were well developed after many years of preaching in the pulpit. Joan had listened to his scream countless times at the dinner table or in the car or before sending her off to bed. As she would watch his lips and puffy face quiver in rage, she had learned to detach herself from his anger and allow herself to float into another world, where she would hear only the smooth sounds of the classical music her mother listened to when her father wasn't home. She liked the distant musical sphere. It was in a safe space. No voices screamed. No one else could come in.

As Joan sat at the piano and listened to her father shout in her mind, her fingers played up to the bar at which she had stopped the first time. Then her hands stopped again. She couldn't remember a single note beyond that point.

This time when she stopped, she turned to the audience, smiled innocently, and shrugged. The audience—quiet, intense, and straining for her victory—immediately relaxed and began to clap for her. The teacher bounded up the stairs and put the music in front of Joan. In an instant, barely looking at the sheets, she played a spirited ending to the piece. She even added a few concluding bars that were not part of the original piece. She descended to the front row to sounds of applause and one older man who whooped with a sporting-event cheer.

After the conclusion of the recital, Joan knew she would pay, not only for humiliating her father, but also for garnering more applause than he had ever gained through his pulpit. She quickly walked through the crowd to her parents and then followed behind her father. He moved briskly, barely speaking to some of the people who greeted him with a smile, a pat on the back, and some remarks about his daughter's sweetness.

Joan and her parents descended into the night. Her father's pace quickened. They were walking in a straight line—her father, her mother, and herself.

After he found the right key and unlocked the car door, he yanked it open. He said nothing. He was ready to explode at her, but he couldn't because some of the people in the parking lot were his parishioners. But the look in his eyes indicated he could have struck her. Instead of hitting her, he screamed through his bulging eyes. She looked beyond his eyes and heard the distant music. Her heart moved toward the music. He would not be allowed in. The door shut, and she settled into the car.

THE radio came on, and Joan was shaken to realize she was not listening to her father's hymns. She was not in her father's car. She was in Noah's Audi, and Noah had just turned on a rock station. The sounds of Shawn Colvin brought her back to the real world. She looked at Noah. She knew he would not explode or even ask a single question. He would stare out the window and count the minutes until he could be in bed.

She smiled and thought about the recital piece she had not finished. She could play it backward if she wanted, but she was not sure whether she could play it the way it was written. Maybe she wasn't spacey, just different.

Everything is meaningless, utterly meaningless.

She had tried so often to be what Noah wanted her to be—and every time she failed. She had also failed to be what her father wanted her to be. She was the one the whole family treated like a slightly daffy nowhere child. Maybe, just maybe, she was a melodious child who heard the music of other spheres, not the chords that most others heard.

Everything is meaningless, utterly meaningless.

Maybe there was meaning, maybe. Maybe it was not to be approached directly, straight on, as if life were a jigsaw puzzle that required mere perseverance and minimal imagination to figure out the picture.

Her heart swelled with the hope that maybe life didn't have the meaning that Noah, her father, even Jack brought to it. Maybe the meaninglessness was the silly bantering of Noah and Jack, the puffy-rage face of her father, her mother's dutiful silence. Maybe the audience's surprising applause, full of humanity in response to her sweet shrug, was a better hope than all the pious words and all the patronizing pats she had endured through her life. It was more than she could bear thinking.

Noah drove on in silence, simply counting the minutes until he would be swallowed up by the warm arms of the down comforter.

7

"Relationships Ought to Bring Me Fulfillment"

WE OFTEN look to relationships to give our lives meaning. We may think that if only we were married or if only we had a close friend, life would be so much better. We yearn for closeness with friends, family members, and people at our workplace or at school. Relationships are a hedge against loneliness, and we often will do anything to gain friends and keep relationships harmonious.

Do any of these scenarios sound familiar to you?

"SOMETIMES it all seems to click between Debbie and me. Those times are so meaningful! But at other times it is as if we hardly know each other. Just last week she was in town and didn't even give me a call. I thought

she was my best friend. I heard about her visit through a common
"friend" who seemed a bit too eager to let me know that I was forgotten.
I was crushed. I cried for an hour. I wonder what's wrong with me. Do I
give off negative messages that I am not aware of? Maybe it's uncon-
scious facial expressions. I sometimes do get caught up in my own world.
I know that, but I really want friends."

- *"Talking to my wife last week about our finances was so embarrassing.
  I made myself vulnerable about my fears and hopes, and she seemed to
  mock me. I understand her disappointment about how much I earn, but if
  only she would support me more, I might have the confidence to step out
  more boldly in my work. I thought that's what marriage was all about.
  She seems to have other ideas about that. I'll never share myself with her
  like that again."*

- *"I'll never trust them again! They certainly don't trust me. I can't believe
  they made me take a drug test. I didn't even know parents could find a
  drug-test kit. And, the nerve, they told me it was for my own good. Well,
  if they don't trust me, I might as well give them some reason for it.
  They'll be sorry."*

WE ALL struggle with relationships in one form or another. We all crave
closeness with our friends, spouse, children, parents, and others. We don't
want to feel alone. We want to connect with others. Most of the time,
though, having good relationships is as difficult as chasing the wind.

Consider Noah and Joan. Noah is an extraordinarily competent man.
He is involved with others when he needs to be, but the bridge to his
heart is closed. He lives with a great hunger to succeed; he lives with an
equally great commitment to make sure no one sees his inner world. He
struggles with Jack. He is drawn to Marcia. He patronizes his wife. He
thinks it works—until Joan breaks the silence with the truth.

Most relationships, even ones that have lasted for years, survive on the
truth's being hidden, left unspoken. To the degree that we live in silence
with one another, we can feel the illusion of peace and even intimacy.
Once we speak words that reveal disappointment, hurt, or desire, then
the tenor of the relationship changes from the status quo to a new level
of tension. And most people choose relationships in which they will find
little conflict or tension, little commitment to change.

Noah is not terribly interested in the book of Ecclesiastes, except to make sure he is not exposed as a slacker or as biblically incompetent. His mind is more attached to Marcia and the oddities of the apartment in which the Bible study was held. He is not moved by the Bible study; he is moved by the injustice of his car being towed. His heart is not moved by life; it is moved by a demand to find peace, satisfaction, and pleasure in a life bound by unpredictable chaos.

For this reason he loves sleep more than his life. His heart is far from considering truth in his marriage or the truth about himself as he studies the Word of God.

Joan unwittingly opens up a hornet's nest. She has been a meek and pleasant woman who has chosen not to engage in interactions that might cause conflict. Her present is to some degree haunted by her past. She doesn't want to relive the sorrow, shame, and anger of an emotionally abusive father. Our relationships in the present often reflect commitments, oaths we have made in the past. Apparently, one oath Joan has made is never to rock the boat. For whatever reason, perhaps due to Jack's remark that Noah is difficult to know, she opens her mouth and rocks their lives with her honesty. It is in relationship, especially our closest friendships and marriage, where our lives will be most deeply disturbed and drawn to the depths of truth about ourselves and God.

Can't Live without Them

Recently, my wife and I (Tremper) took our oldest son, Tremper (IV), to Clemson University to begin his college career. All year long the three of us had anticipated the change and looked forward to it with excitement. Clemson is approximately seven hundred miles away from our home, so we knew that we would not see him as often. Alice and I had prepared ourselves for the moment of departure. We were ready for the big event.

Or so we thought. As we hugged in his new dorm room before we left to return home, I was overwhelmed with emotion, thinking that life in one sense would never be the same. After eighteen years together, our lives were taking different directions, and though our love for one another would not lessen because of it, the separation meant fewer opportunities to share in each others' lives. It was a painful and traumatic moment. I have never wept so deeply in my life.

But the separation was also a positive moment. That's the staggering part. The three of us wouldn't have wanted it any other way. Alice and I were proud that our son had come to a point of independence, a point at which he could leave home and begin to carve out an existence increasingly on his own. We were happy that he was attending a fine and attractive university like Clemson. We were particularly pleased that there was a good church nearby, pastored by one of my favorite former students. Nonetheless, the sense of loss was almost overwhelming.

Relationships are crucial to navigating life successfully. Perhaps it is here that we can find the significance that makes life worth living.

Like all living creatures, human beings need water, food, and shelter to survive. However, if you take a baby and place it in the forest with water, food, and shelter, that baby will die if it has no contact with people. If we put an adult through repeated betrayals, abuse, and loss, that person will often experience an inner death.

Examine your own life. Think of the times in which you have had a number of close friends and family members who have cared about you as you have cared about them. Then think of those dark times when you have found yourself without support, without someone with whom you could share your heart. In the former times, life seemed vital, interesting, exciting, worth living. In the latter, life was dark, depressing, empty.

The three most traumatic events a person can undergo are a move, a divorce, and the death of someone close. These are three quite different events, but the effect is the same. Relational separation is traumatic, whether it is an expected part of life, like our son's moving to college, or an unexpected one.

Imagine if the separation is the result of death or, worse—betrayal. In Psalm 55 King David recalls in confusion and heartache the time before his friend betrayed him. They labored together, suffered for the sake of God, and then inexplicably their relationship was ruptured. In the psalm David dreams of flying away like a bird to escape the pain and the violence of his enemy who was once his friend.

Relationships are obviously important to us, as vital as the air we breathe and the food we eat. Yet, they are also the source of our deepest questions and our darkest despair. If relationships are the route to meaning in life, it is a difficult path. Let's first explore why this is the case.

The Gift of Relationship: Two Can Become One!

We yearn for relationship, the Bible tells us, because God made us that way. Our desire to know and be known intimately by another is not a perversion or sinful desire but rather a God-given trait of our humanity.

According to Genesis 1 and 2, God created Adam alone. Adam could relate to all the animals in the world that God created, but it was not enough. Even though Adam had an intimate relationship with his Maker, God knew that even this was not enough. Genesis records his divine acknowledgment and plan: "It is not good for the man to be alone. I will make a companion who will help him" (Gen. 2:18).

And he did! God created Eve, one who was like Adam but also different. Someone who could enter into a relationship of equals with him. Someone who could labor with him to shape God's good creation into something even more beautiful. And yet someone who was different enough to draw forth mystery and a depth of intrigue that would require both Adam and Eve to spend eternity exploring the differences.

So we see that even before the Fall, the desire for relationship with another human being was a legitimate one, one that is not satisfied even by an intimate relationship with God. What an utterly remarkable, almost terrifying reality: God made us so we would be drawn into relationship with another person rather than exclusively need God.

This three-way relationship is at the core of our deepest psychological wiring: God, man, and woman. When any link is missing, we experience a loss that has consequences for the soul.

According to the Bible, marriage is the most potentially intimate form of relationship between humans. But that is not the only relationship that satisfies the soul. The Bible also describes the deep need we have for other friendships. Friendships sustain us in life-giving ways.

Relationship is the core of reality. The very nature of being is wrapped up in the trilogy—you, me, us. I am never enough. You and I—a pair—is closer to what we were made to be, but a pair without any other relationship or purpose will eventually pervert the intimacy initially enjoyed. We were meant for more than intimacy with one person. Even the closest pair are meant to be in relationship with another. And without a larger purpose than itself, every "pair" will eventually lose its intimacy. The "us" is at least a third person and most likely a family, group, and community. But even other human relationships are not enough; we are meant to relate all that exists on a horizontal, human plane to a vertical, supernatural realm.

Relationship is at the core of existence because God is the foundation of all reality. Remember that God's existence is a relationship; he is three persons who have existed in relationship from all eternity. God reveals himself as one who is in perpetual relationship. The Father, the Son, and the Holy Spirit are bound in a relationship of deep love and unity in eternity.

Relationship is at the heart of God and at the heart of the cosmos. In one sense, God did not need to create the universe. And he certainly did not have to create other beings. But he did. He created cherubim, angels, seraphim. And most magnificently, he created creatures made in his own image—he created humanity!

So again, the desire for relationship is not ugly; it is not a sign of weakness. In fact, all psychological pathology can be linked to the urge to flee or dominate relationships. The person who is closed to relationships is equally closed to God.

The most dramatic relationship God gave his human creatures, according to Genesis 2, is the gift of marriage. This is the only human relationship that is exclusive. We can have many relatives, many friends, but only one spouse. And this is the only relationship that can take two separate people and merge them into one. Adam acknowledged this on the occasion of Eve's creation when he cried out: "'At last! . . . She is part of my own flesh and bone! She will be called "woman," because she was taken out of a man.' This explains why a man leaves his father and mother and is joined to his wife, and the two are united into one. Now, although Adam and his wife were both naked, neither of them felt any shame" (Gen. 2:23-25).

Further, the Scriptures are clear that this particular type of human relationship reflects in a special way our relationship with God (see especially Eph. 5:21-33). Both marriage and the divine-human relationship are exclusive and totally vulnerable relationships to another person. Marriage mirrors our relationship with God as no other human relationship does.

Having said this, we must point out that other human relationships, kinship and friendship, are also God's gift to us to help us in the midst of a world in need of shaping. Together we are all to till God's garden into a beautiful and productive world. Our hearts are wired for relationship; the chaos of life requires relationships if we are going to survive, let alone thrive. Yet, relationships burn the deepest brand of the Fall into our hearts. The Teacher recognized as much.

The Triple-Braided Cord: The Solace of Friendship

Even the Teacher, who has little positive to say about much, recognizes the deep significance of relationships:

> *Two people can accomplish more than twice as much as one; they get a better return for their labor. If one person falls, the other can reach out and help. But people who are alone when they fall are in real trouble. And on a cold night, two under the same blanket can gain warmth from each other. But how can one be warm alone? A person standing alone can be attacked and defeated, but two can stand back-to-back and conquer. Three are even better, for a triple-braided cord is not easily broken.* Ecclesiastes 4:9-12

THE VERSES immediately preceding this picture of the blessings of relationships describe the pitiful nature of human existence, a person who works hard to gain wealth but has no friends or relatives. To the Teacher, this person is an example of the futile nature of life on the earth: "I observed yet another example of meaninglessness in our world. This is the case of a man who is all alone, without a child or a brother, yet who works hard to gain as much wealth as he can. But then he asks himself, 'Who am I working for? Why am I giving up so much pleasure now?' It is all so meaningless and depressing" (Eccles. 4:7-8).

It is in the light of this picture of the lonely miser that the Teacher turns his attention to the benefits of companionship. What a blessing to have a friend in this hard and hostile world, to have people with whom we can face troubles and problems.

The Teacher's concluding metaphor of the triple-braided cord caps it off. Through it, he presents the idea that if one friend is a benefit, how much better two, three, or even more.

Most interpreters of Ecclesiastes believe that the Teacher is describing his own struggles when he tells us about the lonely miser. That means that his words about the blessings of friendship are said with longing and desire. He wishes that he had such companionship to help him in the midst of life's struggles.

But we get the impression that even if the Teacher did have many friends, he knew that their importance was limited. Companionship is one of the few topics that the Teacher talks positively about, but even here, the advantages of companionship, though real, are very limited.

As a matter of fact, when we look closely at what the Teacher says, we see that his words are striking by their lack of enthusiasm. According to the Teacher, though friends are a positive thing in this world, they certainly do not give life ultimate significance. Indeed, friendship, even when one can find it, often lets us down. It has a dark side.

The Dark Side of Relationship: Grasping at Relational Fulfillment

The first few chapters of Genesis are foundational as we seek to understand our relationships. We have seen how Genesis 1–2 describes the creation of relationship and the joy and contentment that are found in our marriages and friendships.

But if this is so, why are we so rarely content? Why are we lonely and frustrated in our relationships? If Genesis 1–2 were all that we had, then it would not be true to the reality of our everyday life.

Theologians rightly call Genesis 3 the story of the Fall. It narrates the fall of the human race from grace, from intimate relationship with God. Adam and Eve chose to rebel against God, kick against his authority, and question his infinite wisdom. This immediately introduced a breach in their relationship with God.

But the Fall had a further result, one that is emphasized by the biblical account. It was only after they sinned that Adam and Eve felt shame, heartache, and enmity with each other. Before the Fall, their union could be described as two people becoming one (Gen. 2:24). After the Fall, they look at each other and head for the hills. Their naked vulnerability became a source of shame.

Physical and emotional nakedness is a wonderful thing. God created Eve so that Adam could look at her naked body and say, "Incredible! I desire to be intimate with her." The man's body was shaped in such a way as to exert a powerful attraction on the woman. To think that the nude human body is crude or to think that the desire to look at a naked body is perverse is a criticism of God, the One who made us that way.

Remember, though, what happened after the Fall. Adam and Eve hid themselves from each other. Similarly today, we withdraw emotionally from one another. We hide our inner feelings and resist truly knowing another person. In effect, we are still hiding "among the trees" (Gen.

3:8). After the Fall, Adam and Eve were no longer intimate allies as they sought to shape the Garden together. Instead, they became hostile rivals. We see this especially in their blameshifting. Once God confronted them, Adam was quick to point the finger at Eve. "It was the woman you gave me who brought me the fruit, and I ate it" (Gen. 3:12).

Forever after, no marriage or any other relationship has escaped the effects of the fall into sin. Though, as we will soon see, God gives hope for relationships, most relationships are marred by fights, abuse, neglect, and loneliness. The two key issues that are played out in all relationships are *lust* and *violence.*

Normally, we think of lust as sexual. It certainly can include sexual lust, but lust involves a far bigger dynamic. Lust is the demand to fill a soul emptiness that craves satisfaction but will not turn to God for fullness. The dilemma is that even turning to God does not take away the pain or the desire, which can be satisfied only when we reach heaven. C. S. Lewis calls this our "inconsolable desire." That is not to say that relationship with the Lord does not melt away enormous fear, loneliness, and pain, but it is not biblical to think that relationship with God now is as rich, fulfilling, or freeing as it will be in heaven. Those who know God most deeply feel the inconsolable desire even more acutely. We ache now. The ache inside is often used to justify rebellion and turning away from God to find satisfaction in our own devices, through serving other gods, like money or safety from pain.

Lust exposes our dark intention to find a lover—any object, person, or idea that will take away our pain. But, in fact, all false lovers eventually leave us more empty and more susceptible to shame. We have a problem. We refuse to be humbled by our attachment to false gods; instead, we get caught serving other lovers, and we turn violent against those who catch us in our refusal to trust God.

Violence involves our effort to demand satisfaction and protect ourselves from the scrutiny of others. Violence may involve physical harm of others, but it is far more often seen in the way we use words or even turn a "cold shoulder" to those who have hurt us. It is our effort to blind others to what is true about us and bind them to us in order to fulfill our demand for satisfaction.

Violence begins by placing the blame for our sin and shame on a scapegoat. Once the sin bearer takes our place, then we are free and absolved of responsibility. We can stand in our world without guilt or sorrow because our anger is self-righteously directed toward destroying something bad. Not only do we feel absolved, but we feel blessed for destroying that which brought harm to others/ourselves.

Noah is a violent man. The greatest thrill in his day was thwarting the ignorance and arrogance of people who did not have the wisdom to see that their assessment about the Pearson stock was wrong. He hated their presumption and self-righteousness. He was a warrior for truth, for right thinking. But he was blind to the truth about his disdain for Joan. Contempt for another person is violent and demeaning. It makes the other person feel small and worthless. The phrase *cutting a person down to size* gives an idea of the inherent violence in disdain.

JOAN, on the other hand, had lived her role of being a flighty, nonsubstantial person to convenient perfection. Her lust, or consuming desire, was to avoid conflict. She did not want to be yelled at or made to feel small by failing as she had done at the piano recital. Therefore, she avoided any activity that was risky or might provoke greater contempt from Noah. It may not be easy to see lust in her heart; her passion was not to get something, which is how we often think of lust, but to escape any experience that triggered her painful past.

But the Bible study, and in particular the phrase "meaningless, meaningless," had seeped deeply into her heart. She did not think it through. She did not know the direction of her words. She did not have a well-worked plan. She simply spoke on the prompting of Jack and Marcia. In the car, her heart wanted more from Noah. Her hunger for a more intimate and real relationship with Noah broke through her spaciness. For decades, she had depended more on her ability not to rock the boat than she did on God. But her safe inner space was not enough to contain the words that welled up in her hungry soul. She disrupted the pleasant ride; she broke the comfort of the convivial conversation.

Joan disrupted life, in the positive sense. Disruption exposes and illumines the sinful paths of those who are moving to personal and spiritual harm. Disruption is violent, but it is a biblical violence, not a sinful one. In the same way, lust can also be positive; lust can be a strong desire to see God's will done on earth as it is in heaven. Joan had often lusted for an avoidance of rage and rejection, and in that she had been violent. She had killed her soul, her desire for more, and in doing so, she thwarted all relationships with others. But lust redeemed turns into a desire for a loving relationship, and violence redeemed energizes a commitment to sacrifice one's comfort to fight for love.

It is not only in marriage that we struggle with lust and violence. Marriage is not the only relationship that has a dark side; friends and other close relatives often are a source of pain rather than support. Kids learn that at a young age.

Charles was shocked when he learned that a job change would move his family from New Jersey to Ohio. Only eleven years old, Charles did not really comprehend the magnitude of the move. He realized only that he would be miles from old friends and familiar surroundings. His mother assured him that they had relatives in the new town and that they would live down the road from his uncle and aunt, who had three children, one Charles's own age.

Charles did not know his cousin James well, but he had always enjoyed the short vacations they spent together at their grandparents' cottage on the lake. James was very popular, and Charles thought that maybe that would help him adjust to school life.

For this reason, Charles went through the move with some enthusiasm, but he was nervous and lonely during his first day at school. At the first recess, he saw his cousin with a group of other boys playing kickball. He ran over to join in. As James saw his cousin, he yelled, "Hey, stupid, what do you want? There's no room for you here!" He emphasized his last point with a shove.

Charles quickly moved away. He was confused, and his eyes started to swell. Before the tears hit, he had found a secluded place.

The rest of the year was more of the same. Since James was popular, the other kids assumed James's attitude toward Charles and avoided him—or, worse, taunted him. Charles was too ashamed to talk to his parents about it. He had nowhere to turn. His life was a nightmare of loneliness, which led him further into withdrawal.

SOME of us identify with Charles. The false friends in our lives may not be as blatantly nasty as James was to Charles, but people can be cruel. When we are honest, we realize that even our good relationships can't fulfill our needs for intimacy. Friends let us down. They use us, as the Teacher recognized in 5:11: "The more you have, the more people come to help you spend it." We react to this disappointment and exploitation with anger and frustration.

If we take a close look at ourselves, we also realize that we can't fulfill the needs of others. We let our friends down. Relationships thus are a prime breeding ground for lust and violence.

A life without friends is barren and dangerous, but friends are also a source of considerable pain. It seems like a no-win situation. To broaden the popular saying, "Friends—can't live with them, can't live without them."

We often react by making either an idol or a taboo of our relationships. The former may be illustrated by my friend Stephanie, who constantly complains that her husband and children take her for granted. She does work hard to keep them happy, but her whole mental state depends on whether or not she gets the strokes she feels she deserves. If her husband and children don't affirm her in the right way, with the right gesture or the right word, she is devastated.

While Stephanie places too much importance on her relationships, Ham doesn't see them as valuable enough. He deals with difficult customers and coworkers all day, but when it comes to going out socially, he balks, even though his wife is quite gregarious. One day Ham confided to me that he was sick and tired of people in general; they brought one headache after another. The only course that brought relief to his pain was simply to refuse to have anything to do with people unless his work depended on it. As a result, he became a near recluse, deeply wounding his wife.

We can all relate to the problems of relationship. We desire to be close to others, but when we sinners come together, the problems intensify; they don't go away. We feel not only the frustration created by the inadequacy of another person but also the guilt in our failures as a spouse, a relative, or a friend.

Perhaps no other area in our life raises more questions than our relationships. Perhaps no other area in our life causes more anger, jealousy, disappointment, and stress than other people. The Teacher, though he had some positive things to say about relationships, recognized this frustration: "'This is my conclusion,' says the Teacher. 'I came to this result after looking into the matter from every possible angle. Just one out of every thousand men I interviewed can be said to be upright, but not one woman! I discovered that God created people to be upright, but they have each turned to follow their own downward path'" (Eccles. 7:27-29).

We should not be put off by the Teacher's obvious sexist attitude here.

In the first place, the Teacher does not reflect normative teaching. We have made that point before. The Teacher's words are quoted by the second wise man, who uses them as a foil to teach his son. And remember that the Teacher reflects life under the sun. Note, too, that the Teacher prizes men only a tad better than women. If the Teacher were a woman, she would just reverse the proportion from her perspective under the sun.

The point is that relationships ultimately are unsatisfactory. And further, even if friendships are good, the Teacher ruthlessly points out, they all end in death: "Whatever they did in their lifetime—loving, hating, envying—is all long gone. They no longer have a part in anything here on earth" (Eccles. 9:6).

So what do we do? Should we plod away at relationships? Should we adopt the devil-may-care attitude to which the Teacher resigns himself?

So go ahead. Eat your food and drink your wine with a happy heart, for God approves of this! Wear fine clothes, with a dash of cologne!

Live happily with the woman you love through all the meaningless days of life that God has given you in this world. The wife God gives you is your reward for all your earthly toil. Whatever you do, do well. For when you go to the grave, there will be no work or planning or knowledge or wisdom. Ecclesiastes 9:7-10

SHOULD we then conclude that relationships will not endure and always disappoint? Or is there a better way?

8

Restoring Relationships through Giving Ourselves Away

RELATIONSHIPS aren't the final answer. They can't supply us with ultimate meaning or purpose in life. Disappointments, rejections, betrayals make this clear. This is life under the sun. But is there something more? Can we move from relational frustration under the sun to something better above the sun? If relationships cannot provide total fulfillment, can they at least provide us some solace in a harsh world? And further, does the "fear of God" advised by the unnamed wise man at the end of the book of Ecclesiastes move us in the right direction? Let's start in an unlikely place, the Song of Songs.

The Song of Songs: The Possibility of True Love
The Song of Songs gives us hope for our relationships. While the message of that book speaks most directly to marriage, it has implications for all relationships.

The story of human relationship, we noted earlier, began in the Garden of Eden. God created Eve to be Adam's intimate companion. They were one in spirit and one in body. But as the story continued, sin constructed a barrier between Adam and Eve as it did between God and his human creatures. The man and the woman could no longer stand naked in the Garden without shame. Indeed, God sent them out of the Garden.

The Song of Songs is widely recognized today as a love poem. It is an allegory that speaks not only of our relationship with God but also a celebration of the love that can exist between a man and a woman.

Some people believe that the Song is a story about love; others say it is more like a collection of related poems about love. This issue is not important for our point. The significant observation to make about the Song of Songs is that once again the man and the woman are in the Garden, naked and feeling anything but shame. The following passage is one of many scenes in which the two find passion in the Garden:

YOUNG MAN: *You are like a private garden, my treasure, my bride! You are like a spring that no one else can drink from, a fountain of my own. You are like a lovely orchard bearing precious fruit, with the rarest of perfumes: nard and saffron, calamus and cinnamon, myrrh and aloes, perfume from every incense tree, and every other lovely spice. You are a garden fountain, a well of living water, as refreshing as the streams from the Lebanon mountains.*

YOUNG WOMAN: *Awake, north wind! Come, south wind! Blow on my garden and waft its lovely perfume to my lover. Let him come into his garden and eat its choicest fruits.*

YOUNG MAN: *I am here in my garden, my treasure, my bride! I gather my myrrh with my spices and eat my honeycomb with my honey. I drink my wine with my milk.* Song of Songs 4:12–5:1

As PHYLLIS Trible, an Old Testament scholar, and others have observed, when the Song of Songs is read in the context of the whole Bible, one cannot miss the allusion to the Garden of Eden. One of the important messages that God gives us in this book, therefore, is that God redeems relationships. Not that any relationship is perfect (even in the Song there are troubles between the man and the woman [see 5:2-8]), but there is the possibility of meaningful and fulfilling connection between two human beings. But where do we find it in this hostile world?

Love of Self and Love of the Other

Why is it so hard to find true love? The Bible's answer to that question is that deep down we love only ourselves. Love of self conflicts with loving another person. We want love; we find it hard to give love to another unless we get something in return. Indeed, we often give only as a way of filling our own needs. How often have we withdrawn from people to whom we have been close because we were getting nothing out of a relationship, and how often have we wanted to be with another person because that person was making us feel good and was serving our own needs?

In 1 Corinthians 13 Paul teaches us that love sacrifices safety ("I won't let myself be hurt again") and deals a death blow to self-righteousness ("I deserve better after all I have done for them"). Love seeks the good of the other without denying the hunger of our heart or demanding that desire be satisfied. We often think of this chapter in the context of marriage, and indeed it is appropriately applied in that most intimate of human relationships, but the truth is that Paul does not restrict love in that way. He is talking about a love that should characterize all relationships.

After asserting the preeminence of love (1 Cor. 12:31–13:3), Paul gets to the heart of the matter. He describes a heart that loves with passion and depth:

> Love is patient and kind. Love is not jealous or boastful or proud or rude. Love does not demand its own way. Love is not irritable, and it keeps no record of when it has been wronged. It is never glad about injustice but rejoices whenever the truth wins out. Love never gives up, never loses faith, is always hopeful, and endures through every circumstance.
> 1 Corinthians 13:4-7

FIRST, the apostle tells us that love is patient and kind. It waits for the other, and it does so with concern, not irritability. It waits. It hopes. It loves beauty and justice and does not give in to the petty pleasure of seeing the one who hurt us stumble. Love is the Atlas of the soul; it keeps holding us up; it does not quit; it does not lose the memory of connection; it does not kill the dreams of reconciliation.

On the other hand, love wants nothing to do with jealousy or pride, which seek their own good at the expense of the other. Instead, love cares for the other, not for the self. Love does not keep accounts. That is, in our relationships we do not weigh the personal advantage that we might gain from a relationship. It is not based on what we can get out of it. In another place, Paul puts it well: "Don't be selfish; don't live to make a good impression on others. Be humble, thinking of others as better than yourself. Don't think only about your own affairs, but be interested in others, too, and what they are doing" (Phil. 2:3-4).

It is this high call to other-centered love that strips us of any pretense that we love well. In light of the standard Paul describes, we fall woefully short. Yet, it is his vision of what *could be* that allures our hearts to dream and to desire to grasp and be held by this kind of love. It is in the midst of facing how little we love that we are drawn to the wonder of being forgiven. The one who is forgiven little loves little; the one who is forgiven much loves much (Luke 7:47). The point is painfully clear: To the degree • that I think I know how to love, I am deceived. The paradox is utterly baffling: If I know I don't love well and need to be deeply forgiven for my failures, then I will offer others the greatest gift of love—forgiveness. •

God does not quit on us. He does not lose hope or faith in us. He will not respond to us according to our sin; he will not merely overlook our failure but will work to see us grow to be like him. As we marvel about his love for us, we are drawn to love a little more as he does.

We are given a picture of this radical kind of love in the relationship between David and Jonathan.

A Biblical Example: David and Jonathan

The story of David and Jonathan is an example of selfless love between two powerful young men. Both had important responsibilities in their society, and both carried them out heroically. They illustrate that godly relationships can bring us a measure of satisfaction.

Jonathan's position was given to him by birth. God had chosen his father, Saul, to be the first king in Israel. As the king's son, Jonathan played an important role in the army. In the war against the Philistines, Jonathan showed his courage and creativity (1 Sam. 14). While God had not assured Saul that his descendants would automatically inherit the throne, Jonathan probably hoped that one day he would rule all of Israel. Certainly his father held that expectation.

David, on the other hand, was born to a sheepherder near the small village of Bethlehem. Due to the repeated sins of Saul (1 Sam. 13, 15), God instructed the prophet Samuel to anoint the young man as the future king. Soon, through circumstances under God's control, David found himself on the battlefield with Goliath, the Philistine giant (1 Sam. 17), and in the court as a servant of Saul (1 Sam. 16:14-23).

The situation was ripe to create incredible hatred between David and Jonathan. Jonathan was brave and courageous, but the people sang songs of honor about David. Jonathan was the logical next king, but David was clearly the people's favorite and God's anointed. Though it is unclear whether Jonathan knew about David's anointing, he did know that David would become the next king. Jonathan gave up his own prerogative to be king.

It would be very understandable if Jonathan had been envious of David. Envy and jealousy ruin nearly every relationship. Envy is a mad craving that will kill or destroy any usurper that would take what we have determined will fill our emptiness. For this reason, envy, far less than hatred, is the opposite of love. Love will never grow until we see our envy pulled out at the roots through comprehending the jealous love of God that pursues us even to his own pain through the cross. Love will never grow until we see our envy as paltry and wasted in light of God's holy jealousy for us, his bride. This great jealousy to regain his bride took God's Son to the cross. No other jealousy for a person, a reputation, or object can stand against the wilting force of his desire to reclaim us as his own.

Jonathan loved David with a selfless love. And that love cost him a great deal. The friendship cost Jonathan his relationship with his father, and conceivably it could have resulted in his death. To love David meant Jonathan had to confront his father's envy. At a crucial moment, Jonathan helped David escape Saul's plan to kill him, and when Saul discovered Jonathan's plot, he lashed out, "You stupid son of a whore! . . . Do you think I don't know that you want David to be king in your place, shaming yourself and your mother? As long as that son of Jesse is alive, you'll never be king. Now go and get him so I can kill him!" (1 Sam. 20:30-31).

But instead of bringing David to his father, Jonathan met with David and renewed their vow of friendship. Jonathan's last words to David were, "Go in peace, for we have made a pact in the Lord's name. We have

entrusted each other and each other's children into the Lord's hands forever" (1 Sam. 20:42).

Jonathan and David illustrate what friendship is all about. It does not
seek its own advantage but, rather, glories in the good of the other and
does all it can do to see the other's glory grow. It is an attitude of generous care, not exploitation.

The Power to Care
We desire intimate relationships. We want our marriages and our friendships to be vulnerable, supportive, and warm. We may have a number of
good relationships in our lives, but they don't seem to satisfy us the way
that we want.

We know that part of the problem lies with us. At heart we are selfish
people. The teaching of Paul and the example of David and Jonathan lead
us away from selfishness in our relationships and toward a depth of sacrifice, passionate regard, and incarnational care.

How can we adopt such an attitude? It is so foreign to our nature.
However, because of God's Spirit in us, we are drawn not only to Christ's
example of sacrifice but also to imagine what it means for us to love as he
loved.

The Spirit warms our heart to love. He also deepens our awareness that
our hearts ache for what only heaven can provide. In turn, the Spirit
points our hungry hearts to the One who can both satisfy our hunger and
empower us to live for love.

ONLY one person can satisfy us and empower us to love—Jesus Christ.
Jesus, through his amazing love for us, reestablished our relationship
with God. This is the message of Romans 5:6-11:

*When we were utterly helpless, Christ came at just the right time and died
for us sinners. Now, no one is likely to die for a good person, though someone might be willing to die for a person who is especially good. But God
showed his great love for us by sending Christ to die for us while we were
still sinners. And since we have been made right in God's sight by the
blood of Christ, he will certainly save us from God's judgment. For since
we were restored to friendship with God by the death of his Son while we
were still his enemies, we will certainly be delivered from eternal punishment by his life. So now we can rejoice in our wonderful new relationship*

*with God—all because of what our Lord Jesus Christ has done for us in
making us friends of God.*

HOW did Christ do this? Through the totally selfless act of dying on the
cross. He gave his life for us so we can have an intimate relationship with
God. He introduced us to his Father. In the face of Christ we see the
heart of the Father. He aches. He pursues. The Father relentlessly and
with abandon seeks the lost even to the point of being willing to lose his
Son to gain his flock of straying, obstinate sons and daughters. It is
through Christ we see the Father's desperate passion that waits and plots
and pursues his children. It is God's heart that thaws my cold heart and
draws me to be willing to risk and sacrifice for love.

Christ's death not only creates a relationship with God but also allows
us to have meaningful relationships with other people. Just as the status
of Adam and Eve's relationship with God determined their relationship
with others, so our relationship with Christ provides the foundation of
our relationship with others.

The message of the gospel is that we can stop running after love; we
have already been grasped by the Great Lover. The wild news of the gospel is that I no longer bear any condemnation and I have been invited to
be to others what the Father has become to me: an unnerving, persistent,
passionate lover.

The remarkable aspect of relationship is that the more aware we
become of the inconceivable glory of being forgiven, the more we hunger
to offer to others a taste of the same banquet. The more we see the petti-
ness and darkness of our hearts, the more aware we are of God's everlasting pursuit of our souls. It is then we hear God's voice, which invites us
never to forsake relationship any more than he has forsaken us.

Relationships: Above the Sun
We have found that healthy relationships can be found in our difficult
world, but not by seeking fulfillment and self-satisfaction. Rather, we
must give ourselves to others.

But we are a selfish people. Why in the world would we act in such a
selfless way? The second wise man would quickly chime in: "Fear God!"

The fear of God helps us to see that we have one and only one certain
relationship in which the other loves us unconditionally, even after knowing us with all our faults. Jesus Christ knows our ugly side, and he loves us

anyway. Instead of recoiling from us, he moves more passionately into our lives. If we open our hearts to both his unfailing love and the certain failure of all other love, then we will no longer be surprised by betrayal, but we will anticipate how the failure of others will deepen our love for Christ. And enjoying his love for us will always take us back into our struggle to love others, since he loves them as much as he loves us.

Our relationship with Christ is the footing that makes all other imperfect relationships possible and even potentially rich. It also enables us to endure harmful relationships in which physical and mental abuse has wreaked havoc in our lives.

After all, Christ loves us in spite of our rebellion against him. He has forgiven us, and that gives us the will to forgive others and move toward reconciliation. It also gives us the freedom to recognize our own faults and allows us to "remove the plank" from our own eyes. What else could motivate us to do anything but look out for our own interests?

Looking at relationship from Christ's perspective (above the sun) gives us hope because we know that heaven will be a time of wonderful community, a time of perfect intimacy. The perfect relationships of Eden will be restored. It is from this "eternal" perspective that we are to endure all failures and betrayals. There will be a day of reconciliation for those whose lives are covered by the hope of the cross. Our deepest desire in relationship, intimate oneness, will be perfectly and gloriously fulfilled.

But not all is dark even in our present relationships. We get glimpses of heaven even now. We can't find our ultimate meaning here, but with Christ as our foundation, we can find some measure of fulfillment and support in marriage, friendships, and other relationships. The wonder is that the more relationships grow, the more we care for others. Only relationship with Christ can give us that above-the-sun perspective.

THE piece she had learned bored her. She had played it so often that she could play it backward. She had tried to do it once and got through at least half the song before she quit and played it through the right way. She liked it better backward.

➤ *How Do We Chase after* **Relationships**?

1. Think about the relationships you presently enjoy. Would you characterize them as healthy? destructive? nurturing? abusive? trusting? suspicious? supportive?

2. How important are your relationships to you? Do you consider yourself a social person? a loner? a family-oriented person?
3. Does God matter in your relationships? Which ones and how?
4. When a child grows up and leaves or a friend moves out of town or a spouse goes on a short business trip, do you find yourself devastated? Why or why not?
5. Whom do you put first in a relationship—yourself or the other person?
6. Would you consider yourself a jealous person or an indifferent person in relationships? If either one, why do you think that is the case?
7. What does it mean to have a relationship with Jesus? How does a strong relationship with him flavor your other relationships—marriage, friendship, children, business associates, etc.?
8. What Scripture passages help you anchor your relationship in Christ?

PART THREE

Chasing after
WORK AND MONEY

9

The Grind

THE PHONE rang early and Joan turned over, only to find that Noah was gone. Normally, he would be just rising from bed and beginning his elaborate series of early morning rituals. But he was gone!

They had driven home the night before in silence. Noah counted the minutes, plotting ways to shave a few from the drive. Joan had simply stared out the window, alternately waiting for the blast to come and sorely disappointed when Noah seemed oblivious to her presence. She hated his anger, but somehow she had come to hate being ignored even more.

The phone kept ringing. Joan stared at it, willing it to stop. But she reached over and silenced its irritating ring.

"Hello."

"Hi, Joan, this is Jessie. You know, from the Bible study." Joan's pause after Jessie had identified herself made both women feel uncomfortable. Joan was still fogged with sleep and worried about why Noah had slipped away so early. She simply had no context for Jessie's voice.

"I'm so sorry, Jessie. Of course I know you. I should have been up earlier, but I just woke up. Sorry."

Jessie stammered as well. "Oh, no problem, Joan. I should have realized how early it is, but I'm off to work in a few minutes, and Erin is sick. I either have to drop her off at the day care center, find someone to care for her, or stay home from work. I guess I am sort of caught up in my own day, and I wasn't thinking you'd be in bed."

Joan suddenly felt even more guilty. Not only had she not recognized Jessie's voice, but she also unknowingly had rubbed in the fact that she could sleep late, an option Jessie didn't have as a single mom. She needed to keep her job at the Doggie Do Drop Inn. Every time Joan thought of that name, she wanted to scream. *Who in the world would be dumb enough to name a pet store the Doggie Do Drop Inn? Doggie Do. Oh, brother!* But her irritation always moved to sadness when she thought of Jessie.

Jessie had been married for ten years to a violent alcoholic. Jim got drunk only a few times a month and rarely hit her or Erin, but he did frequently break things that Jessie valued. He felt terrible in the morning when he could remember his rampage, but most of the time he acted as if nothing had occurred. Jessie had learned to live with the rage, but she couldn't live with the disparity between Jim's home life and his life as a deacon and leader in the men's ministry at their church. No one knew or wanted to know about his bouts with alcohol because at church he was seen as a good man, warm, friendly, and always helpful.

Jessie had gone to the pastor and a few of the leading deacons to ask for help, but each time she had been told to trust God, remain submissive, and encourage her husband to remain involved in ministry. "Sooner or later, Jessie," she was told, "God will get his heart. And it's best not to bring this up again because it will only cause Jim's reputation to be questioned and cause more trouble for you in the long run." She had followed this advice for many years. Jim's reputation soared; he was well respected and liked. But she was slowly spiraling into a significant depression.

The breakup finally came when Jim left her for a woman he had met at a business meeting. Jessie was relieved beyond words. He had left her. She was free, and no one told her to be silent. She was ignored, subtly blamed, but free to live without the horror of wondering what would happen when Jim drank too much. But a new sadness replaced her old fears. She had to leave her daughter at a day care center. It broke Jessie's heart to see Erin cry as she left every morning.

Jessie was free from a cruel man, but she had the singular burden to provide for their daughter. Jessie alone stood between food and shelter—and utter poverty. Many mornings Jessie wondered if surviving Jim's rage and violence would be easier than working at a go-nowhere job.

This morning, Erin was sick. Not so sick she had to have her mom with her, just sick enough that Jessie could not take her to the day care center. On a whim, Jessie called Joan, hoping that she could watch Erin or simply turn on the TV and let her sleep in her cozy Big Bird sleeping bag.

Joan felt sufficiently guilty that she would have agreed to watch Erin even if she had had to postpone surgery or turn down an invitation to meet the queen.

Twenty minutes later Jessie and Erin were at the door. The conversation with Jessie was brief, but one interaction kept swimming in Joan's mind. Jessie was grateful beyond words, and Joan could feel no hint of the envy or the stiff tone that had slipped into the phone conversation. Instead, Jessie seemed preoccupied and resolute. It was as if she had put on her work face and was preparing herself for battle.

Just as Jessie turned to leave, she said, "I used to like pets. Then again, I used to like people. But now I live for payday. That's why I have to be there today. If I don't show up, he puts the check in the mail, and I won't see a dime for three days. Some days, I don't think I am a whole lot different from the horse meat they put in those little cans of dog food. So with that good cheer, I am off to work." She walked to her brown twelve-year-old Buick. She was off to work.

Joan got Erin nestled with her blanket on the family-room floor and turned on the television. Joan sat on the nearby couch and turned her attention to the cartoon. She watched as a superhero flew in the air to rescue a woman who had just fallen out of a window. She thought about God, wondering, *Does he fly? Or does he just watch little girls get sick and their mothers free-fall and then avert his eyes to avoid their sickening thud?* She was shocked at her own thought. Why had it come within seconds of seeing a red-caped superhero? The turn inside of her was all too strange.

It was equally strange that Noah had left no note or mentioned to her last night that he would be leaving early. But then maybe he had run away from home after the hassle with the car and the conversation with Jack and Marcia.

The phone rang again before Joan could finish the thought. It was Noah's secretary, Janet. "Hi, Joan. Noah asked me to call you. He had an emergency at work. The proposal Noah made yesterday has caused quite a stir here. The brass have planned another meeting to go over his proposal. It's a big meeting, Joan. Noah asked me to let you know not to worry. He will be back late tonight."

Joan was stunned. She didn't know whether to be upset or grateful that Noah had asked Janet to call. His secretary had never before relayed a personal message from Noah.

"Thanks, Janet. I'll wait to hear the news." She went back to the couch and tucked her knees under her chin. Tears cascaded down her cheeks. She didn't know why.

Since last night's Bible study and the conversation in the car, her life seemed to be sliding on black ice. She didn't see the ice, and there was nothing to be done. If she put on the brakes, she would spin more violently. She saw no point in turning the wheel, so she held on and waited to see what would happen next.

On the television the superhero was now wearing a suit and glasses. Somehow he looked much more like her vision of God: proper, well groomed, distant.

She could not sit for long. She had to rouse her two boys, make them breakfast, get them ready for the car pool, and then make a half dozen phone calls, snag several service people, and run a truckload of errands. She had planned to meet a friend for lunch, but she would cancel that in case Jessie didn't return soon enough to pick up Erin. The day was all penciled in on her daily planner. She looked over all the hours that were filled with mundane but necessary duties, and she thought about Noah winging his way to an important meeting she knew nothing about. *Why such a panic? Why such a quick demand to be in New York? He had to have known after he checked his E-mail last night. Why didn't he tell me?*

She sat back and looked at her life as it was sketched in her planner. Nothing *had* to be done. No corporation would quake if her prognostications were right or wrong. If she chose to stay in bed, the kids could fix their own cereal and drag their disheveled bodies to the corner to get a ride with Jimmy's mother. Even Erin would likely watch TV for hours and not need her to do a thing.

Joan was important for all the mundane matters that keep a home percolating along, but she felt as if her life were not crucial to anyone. If she just sat at the piano and did not finish the piece she was to play, what difference did it make?

Meaningless, meaningless.

The electricity in Timmy's room didn't work. She had to wait for the electrician, who said he would call sometime between one and four o'clock in the afternoon. Her time was not that important; the electrician could have said that he would be there between Tuesday and Friday, and she would wait. It was her job. She was not paid, but her room and board, the privilege to herd two wild boys who squawked like wild animals, and the meaningful opportunity to sleep with a man who did not even bother to inform his wife that he would need to go out of town, all came with the one requirement: waiting. She was a capital, first-class waiter. She waited on phones for credit-card personnel to clarify a charge no one in the house had made. She waited in line to pick up Noah's impeccably ironed, properly starched shirts.

The superhero made another bold leap into the air to save another damsel in distress. *Why are so many women falling out of windows in New York?* She thought, *Maybe they hate their jobs too and are either testing God or just giving someone else the chance to clean up the mess. At least the day wouldn't end in a fog of exhaustion and a sense of incompleteness that meant that many of the penciled plans had to be carried over to the next day's endless trail of tasks to be done.*

Joan rarely allowed herself to think about her life. She found it too disturbing. She had learned through her father and the daily drudgery of life that it is better to focus on the task, not meaning, not desire, and certainly not the pain that pulsed just below the surface.

She looked at Erin, tucked away in the yellow sleeping bag, sucking her thumb, her brown ponytail tied back by a green rubber band. Erin looked contented; she was lost in the flurry of danger and rescue, evil and good locked into the daily war of Gotham. *The two of us are the same,* thought Joan. *I'm just as wrapped up in my little world as Erin is in hers, and it all feels meaningless.*

Erin didn't think it was all meaningless. Her only job was not to whimper too loudly when her mommy left. She wasn't good at her job, but no one had complained yet.

Erin's mother was not so confident about her job. Jessie was like all employees who worked for the Doggie Do Drop Inn—ashamed of the name, uncertain about how much longer their work would last, and irritated by the petty mind-game politics the manager played with all the employees, especially the young or unmarried women.

The Doggie Do Drop Inn offered a combination of grooming services, pet supplies, and boarding kennels for the pets of yuppies. The Doggie Do, as the employees called it, was a strange combination of a Southern beauty parlor, pet convenience store, and animal jail. It was owned by an older woman who loved pets and dedicated her life to caring for as many animals on her five-acre ranch as the health department would permit.

She was a dear woman but had little business sense and even less desire to learn. She was involved enough to keep the shop going but relied on her nephew George to keep the place afloat. What the owner didn't know was that George siphoned off profits for his lecherous pursuits. The dark leather interior of his company-paid blue sports car had been the close quarters for many employee "conferences." Not many employees had slept with George, but those who did clearly had the best jobs, largest raises, and the choice vacation times.

George was clever enough never to cross the line of propriety in public and provoke a charge of sexual harassment, but he pushed the limit with his double entendres and lustful looks. Jessie had grown accustomed to being used by her husband on command and under conditions that made George look like a choirboy. But like all daily grinds, listening to George's remarks about her hair and the neckline of her dresses was like walking with a stone in her shoe. It was possible to continue, but at the same time the distraction and numbing pain made the journey almost impossible.

At times Jessie thought about slapping him, reporting him, or quitting. But each time she came to that point, she would envision her daughter Erin. She knew she would not be able to find a job that paid more unless she got some technical training or even a college degree. She was stuck. She made a decent living at her job, but she couldn't stand her life if she stayed at the Doggie Do.

She felt trapped, just as she had when she was in junior high school. Jessie was in seventh grade when a ninth grader discovered her alone in the band room. No one was near. She had to return a music score that she had accidentally taken from band to her next class. She knew enough not to wait until the next day to return the music and face the band director's shaming ridicule.

Just as Jessie had slid the music under the band-room door with a note about her failure and a sincere apology for any inconvenience she had caused, she saw Todd looking up the stairs at her. She blushed when she realized that the large drummer had been looking up her skirt as she had bent over to slide the score under the door. She tensed as she walked down the stairs. Todd blocked her path and began to move against her motion.

She backed up a stair. He moved forward. They continued this dance until she was pressed against the band-room door. Todd snarled, "If you open your mouth, you will pay. Just shut up." She had not even thought about screaming. Her heart had stopped as soon as she had realized he was going to push her against the wall and touch her the way her older brother had done for years.

Jessie knew to stop breathing, to stop thinking, and to stop feeling. She let him grope her, and she bit her lip and closed her eyes to go where boys could not imprison her with their looks, their sly words, and their roaming hands. When he finished, he looked into her eyes. She would not look back. He grabbed her face and put his face inches from hers. "See you again, baby. Hope you had fun." He turned and bounced down the stairs, laughing. Jessie straightened her blouse and skirt and wiped away a tear that had slipped down her cheek.

Another day at school. Another day of walking into another trap. She would do better tomorrow. She would be smarter, quicker. She wouldn't be caught alone next time. She knew she was as helpless as a doe blinded by headlights, its heart beating until it was ready to explode, ready for the flesh-ripping impact. Helpless to move out of the way, she just wanted someone to swoop down and take her away.

Help never came.

George was just another Todd. Work was just another day at school. Jessie wanted to quit, but there was no escape. And so she waited until George dropped her check on the floor so that she would have to bend down to get it. Then he would either crouch down so he could look at her in this compromising position or wait until she bent over and watch her bow before his mocking prank.

Was it worth it? Why work and be humiliated when all she wanted was to provide for her child? All she wanted was to be treated with respect, and all she got was mindless, soulless work and demeaning mockery. She didn't know if it was because she was a Christian, a divorced woman, or merely a woman. She did know there were no safe places.

AT THREE o'clock Jessie called Joan to report apologetically that she had to work overtime in the warehouse. She said her boss would press her hard if she didn't do it. Her voice, which sounded frantic, became very faint, and Joan thought she heard someone laughing in the background. She assured Jessie everything would be just fine.

Jessie responded, "Yes, Joan. Someday it will. Thank you."

Jessie's voice made Joan want to cry, but she held back her tears and told her again, "Take your time. Erin and I will be here when you get done at work."

Joan had spent the day watching Erin watch television. She could not even recall if she had made lunch for her boys. Somehow they had gotten off to school. All the phone calls, errands, and other to-do-list demands had been lost in the wake of the meaninglessness of the day. She liked listening to Erin laugh. Joan wanted to crawl into the Big Bird sleeping bag with Erin, but she decided it would be an unlikely fit.

When the phone rang again, Joan jumped off the couch to get it. All day long she had expected Noah to call. She caught her breath and tried to slow down to sound as normal as her racing heart would allow. "Hello."

"Hi, Joan. This is Jack."

"Jack, I . . . I was not expecting you."

"Well, Joan, you don't need to sound so disappointed it's me. But were you expecting another call?"

Joan didn't know what to say. She felt exposed. She bit her lip, and then spoke quietly: "Yes, Jack. I haven't heard from Noah all day, and he left this morning so early I didn't talk with him. I'm afraid. I'm afraid about—"

"Last night," Jack spoke with equal quiet and intensity.

"Yes."

Jack must have leaned back in his leather-covered desk chair because Joan could hear the squeak and groan of the swivel. Jack's voice was reassuring. "Joan, I'm not surprised, but obviously I'm disappointed. I had prayed Noah wouldn't ignore the discussion in the car or turn it on you.

But I want you to know we will not leave you alone in this situation. You spoke boldly and kindly last night to him. I suspected you would suffer either guilt or loneliness today. Marcia and I plan to fight this battle with you. I plan to call Noah this week to set up a time to have a meal with him before the next Bible study. Marcia and I wanted you to know we will be praying for you."

Joan felt light-headed and speechless. She didn't know what to say. She looked down at the multicolored pad of paper next to the phone. The pad was wet with a pool of tears. She had not even been aware she was crying. Somehow she thanked Jack and told him she appreciated his willingness to pray and meet with Noah.

Joan walked back to the couch. She looked at the TV, hoping against hope that the caped crusader was still rescuing Gotham's citizens. She so wanted to see him rescue someone.

10
"Money Ought to Make Me Feel Free"

OUR advertising-heavy culture screams at us in countless ways that if only we have enough money, life will be meaningful. We look to money to bring us security, freedom, pleasure, and power.

Do any of these scenarios sound familiar to you?

"FOURTEEN hundred in the account and fifteen hundred in bills! How's that going to work? I guess I can wait a month to pay a couple hundred on the credit card, but I hate to do that. I promised myself I would not let the balance get over two thousand. But what else can I do?"

- *"It's not as if we are living extravagantly. Can we hold back on food? house payments? kids' braces? Maybe Christian-school tuition or giving to the church, but that would be a compromise with another commitment."*

- *"It makes me feel small, and not just me but my wife as well. Once all the kids were in school, she started back as a part-time accountant. We both work hard. We thought the two incomes would do it, but it seems that no matter how hard we work and how much money we earn, the bills just get larger and larger. Is it my imagination? We just never seem to have enough. We've all but given up on our dream of a small cabin on the lake."*

- *"My boss—he seems to have enough. That car he drives sure flaunts it, and so do his clothes. I'll bet he even has his secretary take care of his bills; he probably doesn't have to write the checks himself. I'd sure like his money, but not his life. He probably never sees his family. Maybe he doesn't care, but I couldn't stand it."*

DOES this sound familiar to you? Do you have similar thoughts at bill-paying time? Whether you earn minimum wage or pull in a six-figure salary, you likely have the feeling that just a little more would be enough. But when that little more comes, it seems to run through your hands so quickly that it feels as if you are trying to grab the wind.

Work can be a despairing reality. Most people spend nearly half of their waking life commuting and working. As E-mail, faxes, beepers, and car phones increase, so does our workweek.

Noah loves work and the challenge of the hunt and kill. Jessie is stuck. She is untrained and ill equipped to meet the challenges of the nineties. She can be easily replaced; consequently, she feels compelled to endure the abusive working conditions of her job. Joan feels lost in the mundane, routine tasks of remaining at home. She feels unappreciated. Her emptiness is complicated by a husband who loves his work more than his wife.

Few people are happy with work. Few feel as if they have enough financial wherewithal to survive, let alone thrive.

Let's Be Honest

People who say that money is not important to them are either liars or fools. The truth is we can't live without it in our modern society.

All of us are vitally concerned about the issue of money, even people who can get by with little in life. After all, without money we can't eat or have a roof over our heads. So most of us work to earn money just to be able to live in modern society.

Certainly, some people are satisfied with the money they have, but then they yearn for more than money for their labor. As a professor at a seminary, I (Tremper) have met many devoted men and women who have left lucrative careers because they are not happy with their work in spite of the high pay. They desire more than money; they want to make a difference in life. Some of these people, as devoted as they are, go into the ministry and are surprised to find that their work life is still filled with anguish and frustration. The sense of meaning and fulfillment they expected to find in the ministry seems to be as fleeting and temporary as wealth itself.

But many people are like Noah. He loves his work and is adept, driven, and well paid. Noah lives for whatever brings a sense of control and reward—now.

Noah's life is so different from Joan's. Joan is a stay-at-home mom. Her work is without pay, most often unappreciated, and noticed only if it's not done to Noah's expectations. She feels ambivalent. She loves her kids; she loves the freedom not to be pressed each day to work outside the home. But Joan is overwhelmed at times with the routine and isolation she faces. When she looks at Noah's life, she envies his freedom and sense of power; on the other hand, when she looks at Jessie's life, she thanks God she does not live a trapped existence.

Jessie's life reveals the dark side of work. She earns just enough to survive—but not well. She suffers at the whim of her boss and is too poor and powerless to object to his sexual harassment. Each day she suffers not only a boring routine and meaningless interactions but also demeaning intrusions that make her life miserable. For Jessie, money is scarce, and work is a labor of survival. For love of her daughter she suffers daily degradation.

Most people fit somewhere between Noah and Jessie. We live for work, feel ambivalent about our situation, or hate our jobs and work solely to survive.

Money, wealth, and work. They are important to us and take up most of our time and energy. We pursue them, expecting to find meaning and purpose through them. It's not surprising that the Bible and, in particular, the books of Proverbs and Ecclesiastes have much to say about these topics.

The Value of Money

Most people think that the Bible frowns on wealth and hard work. They commonly quote the saying, "Money is the root of all evil," forgetting that the verse actually says, "The *love* of money is at the root of all kinds of evil" (1 Tim. 6:10, italics added).

The book of Proverbs informs us of the value of money:

The wealth of the rich is their fortress;
   the poverty of the poor is their calamity. Proverbs 10:15

The earnings of the godly enhance their lives,
   but evil people squander their money on sin. Proverbs 10:16

Wealth makes many "friends";
   poverty drives them away. Proverbs 19:4

The wise have wealth and luxury,
   but fools spend whatever they get. Proverbs 21:20

NOWHERE does the Bible say that the rich are heading toward perdition by virtue of their wealth. Indeed, many of the "heroes" of the Bible were fabulously rich people. Think of Abraham, Jacob, Joseph, David, Solomon, and Joseph of Arimathea. Job was an exceedingly wealthy man for his day. God took away his wealth in order to test him, but after the test, God gave Job even greater wealth.

The Teacher of Ecclesiastes knew well that wealth gives people authentic enjoyment and is something to be desired. In Ecclesiastes 7:11-12, he talks about how wisdom is superior to money, but he does so in a way that, far from denigrating money, recognizes its value: "Being wise is as good as being rich; in fact, it is better. Wisdom or money can get you almost anything, but it's important to know that only wisdom can save your life."

And then hear what he says in Ecclesiastes 10:19: "A party gives laughter, and wine gives happiness, and money gives everything!" After all, one can't have a party or drink wine unless one has the money to pay for them.

In the early church and during medieval times, it was felt that money, like sex, was inherently evil. Spiritual people avoided both. The monastic life was the ideal of great spirituality. Those who followed God were both poor and chaste. Remnants of these ideas continue down to the present day.

But these ideas are foreign to the Bible and reflect Greek philosophy, which separated the body and the spirit. According to the Bible, money is not evil; it is a necessity and blessing from God. Hard work is not a sign of godlessness; it is a virtue.

Work was a part of the world that God created for Adam and Eve. Genesis 2:15 states this clearly: "The Lord God placed the man in the Garden of Eden to tend and care for it." Work was not the result of sin but a God-given responsibility that human beings were to enjoy and from which they were to derive satisfaction.

Indeed, in their work, Adam and Eve—created in the image of God—were reflections of their Creator. The Bible opens with a magnificent portrait of God, the Worker. Through his Word, he brought the cosmos into existence. He shaped it into a thing of great beauty. At the end of his work, then, God rested (Gen. 2:2). God intends our labor to be the place where we live out the same creativity he exhibited when he created the cosmos. Work is to be beautiful and thrilling. But for most people, work is a place of boredom or humiliation, frustration or failure.

The picture of work that we get from Genesis 1 and 2 is an extremely positive one. Adam and Eve labor together to develop what God has created. They "subdue" the earth, becoming "masters over the fish and birds and all the animals" (Gen. 1:28). They "tend and care" for the beautiful garden that God has given them (Gen. 2:15). And they do it together, in harmony with each other and with God.

The Futility of Work

Why then is our experience of work so difficult, its results so unsatisfying? Why do some people struggle to get a job and then, once they get it, dislike it so much? At the very least, we all view work as an obstacle to overcome rather than a purely wonderful and completely fulfilling part of our lives.

I write these words as someone who passionately enjoys his work as a teacher and a writer. I often can allow work to consume more of my heart and soul than it deserves. Indeed, I find it hard to contemplate anyone's relishing work as much as I do. However, those of us who like our work must honestly acknowledge its frustrations.

Just yesterday I got a small reminder of the pain of labor. I was writing this section about the irritations and setbacks of work when my computer screen went blank. I was working on my laptop computer out on my porch, using battery power. I knew that I might run out of power, but my computer automatically saves the file before it switches off. Under normal circumstances, though, it gives me a message that the file was saved. Ominously, no message appeared, and I was left staring at the screen.

Holding my breath, I quickly got the adapter cord and plugged it in. I turned the computer on and was greeted by a harsh grinding noise and blackness. My heart sank.

Hours later, after the battery was completely recharged, the screen flickered on. But when I searched for my file, I discovered that my morning's work had vanished into cyberspace.

Disappointment changed to anger. I had wasted a whole morning of valuable time! But then I remembered the topic of my writing. What else should I expect? Work, far from being an experience of joy and fulfillment, is fraught with obstacles and frustrations.

But why? The book of Ecclesiastes again articulates and explains the feelings that we have on a daily basis. The Teacher, mirroring the futility of the curse in Genesis 3, reminds us that all our labor is thwarted by the thorns and thistles of life. The Teacher did not anticipate computers or the computer demons that would snag a day's labor, but he did understand that all our work turns to dust and that all our labor is impeded by a world that doesn't easily respond to our touch. This is the inanimate enemy of work; there are other enemies that have faces.

The Teacher also recognizes that much of our work is motivated by envy. "Most people are motivated to success by their envy of their neighbors" (Eccles. 4:4). Envy is the lust to have what others possess.

This is a staggering truth. The Teacher suggests that we go to work with one central motive—envy. We see a coworker or a boss getting more money, more perks than we get, and we set out in hot pursuit to gain the same advantages. The kind of envy that the Teacher describes here is extremely destructive since it encourages people to get what they want at the expense of others. Envy creates a competitive rather than cooperative environment.

However, the Teacher notes that those who have the right motives don't always win. "I have observed something else in this world of ours. The fastest runner doesn't always win the race, and the strongest warrior doesn't always win the battle. The wise are often poor, and the skillful are not necessarily wealthy. And those who are educated don't always lead successful lives. It is all decided by chance, by being at the right place at the right time" (Eccles. 9:11).

This observation about life in general has obvious implications for our work. No matter how gifted, prepared, and honorable we are in carrying out our labor, we have absolutely no assurance that our work is going to be rewarded, financially or in any other way. Life is run by what appears to be brute luck. One person stumbles onto good fortune; another works a lifetime and doesn't seem to get a break. This insight often leads us to give up or live a life of daily disappointment.

But if the wise and the diligent don't win the day, who does? Here a proverb clues us in: "Beautiful women obtain wealth, and violent men get rich" (Prov. 11:16). This proverb, composed thousands of years ago, retains its validity today. The proverb is not saying that feminine or masculine beauty is inherently evil or wrong; it is just observing that physical attractiveness, a superficial quality, does give people an unfair advantage. In our surface-oriented culture, who is more likely to get a job or attention that leads to wealth? Someone who is fit and good looking.

We want to scream, "That's unfair!" or "It can't be true!" But we can see it in our own workplaces; violent people often prosper, while those struggling to serve God and help others often suffer. No wonder we envy those who succeed.

The Teacher does not say that the violent always prosper or that the godly are always held back. He would admit that it is possible to be righteous and to prosper, though he would probably suggest that it is rarely the case. But even occasional prosperity would not make him happy or temporarily relieved from his anxiety. The Teacher informs us that even the success of the godly has its sorrow.

He wants us to know that the frustration of work goes even deeper than failure. The tragic news is that success itself is unfulfilling. Even rising to the top of the ladder doesn't bring the fulfillment we might have expected. Once again, hear the wise words of the Teacher:

So now I hate life because everything done here under the sun is so irrational. Everything is meaningless, like chasing the wind. I am disgusted that I must leave the fruits of my hard work to others. And who can tell whether my successors will be wise or foolish? And yet they will control everything I have gained by my skill and hard work. How meaning-less!

So I turned in despair from hard work. It was not the answer to my search for satisfaction in this life. For though I do my work with wisdom, knowledge, and skill, I must leave everything I gain to people who haven't worked to earn it. This is not only foolish but highly unfair. So what do people get for all their hard work? Their days of labor are filled with pain and grief; even at night they cannot rest. It is all utterly meaningless. Ecclesiastes 2:17-23

THE TEACHER thinks deeply and takes things further than we often do in our need to survive day-to-day. But he is certainly right. We work hard and with integrity, but, as the Teacher tellingly observes, we will one day die. What will we leave behind, and to whom will we leave it? Possibly to people who will waste it, squander it. Who knows? We can't control it. So we work hard, but work always frustrates.

Futility of Money

Closely connected to work is money. One of the chief motivations for going through the agony of work is the need to get money. And why do we need money? As we mentioned earlier, money allows us to survive in modern society. We have to have money to buy food, shelter, and clothing.

However, it does not take a great deal of money to obtain these basic essentials, and even when we have enough food to sustain our bodies and adequate shelter to protect our bodies from the elements, we want more. Why?

At bottom, money is a refuge against fear and a weapon of our anger. We are afraid of what might happen to us, so money gives us the power and control that we need to fend off assaults.

We may be disgusted, for instance, by the O. J. Simpson trial. However, we also became witnesses to how huge wealth probably protected him from conviction and imprisonment, even if not from liability in a civil trial. People of lesser means would have been locked up or even given the death penalty for their crimes. If we are honest with ourselves, part of our aversion to the outcome comes from our realization that we don't have that kind of wealth to buy such protection for ourselves or our families.

Just this week, my father had major heart surgery. But he almost didn't get to the doctor on time. He tried, but the cardiologist he was supposed to see never returned his phone calls to schedule a catheterization. Finally, my mother asked another cardiologist friend to intervene and get my father in to have his heart checked. When my father went in for the appointment, the cardiologist determined that he needed to have surgery within the next few hours! The unreturned phone calls almost killed my dad. It made us all think. What would have happened if my parents had not had a friend with connections? What about poor people who have no connections, who have no one who can intervene for them?

Without money, we fear that we might be left alone, ignored, or mistreated in life. Money becomes a hedge against such treatment. In the case of Jessie, it is a simple and obvious fact. She is powerless because she lacks the financial means to report her lecherous boss to the owners of the Doggie Do or to a governmental agency. She might eventually gain legal redress, but in the meantime she would not be able to survive without an income. She is trapped by her poverty. Money is a shield against the ever present cruelty of life. Those without financial means not only are treated poorly but also are helpless to stop the harm.

Money is also the means by which "good care" is extended. My wife has noticed, for example, that department store clerks treat her better when she is wearing an expensive outfit than they do when she is wearing slightly worn jeans. This happens even among Christians. The New Testament writer James noticed that believers were more welcoming and supportive of well-to-do visitors than they were of those who came from the lower strata of society. He rightly reprimanded the church for this unfair treatment (James 2:1-13). James reminds us of our natural, though sinful, human tendencies. Consciously or unconsciously we envy people who have more than we do.

The Teacher recognized that people are attracted to the rich. We want to be around those who have money. Thus, one reason we desire lots of money is so that people will pay attention to us and give us the best treatment. It is a matter of control and power.

The control and power that money brings also serves the interest of our anger. We can display our anger toward others by withholding our money. If children do not live up to our expectations, we can withhold their allowance or cut them off from our will. If pastors make us mad in their sermons, we can quit tithing. If a leader doesn't please us, we express our anger by giving our support to another organization. Money becomes an avenue for distributing blessing and curses. Instead of feeling fear, we can create fear. Instead of stewing, we can vent our anger in a tangible way.

IN SUMMARY, we all need money to survive, but we don't stop there. We want more. We are all tempted to pursue money, even riches and wealth, for a variety of reasons: independence, fear, control, and anger. And that is why, in the final analysis, we feel that we can never get enough money. Wealth can never completely satisfy. Wealth can never fully protect us, enable us to have friends, or keep back the effects of the Fall. The Teacher speaks frankly about this when he laments:

> *Those who love money will never have enough. How absurd to think that wealth brings true happiness! The more you have, the more people come to help you spend it. So what is the advantage of wealth—except perhaps to watch it run through your fingers!*
>
> *People who work hard sleep well, whether they eat little or much. But the rich are always worrying and seldom get a good night's sleep.*
>
> *There is another serious problem I have seen in the world. Riches are sometimes hoarded to the harm of the saver, or they are put into risky investments that turn sour, and everything is lost. In the end, there is nothing left to pass on to one's children. People who live only for wealth come to the end of their lives as naked and empty-handed as on the day they were born.*
>
> *And this, too, is a very serious problem. As people come into this world, so they depart. All their hard work is for nothing. They have been working for the wind, and everything will be swept away. Throughout their lives, they live under a cloud—frustrated, discouraged, and angry.*
> Ecclesiastes 5:10-17

IN THESE verses, the Teacher specifies a few reasons why money, no matter how much we have, never satisfies and always leaves us craving more. For one thing, people latch on to rich people and take advantage of them. Those who have money must be hypervigilant against those who have targeted them for their money. A close friend of mine lives in a wealthy part of town and has found that service people often raise their prices when they see the size of her house. She ends up having to pay more for the same quality and quantity of work that other people get. It's hard for the middle class and the poor to feel sorry for the rich, but this does illustrate the Teacher's point that increased income results in increased expenses.

And, the Teacher knows well that hard-earned money can also quickly evaporate through wrong investments. In a single day, a dramatic stock-market shift can result in huge losses. There is no real security in a large bank account.

But isn't security what we hope money gives us? We want control and power over our lives. We want independence and a hedge against the changing fortunes of daily living. If anything, the Teacher reasons, money brings worry, not security. The working poor sleep well; the rich toss and turn wondering about their fortunes.

Money never brings ultimate satisfaction. It never gives us what we want. It doesn't give us independence. It lacks the power and control that it promises on the surface. When we get it, it proves to be a false ally and leads to disappointment, even despair. Proverbs articulates this well when it says, "Don't weary yourself trying to get rich. Why waste your time? For riches can disappear as though they had the wings of a bird!" (Prov. 23:4-5).

To think otherwise can lead to great danger and tragedy. Paul remarks that "some people, craving money, have wandered from the faith and pierced themselves with many sorrows" (1 Tim. 6:10b).

11

Restoring Work
through God's Glory

OUR work and money can't give us meaning. The rich are often the most
desperate; the poor are often happier and find greater fulfillment. There
seems to be no correlation between money and fulfillment. I saw this
recently on a ministry trip to Mexico.

Most people outside of Mexico know the Acapulco of glittering
beaches, sunny skies, and luxurious hotels. But over the mountains that
conveniently shield the rich is the real Acapulco, with around one mil-
lion people living in poverty. During the trip I found sad, lonely people
in the rich hotels and confident, happy people living in shacks. I also saw
the opposite, but the point is that it wasn't the money that determined a
person's love or hate of life.

Those of us who aren't wealthy create the illusion that if only we had more . . . But once we realize this, the question still persists, how can we navigate life and not lose purpose?

God created humans to work hard in the Garden and enjoy all of its pleasures. Even so, Scripture and experience tell us that work frustrates and money never satisfies. To put it another way, God's original plan arranged work to reveal our glory as cocreators.

The Lesson of the Fall

To understand our hearts, we have to look at work and money not only in the light of our creation but also through the prism of the Fall. After all, when Adam and Eve sinned, it had serious and explicit repercussions on our work life and on our enjoyment of God's good creation.

We see this specifically in the words that God speaks to Adam after his sin of rebellion: "Because you listened to your wife and ate the fruit I told you not to eat, I have placed a curse on the ground. All your life you will struggle to scratch a living from it. It will grow thorns and thistles for you, though you will eat of its grains. All your life you will sweat to produce food, until your dying day. Then you will return to the ground from which you came. For you were made from dust, and to the dust you will return" (Gen. 3:17-19).

These indeed are harsh words, but they ring true to our experience. We know the sweat and difficulty of working to eke out an existence, the labor that it takes to enjoy creation. Adam, after all, stood in our place. We are not being punished for the sins of another. We would have rebelled exactly as Adam did; our nature is inherently sinful.

In all of this, God is not cruel but actually abundantly gracious. He warned the first human couple that if they sinned, they would die (Gen. 2:17). He gave them (and us) life, and he is perfectly just in taking it away as well. And, indeed, because of our sin, death became a reality—but not immediate death. Death would eventually come, and in the meantime life would be hard.

But that is not the end of God's grace. Because of the curse, work is tough, and money, the modern gateway to enjoy the pleasures of creation, is never enough. But God did something that was totally unexpected. He provided a way out of the mess, at great sacrifice to himself.

He hints at this already in Genesis 3. In the context of the earlier curse on the serpent, whom we know stands for Satan, God says this: "From now on, you and the woman will be enemies, and your offspring and her offspring will be enemies. He will crush your head, and you will strike his heel" (Gen. 3:15).

As the Old Testament unfolds, this prophecy of redemption takes on clearer and clearer shape. Isaiah speaks of this redemption as something that costs us nothing! "For this is what the Lord says: 'When I sold you into exile, I received no payment. Now I can redeem you without paying for you'" (Isa. 52:3). And in Isaiah 55:1-2, the appeal goes out: "Is anyone thirsty? Come and drink—even if you have no money! Come, take your choice of wine or milk—it's all free! Why spend your money on food that does not give you strength? Why pay for food that does you no good? Listen, and I will tell you where to get food that is good for the soul."

The message is that we don't have to work to earn a place in God's heart; we don't have to pay money. Salvation is God's free gift. He is the One who pays for it on our behalf. Paul understood this when he said, "You know how full of love and kindness our Lord Jesus Christ was. Though he was very rich, yet for your sakes he became poor, so that by his poverty he could make you rich" (2 Cor. 8:9).

The riches Christ gave up for us far surpassed the riches of money or material things. Hear Paul again: "Though he was God, he did not demand and cling to his rights as God. He made himself nothing; he took the humble position of a slave and appeared in human form" (Phil. 2:6-7).

The bottom line is that as long as we strive to find our satisfaction and purpose in work or money, we are doomed to a life of meaningless futility. We are built for Eden, after all. Billions and billions of dollars cannot be enough for those of us who have been ejected from God's Paradise. We can never be happy with anything short of the restoration of that Garden, and only heaven can provide that. This knowledge is the best news of all.

Among the fascinating people that my wife, Alice, and I met in Acapulco were Willie and Bruni Bezemer. Willie works at the luxurious Princess Hotel as the head pastry cook, a prestigious job. While Willie was giving us a tour of the hotel and showing us many of his wonderful edible creations, he told us the story of his life.

Willie poured himself into his profession, working hard to achieve his international reputation. Though his wife was a Christian, he was more interested in cultivating his jet-set lifestyle. When he heard that the fabulously wealthy Howard Hughes was taking up residence in the top two floors of the hotel, Willie thought he had reached the crown of his career. He would create the most fabulous baked goods for the wealthiest man in the world.

When Hughes arrived at the hotel, he ordered a cinnamon bun. Willie did the work himself, using the best ingredients and giving the order his best attention. He sent up the pastry with great expectation, only to have it returned with the message that it was inadequate. Willie sent another, but again Hughes rejected the creation. After Hughes sent back Willie's third attempt at creating the perfect cinnamon bun, Hughes sent his private jet to his previous place of residence to retrieve an example of the type of cinnamon bun he wanted. When Hughes' servant brought Willie the bun, he couldn't believe his eyes. It was a piece of junk, the type of bun that anyone could pick up at a grocery store.

This experience brought Willie's world crashing around him. His life, which was wrapped up in his work, had no meaning. His years of dedication to his craft had no purpose.

But God had a purpose beyond anything Willie could imagine. Willie's crisis opened his eyes to Christ's love, which he saw displayed in his wife's love for him and for other people. After a time of questioning and exploration, Willie found his satisfaction in Christ. After that happened, he once again found joy in his work.

Purposeful and Redemptive Futility

What, then, is the proper attitude toward work and money? How does our fear of God drive us to a healthy view of our labor and material blessings?

Our work in a fallen world will always frustrate us, and we will be continually tempted to shield ourselves from cruelty, sorrow, and loneliness through money and work. But is this the final word? Of course not. God has a good purpose for our struggles with work and money.

God wants us to face our illusion that we can find any level of real happiness in what we do or how much we earn. The message is the same through failure or success—no "it" is enough. Work is an "it"; money is an "it." Both involve objects and gain the benefit of buying objects. But acquiring things is a slippery slope. The more you get, the more you want. The more you want, the more dissatisfied you feel when you can't get it.

Money and work expose the depths of our depravity. Like relationships, work and money satisfy us initially but then leave us disillusioned, hungry for what no person or object can give us. Money and work are like a purgative that brings up all the ill inside of us, leaving us hungry for good food—a food that money and work can't possibly provide.

As Jesus taught, "You shouldn't be so concerned about perishable things like food. Spend your energy seeking the eternal life that I, the Son of Man, can give you. For God the Father has sent me for that very purpose" (John 6:27).

Once we begin to grapple with our illusions about work and money, we can pursue our daily labor in a way that leads perhaps not to satisfaction but at least to personal change. God's intention in work is to draw forth our sense of godlikeness in the joy of creating, making, shaping, and working.

In a fallen world, this joy is never complete. We always bump up against futility. But even futility is not the end of the story. Futility can serve the positive function of keeping us from making our work and money into idols. Our sense of futility also draws our hearts to the basis of true riches—Jesus Christ—and to the greatest work of all time—his labor of dying to pay our penalty of sin and rebellion.

This attitude can lead to an anticipation that asks, What is God going to do today in my work? How will he unnerve me, expose me, allure me, use me, bless me through my labor? We will be ambivalent about our work—hating it and loving it—but at least it will arouse us to look to the heavens to ask the question: God, what are you doing in my life?

After all, we now know that our work is not the most important thing in the world. If we falter in our work, we are not complete failures. If we are not rich in material possessions, it is not the end of the world. God loves us whether we are poor, middle class, or rich.

But even once we are purchased by the salvation that costs no money, we have to be on guard that we don't fall back on our idols of money and work. The Old and New Testaments are full of such warnings:

Trust in your money and down you go! But the godly flourish like leaves in spring. Proverbs 11:28

"No one can serve two masters. For you will hate one and love the other, or be devoted to one and despise the other. You cannot serve both God and money." Matthew 6:24

Stay away from the love of money; be satisfied with what you have. For God has said, "I will never fail you. I will never forsake you."
Hebrews 13:5

THE last passage tells us again why we don't need to be obsessed with money. God is the source of true riches. We always have him with us, even if we don't have a dime.

This does not mean it is wrong to work hard for a good salary. The Bible never condemns riches as such. It never discourages hard work either. Indeed, the Bible's harshest warnings are directed toward the lazy. Paul tells Christians to avoid those in the church who are lazy and those who don't "follow the tradition of hard work we gave you" (2 Thess. 3:6).

We are to be content with what we have. We may pursue a better job or a raise, but if we don't get it, we should never become angry or bitter. In the words of the Teacher, "Enjoy prosperity while you can. But when hard times strike, realize that both come from God. That way you will realize that nothing is certain in this life" (Eccles. 7:14). Riches, after all, will not help us at the end of our lives (Prov. 11:4).

Purposeful and Redemptive Blessing

But our "fear of God" drives us to concerns that transcend our needs and the needs of those nearest us. One of the surest signs of the heart's redemption is the desire to bless others with the fruit of our labors. Our attitude should always be one of generosity with what we have. Our ultimate goal, after all, is not to get financially independent or to be the richest person in our community. Our goal is to hear these words from our God: "Well done! . . . You are a trustworthy servant" (Luke 19:17). We live for our Father's blessing; it is to be the sweet, alluring energy behind all our labor.

We are not to work for power, protection, or the pleasures of this earth; we are to work for the words "Well done!" One of the most basic decisions about work is this: Do I work for *this* world, or do I work for the world to come? As the Scripture has made clear, there is nothing wrong with being rich, wanting more money, or working diligently with a thoughtful plan. The battle is simple: Will I work for myself or for

God? Even the middle ground of saying, "Well, I'm working for my kids' education" or "I'm working for our retirement so we are not a burden to the kids" or "I'm working for a small piece of the pie and a few earthly pleasures" can easily be a smoke screen to avoid the more basic issue of whether we are working for ourselves or for God.

One way to determine for whom you work is to ask yourself this question: Do I pray, plan, and perspire in my work to make more money so I can give more away? As you see needs in your community, do you ache to earn more to help a poor child get a week in the country and purchase a computer to join the world of knowledge and competency? Are you driven to earn more so that you can help a needy neighbor?

Don't misunderstand us here. It is not wrong to dream about getting yourself a new fly-fishing rod, a new car, or a new piece of furniture. None of these objects is wrong; all may lead to a small taste of heaven and can be used redemptively for the purposes of God. But wealth has one true, eternal purpose: to invite others to know God.

One man I know threw a staggeringly lavish Christmas party in order to attract his extremely well-to-do neighbors, business associates, and friends to join him in celebration. He also invited a few people from different countries, races, and socioeconomic settings to talk about their Christmas experiences. The wealthy guests were enchanted by the cultural diversity represented. What they weren't prepared for was having the African-American pastor talk about the poverty, heartache, and confusion of having to grow up with a white Santa who didn't deliver presents to his home.

When white guilt in the room was at its apex, the pastor shared that Christmas is not about Santa but about Jesus, who is neither black nor white, who was a helpless Jewish baby born to a poor family in a setting of squalor, with no future but to flee from the hatred of the ruling class. The pastor passionately described that Jesus' goal was to die—for us, all of us who are humble enough to cry out like the rich publican: Help me.

My friend gives his hard-earned money in order to bless the poor and the rich, the hungry and the well fed. Money is the means to give blessing and eventually to gain the one blessing our souls are most craving to hear: "Welcome home, my son, my daughter. Well done."

Work and Money: Above the Sun
In life under the sun, work is oppressive, and money, though necessary, is frustrating. We never have enough.

But this is the way it is supposed to be. If we were satisfied, we would not long for something better, something that can be satisfied only in heaven, that is, above the sun.

What is really important in life is not for purchase. It's free. It costs us nothing to have our sins completely forgiven and have the God of glory fill our life with spiritual blessings.

Once we have adopted this above-the-sun perspective, our work and money fall into proper perspective. We will no longer hate our work, even though it frustrates us. Work is not where we find our ultimate meaning. But we realize that we do not work for our boss, our company, or even for ourselves. We work for the glory of God. This is as true for those in sales as for those in the ministry; it is as true for the homemaker as for the missionary. All work has eternal significance.

Work also provides the venue for us to reflect our Creator. We are created in God's image, meaning that we have creative impulses that can be exerted in the work of the gardener, the janitor, the parent, the counselor, the politician, the minister, the student, the accountant, the pilot, the pet-store worker.

Money above the sun becomes a tool not for filling the void—it can't since we were made for Eden—but for enjoying God's creation and extending his kingdom. Since money doesn't purchase what is really important, we can hold it more lightly. Our fear of God informs us what is really important. As long as God is the most important thing in our lives, money and work take a proper subordinate significance to us and engender a contentment with what we have and a generosity toward others.

We realize that our lives on earth are a time of frustration, sacrifice, and loss. But the Bible teaches us that even small sacrifices today have eternal ramifications. We have left the riches of Eden and have been cast out into the wasteland. But we look forward to the restoration of Eden, indeed, a place that will make the Garden look bare (Rev. 21–22).

➤ *How Do We Chase after* **Money**?

1. Take a moment to assess your money situation. Would you consider yourself rich? poor? getting by? Are you contented with your present financial situation, or do you find it an occasion for anxiety or even panic?

2. Are you hopeful about the future in terms of your financial security, or are you depressed? Why?

3. Take a moment and assess your work situation, whether that work is outside the home or in it. Are you content with your work? Do you enjoy it or hate it? Why or why not?

4. Would you consider yourself a workaholic? How would your spouse or close friends characterize you?

5. Is your chief motivation in your work to earn money to survive? to thrive? to gain prestige in the eyes of others? to help others?

6. In what ways do you relate Christ to your financial and work situation? In what ways do you tend to keep your finances and work separate from your spiritual life?

7. How can finding your ultimate meaning in Christ help you have a more balanced perspective about money and work?

8. What Scripture passages can help you maintain that balance?

12

The Bible Study

THE REST of the week had passed in silence. Noah never spoke to Joan about his early morning departure or the important meeting. He mentioned he might be traveling to New York again to answer questions raised by his Pearson report. He was neither direct nor evasive. Noah was an efficient and clear reporter about life after the fact. When uncertainty had been resolved, he would report the data and explain why he had made a particular decision. But in the middle of any situation, he was curt and to the point.

He never mentioned to Joan whether Jack had called or whether they had made plans to have a meal together. As she dressed for the Bible study, Joan knew she would not gain any ground by asking Noah why he wanted her to drive by herself to Jack's house. He had merely told her to meet him there, that he would come straight from work, and that he would eat a sandwich in the car.

Joan drove to the study and wondered whether it would be better not to go. She had not called Jessie to find out how Erin was feeling. She had simply let the sorrow of her life pass in the flow of busyness. She had not called Jack to find out whether he had spoken to or met with Noah. She had not returned a call Marcia had left on the answering machine. Driving alone to the Bible study felt like going to a movie by herself. She hoped no one would see her arrive unaccompanied.

Jack greeted her warmly at the door, "Well, stranger, welcome. You are the first to arrive, and I'm thrilled to catch you before anyone else comes." Joan felt her throat tighten. She didn't want to talk. She had already concluded it was best to put last week's conversation on hold. Noah had told her he had a lot on his mind; he was clear he didn't want to be troubled with extraneous matters when his work was so demanding and volatile.

She didn't understand his stress at work, but she knew it was consuming, and it was time to be quiet. She was afraid her heart might side with Jack's desire to see Noah grow, and then she might be seen as an enemy, a betrayer of his secure world by letting Jack in through a side door. She looked away from Jack but followed him into their spacious living room.

She loved the room, which felt like a Colorado ski lodge. The huge stone fireplace blazed with warmth, and the leather couches beckoned her to sit and put up her feet on the antique blanket chests. As she sat, she noticed a strand of Mardi Gras beads that Jack's kids had hung on one antler of a ten-point buck. Joan loved the interplay of refinement and playfulness.

Jack sat down in a red leather Queen Anne chair. He looked regal and intense, younger than his fifty-five years. Joan blushed and again looked away. She hoped the doorbell would ring and save her from the encounter. Marcia was either dressing or aware not to disturb their conversation. "Joan, let me cut to the chase. I could never get Noah to return a call. I chose not to call at home. I will not embarrass him or prod him, but please be assured, I am not easily put off or discouraged." He rose. He seemed to sense there was no need to talk. "Joan, what can I get you to drink? You seem too comfortable to get up. Sit and let me serve you."

As he walked to the kitchen, the bell rang, and Joan felt a slight chill from the wind as Marcia answered the door. She shivered, rose, and turned to see Noah. He seemed immediately perturbed to see only Marcia and Joan and no one else from the study. He quickly regained his composure, but he entered the house with labored steps.

Noah greeted Marcia, then slid past Joan without a touch or any indication of warmth as he walked into the kitchen to talk with Jack. Joan could hear the comfortable chitchat of two men who seemed to enjoy each other but also had no intention of departing from familiar banter.

Within a short time the others arrived. The more people came and sat down in the living room the more the room seemed to breathe an air of gentility and care. Jessie was the last to arrive. Joan had no way of knowing how Jessie felt about their lack of contact through the week. She looked worn and threadbare. Her smile seemed forced. Jack eventually called for everyone to gather in the living room to get things started.

Jack was an expert at beginning a study. After a brief prayer, he began a review of the control, power, and relationship issues they had covered in the previous weeks. Noah looked cautiously at Jack as he talked about the unbidden intrusions that God often sends to remind us we are not the captains of our own fate. He listened intently to see if Jack would hint at or allude to his car being towed or the unpleasant interchange in the car. Noah imagined that many of Jack's references were intended to be heard as pictures of his incessant demand to be in control.

The discussion was lively, and for over an hour Jack elicited thoughts about how each group member attempted to manage the unmanageable and control the direction and speed of the wind. Mimi was the only one clearly unwilling to speak. She finally said, "We've talked about control, relationships, and work. Nothing in any of those areas is going well for me. I can't stop some really bad things I'm doing. I just broke up with another guy. And I haven't been able to find a job that I like or want to keep. I'm at a point where even working at the Doggie Do Drop Inn looks good." Jessie glared at what felt like a swipe at her dead-end life. No one in the room could have missed sensing the immediate and steep tension.

Jack spoke directly, "Good. We finally got to the passage I wanted to talk about. It brings together the issues of control, relationships, and work. Before we address the current tension in the room, look again at Ecclesiastes 4, verses 1 through 4. I'm reading from the New International Version. 'Again I looked and saw all the oppression that was taking place under the sun: I saw the tears of the oppressed—and they have no comforter; power was on the side of their oppressors—and they have no comforter. And I declared that the dead, who had already died, are happier than the living, who are still alive. But better than both is he who has not yet been, who has not seen the evil that is done under the sun. And I saw that all labor and all achievement spring from man's envy of his neighbor. This too is meaningless, a chasing after the wind.'

"Let me be blunt, folks. This room, frankly any room where more than two people sit, is full, just chock-full of jealousy and envy. You may doubt this fact, but every married man in this room is to a degree envious of his wife's life; and the other side of the equation is equally true. Every wife sees her husband living a life she wishes to some extent she lived. You two single women envy the married people; the married couples wonder how much better their lives would be if they could be single and start over. Mimi, no doubt you envy Jessie in part for having a child; Jessie, I can't believe you don't at times wonder how much easier it would be if you didn't have to support Erin and could be as free as Mimi.

"Look at Mark and Suzi. They are still in the glow of the first year of marriage. They both have good jobs. They don't yet have children. They are free and happy. To be honest I can look at your lives and feel a pang of desire—no, envy—that at your age you know so much that most of us didn't even begin thinking about until it seemed as if it was too late. We will never get very far in this study or in relationship with each other unless we can at least acknowledge to ourselves the envy and jealousy that stirs inside of us as we look at each other's lives."

Jessie was near tears. Her eyes did not stray from the carpet. Joan was dry eyed, but she glanced up from looking at her feet and then returned to a faraway gaze as she looked into the eyes of the buck. Mimi sat defiant and stoic.

Jack continued, "I suspect we are at a crossroads of some sort tonight. There are few things more humbling to admit to than envy. It implies we are both desperate and dark. By desperate I mean really, really unhappy and empty. Or, let me put it another way. We feel incomplete and unsatisfied with who we are and what we have. By dark I mean committed to getting what others have, no matter the cost. It's not a pretty picture. Of course, it is easier to believe and promote a different view of ourselves. But the Teacher in Ecclesiastes tells us that we feel unprotected, alone, and powerless. The Teacher cuts to the chase to then say it seems better to be dead. I suspect he means physically dead, but I don't think it is inconceivable also to add that it is easier to be internally dead, numb, silent about our situation."

Jack began to talk about how he had become a successful lawyer. The story was simple. His older brother, who had been a great athlete, had won the acclaim of Jack's dad, who thought intellectual pursuits were for sissies. His father was a hardworking, lower-level executive working for Ivy-League men. He hated their lavish corner offices and their disdain for his pull-yourself-up-by-the-bootstraps work ethic. Jack's brother was stocky, tough, and gritty enough to outdo the bosses' sons. Jack, on the other hand, gravitated to the lifestyle of his father's enemies' sons. Jack was never forgiven, though he was never thwarted from being successful. He was simply ignored.

Jack talked about his battle with envy and the fuel it provided to succeed. He also talked about the effects on Marcia and their children of the hollow benefits of his success. He described how he and Marcia had battled with alcohol. He shared how he had betrayed several good friends in his passion to achieve and gain his father's blessing. Tears streamed down his cheeks as he spoke.

The room was no longer full of tension and disjointed eye contact. Joan stared at Jack. She had lost all awareness of the people around her. She had never, ever thought of herself as envious. She was a happy, contented woman. She knew she was not jealous of the single women, or even Mark and Suzi. She did not want much of anything at all. She suspected her lack of desire, her quiet contentment, was more a flight from sickness, the desperate emptiness that Jack spoke of earlier.

She glanced out of the corner of her eye at Noah's face. It was expressionless; all color had faded from his cheeks. He looked marblesque, frozen. She felt sick.

Jack returned to the text of Ecclesiastes 4. "Look at the key issue. We are alone, lacking someone who will keep us from oppression in the past, present, or future. It weighs heavily on us. We want someone to rescue us from injustice now. God simply doesn't seem to spend too much of his day rescuing people from oppression.

"On the other hand, someone is getting his favor. And of course, we wonder why it's not us. We are terrified and angry. We assume others are happy, and we wish God would either bless us or just not hurt us. Does this seem too strong?"

Mimi had softened. She looked at Jack like a young girl might look at her father the first time she really realized that older people cry, hurt, and are confused too. "Thanks, Jack. And Jessie, I'm sorry. I know life is not a bowl of cherries for you either. I didn't mean . . . I guess I did mean to take a whack at you for working at the Do Drop. I'm sorry." Mimi's brief apology worked a magic on the group. Jessie brightened.

Joan sat forward, and even Noah spoke. "Jack, do you mean to tell me every day when I get up and go off to work, I'm motivated by envy?" Noah's voice was not strained with fight or incredulity. For Noah, the question was both honest and revealing.

"No, Noah. I assume better about you. You are a Christian. You are a man who knows there is something above the sun, or in different language, you actually fear God. At any one point, Noah, we might deny that by the way we live, but the Spirit of God is in you, nudging you, wooing you, convicting you that he is God. But I suspect that like any of us, you have moments that are tinged with envy. True?" Noah smiled and relaxed. He did not feel attacked. He began to think about envy in his life.

Jack spent a few more minutes connecting jealousy and envy to his marriage, friendships, and work. There were many nods of agreement, questions, and the comfortable laughter of a group that had suffered disruption but had been rescued from the brink of disaster. Joan felt oddly cold and warm, relaxed and even more tight than when she had first come in the door. She wanted to feel hope that Noah might talk to her, but she knew it was a dream that felt too dangerous to hold.

PART FOUR

Chasing after
PLEASURE

13

The Dinner

THE NEXT two weeks melted into a routine of early morning departures. Even Noah's ritual presleep routines were disrupted. Many mornings he never bothered to let Joan know whether he was going to be late, and many nights he simply went to bed, without reading a few pages of a financial quarterly.

Days passed. Noah spoke only if Joan or one of his sons asked him a question. Joan had never felt more excluded. She blamed herself for Noah's silence or anger, she didn't know which. She just knew that one unplanned, inadvertent conversation in a car had changed her life for weeks.

Joan sensed that Noah's situation at work was becoming even more tense. One morning he had made a remark indicating that his job might be on the line. Joan knew better than to ask. She found herself checking job ads in the newspaper in case the unthinkable happened. She was more frightened at Noah's silence than at the prospect of having to go back to work.

One morning when Joan walked into the closet, she noticed that Noah's travel bag, his best suits, and several of his most expensive, starched shirts were gone. She immediately looked to see if he had packed his shaving kit. It was gone as well. Her heart sank. Her mind began to race. She could not conceive of his leaving her. She could not even imagine Noah having an affair, let alone a relationship with another woman. Thoughts laced with inconceivable fears pumped through her veins with adrenaline force. It was the longest morning of her life.

Joan waited all morning. Just before lunch, she called Noah's office. She was put on hold before she could get through. She waited, and her hand quivered. Several times she almost hung up.

"Good morning, Brothers Consolidated. This is Noah Adamson's office. How may I help you?" Janet, Noah's secretary, offered.

"Ah, hi. This is Joan. Is Noah available?"

A long pause was followed by a hesitant response: "Joan, I'm sorry. Noah is in New York. He left on the six o'clock flight to La Guardia. He will be in meetings all day. Do you want me to have him call you? He should be calling in for his messages before the day ends."

Joan felt a wave of humiliation that made her pulse beat loudly in her ears. She heard the question, but she could not speak. She could not ask Janet to remind Noah that he had a wife. "Yes, please have him call." She hung up before his secretary could speak.

The day hung in the balance between fear that cut her into jagged pieces and errands that for brief periods enabled her to forget Noah and her dark imagination. Her hope shattered each time the phone rang and it was not Noah.

Just before dinner Noah finally called. Joan was sick and exhausted as she answered the ring.

"Hey, babe. Noah." In nearly fourteen years of marriage, Noah had never called her any endearing nickname, let alone *babe*. Not that babe was endearing, but it was a huge stretch beyond his normal, formal greetings. "Hey, I'm real sorry I didn't—Hold on, Gary, I'll be with you in a minute—I didn't let you know what was happening. But I was too tired to tell you about this trip last night when I found out I had to be in New York. Anyway, the meeting is going to stretch on through tomorrow. I had a flight home, but it isn't going to work. So—Hey, Gary, hang on. Don't leave me here. I don't know where we are eating—Sorry, Joan, but we are heading out to eat and drink away the day. Don't worry. They are drinking. I am their designated taxi hailer. The meeting is still a toss-up. I will either be the goat or the hero. At the moment, I have sprung horns, and if I keep talking and making the big boys wait, I'll have a full-fledged tail. I'll call you when I can. Bye, hon."

Joan put the phone into its cradle. She felt sick, alone, and lost. *Hon.* He had never called her hon. Was he drunk? Was he talking for someone else's benefit?

NOAH felt sick. He had just been cruel to his wife; he knew it. He hung up the phone and turned to look at the three men in nearly identical gray suits. They were differentiated by their ties. Their tan faces marked them as successful and sophisticated players in the game of life. They stole occasional glances at Noah; they were either anxious or furtively hiding their patronizing pity. He could not read them. If he could interpret their fleeting looks, then perhaps he could determine whether he was going to have a job tomorrow or be out on the street.

The meeting had been six hours of territorial marking. The eight big dogs in the room, including the two men who owned Brothers Consolidated, had spent the first few hours analyzing Noah's report on the Pearson Furniture deal. Figures glided around the room like streaking pigeons only to land a few feet further away from their original pecking point. Then another flurry of financial spreadsheets would land after being scattered by one of the big boys. It was a give-and-take, high-stakes poker game whose players were less concerned about winning than merely protecting their gilded chips.

Noah knew he was the interloper—the Chicago hotshot analyst who had stirred up trouble. It was not merely the Pearson deal; Noah was challenging the way Brothers Consolidated had been doing business for years. The firm had been established by the Andrajian brothers, two Armenians who had come to the U.S. soon after their parents had been killed in one of the least-known and least-cared-about holocausts. The Turkish slaughter of the Armenian innocents had never gained the notoriety of other twentieth-century holocausts, in part due to the fierce pride and silence of the Armenian people themselves. They mingled in the society at large, developed immense real-estate holdings, and swore fierce loyalty to their new country, but their hearts beat for their own slaughtered countrymen.

Money for the Andrajian family was not a matter of wealth or privilege; it was the green necessity to honor the savage murder of their mother and cruel torture of their father. It was the bulwark against future holocausts.

Everyone who worked for the Andrajian empire knew unconsciously that money was not a mere commodity but a religious icon that enabled the owners to honor the blood that still cried for justice. To lose money was not a mere failure; it was an assault against a heritage, a country, a family, a memory of suffering.

No one in the meeting wanted to risk his privilege; no one wanted to challenge a system that had been established by the brothers Andrajian and had worked for twenty years to produce one of the strongest, most successful stock firms in the country.

Noah had known he was taking a huge risk; he simply had not known the extent of the peril or the weight of the cultural stream in which he had chosen to throw his small, flat-backed stone. And he could not tell after six hours whether the stone had skipped effortlessly to land on the other side of the stream or had sunk at the first touch of the water.

What he did know was that he could not decline to go out to eat and get a few drinks with his three compatriots. After a day of posturing and plotting, it was required to go out to the watering holes of the city to do the same. At least he would be able to take his coat off. He wanted desperately to go back to his room at the Four Seasons and crawl into the womb of his bed.

Instead, he would follow the flow of money and conversation to learn how to proceed into tomorrow's jousting for place and power. He wondered what Stephen and Sam Andrajian would do this evening. He could never understand why they insisted that their employees stay in one of the most expensive hotels in New York City while they stayed in the same small room at the Algonquin, a writer's hotel full of history, dark corners, and the ghosts of Hemingway and Virginia Woolf.

"C'mon, Noah, it's time to go float your boat. We're going to let you decompress after that marathon," said James, the head analyst over the entire Andrajian empire. "Well, ol' boy, you were fairly subdued after your initial report. What were you doing? Watching us flap about to make sure you were there at the end like a vulture to pick up the pieces? You certainly were a man of few words after you dropped the bomb. A regular Truman. But we'll see tomorrow where the buck stops." James laughed with a hearty but ominously deep-textured roar.

The evening was spent over a multicourse meal at Il Mulinos, a decadent, calorically blind Italian restaurant. Five waiters hovered over the delivery of hors d'oeuvres, fresh olives, breads of Olympian glory, and salads that made even the sophisticated Epicureans swoon. The wine steward had been told to provide for them with little regard to the cost. The first wine cleansed the palate. Their second wine tingled the taste buds and announced the arrival of a passionate repast that could neither be fully eaten nor allowed to be scraped into the holding bin for uneaten food. It was torture, a culinary seduction that could not be resisted even if one were tied to the mast as the sirens began to serve pasta.

By the time the main course arrived, Noah had forgotten about the day. He had forgotten about Joan, the awful phone call. He had even forgotten about the day ahead. Pleasure had erased his past; it had expunged his future. For the first time in a week, he felt free and happy. Noah nipped at his fourth glass of wine. He was not unfamiliar with imbibing, but tonight he consumed far more than normal.

The intense interactions of the last few weeks, from his initial Pearson presentation to Joan's disruptive conversation in the car with Jack and Marcia, faded slowly—as did Noah's focus. He looked at his watch and noticed that he had to stare with intensity to distinguish the small and large hands on his watch.

The evening passed with convivial jocularity, risqué humor, and the boasting of people, places, and privileges. Noah was quiet, but he laughed more than he had in a long time. These men were sharks in the dark eddies of work, but out on the town they were expert conversationalists and fascinating storytellers. For Noah the mealtime passed like a few hours in a hammock when the winds were cool and soft.

The group finished their meal, and after honoring everyone from the waiters to the chef to the maître d', they walked two blocks east to the Blue Note, a popular jazz spot. The streets were ablaze with the strident, cacophonous harmonies of the Village. Noah walked behind the other men and stared at the girls whose body parts were pierced with stones that glittered in the night air like constellations. The fragrance of the cool breeze, the sensuous bodies, and the alcohol-induced euphoria led Noah to an oasis-like refreshment that he usually tasted only in the barely conscious moments right before he fell into a stuporous sleep.

The remainder of the evening was a blur of the piano pyrotechnics of Brad Mehldau, the seamless singing of Julia Stram, and the burning comfort of Laguvulin. Noah did not even remember when he got back to his room or how he undressed or if he called the operator for a wake-up call. Pleasure had endowed him with an Elysian holiday, and he followed his brief respite as far as he could until the inevitable morning light awakened him to the reality he had so effectively escaped.

Chicago, Dinnertime

Joan looked at her two boys stretched out on the carpet, heads on the crunched-up sofa pillows that she had told them a thousand times not to use to prop up their blank-eyed, empty heads as they watched old reruns from the sixties and seventies. Today, she didn't care. She had dinner to prepare, and her mindless day of doing errands had sapped her of energy and initiative.

She sorted through the freezer for a microwave meal but found only the icy remains of a few skeletal dinners—nothing she could beg, pay, or threaten her two boys to eat. She decided to run out to the nearby Boston Market. If she was going to be alone, worried sick about her husband, she at least would treat herself to a meal of exceptional taste for fast food.

She told her boys she would be back in a half hour. They grunted acknowledgment but had no more idea whether she had said she was going to the moon, joining the Marines, or running off with Michael Jackson.

As soon as Joan started the car, she turned on the CD player and began singing softly Nanci Griffith's song "An Inconvenient Time." She loved Griffith's twangy, luscious east-Texas voice and the rich, mournful overtones. It transported her from the fear of where Noah might be, of whom he might be with. Griffith's pain was Joan's anguish too. Griffith's lyrics sang Joan's unspoken words. Somehow the magic of the songs made Joan's feet tap and her heart hope.

Joan hated Noah's occasional travel, but she had never felt so alone. His phone call had been the worst phone call of their marriage. He had not explained why he had not told her about the imminent trip; he had left no message, no apology.

And he had called her babe.

She began to think about the Boston Market creamed spinach. It was rich and moist. She knew the boys hated anything wet and green, but she decided she was going to eat what she wanted. She would salve the wounds of the day in white meat, green spinach, mounds of mashed potatoes, and the piece of chocolate cake she had hidden in the vegetable drawer since her sons' birthday party. Noah may be having an affair, recklessly living the fast life, but she knew how to indulge her senses too. She knew how to throw a wild party for one.

She would check out a weepy video, pick up a *Country Living,* and escape after dinner to a hot bath. She would throw caution to the wind and indulge all her senses.

Joan thought, *I will not purge. I will not purge.* Joan had never told anyone that she occasionally struggled with an old desire and practice of ridding herself of some inner demons by bingeing and purging. The unbidden words came gurgling up from deep inside her. She had not purged for over fifteen years. When she was a junior in college, Joan often ate indiscriminately and then forced herself to throw up. She hated the acidic, unclean taste. She was humiliated by the violence of the act, but somewhere deep in her she felt a relief that was unlike any pleasure she had known in her rigid, angry home.

It was a ritual that for some reason passed away when she began to attend a Bible study on campus that year. She once confessed what she called her "dirty habit" to a male campus leader. He had scrunched up his face and told her to talk to one of the female staff. Joan had never done so, but his response had deepened her disgust for herself. His repulsion also seemed to help her break the pattern over a few months. *Where did that thought come from?* thought Joan. *What is my problem? I think about having a nice evening and somehow surviving this pain, and then I ruin it with the thought of vomiting. Maybe I'm sick and gross.* Joan popped out the CD and turned on a Christian talk-radio show to try to get a handle on her spiraling heart.

"Well, folks, I don't know about you, but I know Jesus takes away the pain of the world. Today, my guest is author and speaker Chuck Richburg, who has written the book *Seven Ways to Get Heaven Now.* Folks, I have been looking forward to this interview for weeks. Chuck, your work gives us hope. Too many books tell us that life is hard. Your book is a great antidote to the depressing perspectives we keep hearing about. Welcome to the show."

"Leonard, great to be with you. You are absolutely right. I wrote *Seven Ways to Get Heaven Now* to let Christians know that we are the victors, the winners of life, and God wants to invest us with the pleasures of heaven now."

"Chuck, tell our listeners what they all are eager to hear. How can we claim our eternal rewards now?"

"Well, Leonard, it is crucial to take what God has for us. Why, think about a meal. If the cook prepares a sumptuous meal but you don't come to the table or pick up your fork, you will never eat what the cook has so painstakingly prepared. Why, we need to expect the Lord to prepare for us each and every day a banquet to be served at a table prepared for us in the green pastures of his love."

"Great word picture from Psalm 23, Chuck. Now, how do we get to the banquet?"

"Leonard, let's go through the seven promises God gives us in his Word. These promises tell us precisely what we need to do to make sure we sit at that great meal. Step number one is—"

JOAN slammed her palm against the radio on-off dial. She cut Dr. Richburg off in midsentence. She had heard enough about provision, pleasure, heavenly food, and doing the "right thing" to secure God's favor. She had read the books. She had attended the seminars that offered anywhere from four to twelve steps for nearly every ill known to humankind. She was angry. She could feel something godless and mean rising up in her heart. She wanted to swear—to whom she did not know, but she wanted to let someone in the universe know she was protesting what was said in the name of Christ.

She drove into the garage and grabbed the food for the kids. She didn't feel like praying. She didn't feel like eating, watching her video, reading her magazine, or even indulging in a warm bath. She felt sick, and if she could find a way to cleanse herself from the words she had heard on the radio show, she would have been willing to purge and taste the acidic contents of her soul. But there was little to be done but to set the table for her boys, fill their plates with just enough spinach to gross them out, and then let them rip apart the defenseless bird.

She went into the study and found her Bible. She knew the psalm the men had been talking about, but she needed to see the words in print. She dropped the thick, leather-covered Bible in her lap and turned to the

Twenty-third Psalm. She read: "Even when I walk through the dark valley of death, I will not be afraid, for you are close beside me. Your rod and your staff protect and comfort me."

She started to laugh. *Amazing,* she thought. *Two great radio Bible teachers and they left out a rather poignant verse. But what in the world is God's comfort when my life feels as if it is dissolving, my husband is gone, and maybe really gone, and I'm sick of being who I am? I am sick of seeing friends suffer. I am just sick, sick, sick.*

Tears, big, full-bodied tears, burst from some unseen dam that had held back her heart. She wept and wept. Her tears coursed down her face and plunked on the dry pages. Her face throbbed with the heat of confusion, wet rage, and relief.

Relief. She gave in to the pleasure of sorrow, and her heart flowed down the river of tears that so many saints before her had cut into the dry earth.

14

"Pleasure Ought to Satisfy Me"

IT MAY BE easy for us to cluck our tongues at Noah's indulgence, but if we are honest with ourselves, many of us look to pleasure to make life worthwhile. We tell ourselves that we work hard and that we ought to be able to enjoy a moment of pleasure now and then. Our pleasure doesn't have to be illicit, but we want it to be satisfying and fun.

Do any of these scenarios sound familiar to you?

"IT is a different world! When I walk into the opera house, my problems disappear. There is no such thing as routine and daily grind as I watch the performers onstage. And when the music starts, I am entranced. I'm not aware of it at the time, but my husband once told me that my eyes widen, my hands clench, and my jaw drops a tad so that my mouth is slightly open. He told me that I don't drool, but I am caught up in a near trancelike state. And when it is Wagner! The four hours seem to pass in a moment. If only we could bottle up whatever makes us feel good so that we could feel it whenever we want. Maybe that's why Prozac is so popular these days!"

- *"I live for this moment! No kids screaming. I put the chores behind me. My husband is even sound asleep. Just blissful quiet. It's especially wonderful in the winter. I open the window a tad, make myself a mug of hot chocolate, and curl up under the thick covers with a good book. What a feeling! And it's not even sinful!"*

- *"I think she's the one! When she kissed me, I got light-headed. I'm in love. I wonder if we'll get married? I hope so because I want to feel this good twenty-four hours a day, seven days a week."*

WE all have pleasures that lift us out of the mundane and make us forget our problems. What does it for you?

If we are honest, however, we know that a good feeling is short lived, and we spend much of our energy looking for the next "high." We never get enough of it. Indeed, holding on to a good feeling is harder than holding on to the wind. . . .

CONSIDER Noah. His real pleasure is work, but after a grueling and uncertain day, he turned from his fear and exhaustion to food and drink. For many people, the best time of day is coming home and getting a drink and some food to relax and forget their troubles through the ritual of indulgent snacking. We crave a break, an intense moment of relief and pleasure.

For some people that pleasure is sex. For some it is food. Others settle for the escape and thrill of a television program. Some people thrive on the adrenaline rush of physically threatening risks. Whatever the pleasure, we know that it is brief and that when it's over, we often feel a deeper ache than before.

Pleasure can also be perverse. Joan, at one point in her life, turned to bulimia for pleasure. The process of vomiting, though painful, brought her momentary relief when her stomach was empty and the unnamed struggle was exorcised.

The Joys of Life
If it tastes good, *it will probably give you cancer.*
If it feels good, *it must be immoral.*
If it's fun, *it's probably dangerous.*
If it smells enticing, *it is likely seductive.*
If it sounds pleasant, *it is probably superficial.*
If it's pleasurable, *it must not be biblical.*

MANY of us grew up with these warnings ringing in our ears. The message came from parents, teachers, and the church. We pass it on to the next generation. Christianity sometimes can seem to be the opposite of pleasure, especially of sensuous pleasures; that is, those that appeal to our sense of smell, touch, taste, sight, and hearing. After all, we are interested in growing our spirit, not our body, which we think anchors us to this present world.

But is the Bible really a killjoy book? Does Christ really want us to flee all worldly pleasures? What are we to think about Noah's flight from the day's battle? His culinary indulgence and imbibing of wine is clearly an effort to put the day behind him. Is that wrong?

Similarly, Joan turned to music to soothe her fragmented heart. She chose to eat a special meal to turn away the fear of what Noah was doing. Is she wrong? Are food, television, videos, or magazines God-given gifts to blunt the full horror of life, or are they simply escapes from facing reality?

The psalmist praises God for pleasure. He writes: "He makes grass grow for the cattle, and plants for man to cultivate—bringing forth food from the earth: wine that gladdens the heart of man, oil to make his face shine, and bread that sustains his heart" (Ps. 104:14-15, NIV). To gladden the heart implies a degree of joy brought through the chemical effects of the wine. There are a number of degrees of intoxication, and the word in this passage implies a slight buzz, a small but pleasant change of mood due to the wine.

The idea that God recognizes the sorrow and desperation of living in a fallen world and provides for an occasional oasis break in our desert journey is not a commonly held Christian perspective. Many Christians will be offended by the psalmist's praise of God for providing wine and its incumbent potential for dulling sorrow and invigorating pleasure. We simply must reconsider our view of pleasure in the light of what the Bible clearly says.

Think back to the promise given to the people of God in the Old Testament time period. God promised to give his people the land, a special land, a land "flowing with milk and honey" (Exod. 3:8; 33:3; Deut. 26:9). The image of milk and honey is intentionally sensuous. These thick, luscious liquids linger long on the palate. They are rich symbols of blessing and enjoyment.

Or take the equally sensuous divine promise found in Jeremiah's "Book of Consolation." After describing the punishment that God's people would receive for their sins, Jeremiah gives them this promise from the Lord: "The Lord has redeemed Israel from those too strong for them. They will come home and sing songs of joy on the heights of Jerusalem. They will be radiant because of the many gifts the Lord has given them—the good crops of wheat, wine, and oil, and the healthy flocks and herds. Their life will be like a watered garden, and all their sorrows will be gone" (Jer. 31:11-12).

God created us with senses and desires for a reason. He created a beautiful and enjoyable world for our pleasure. Our bodies are not a trap that we need to ignore or abuse to achieve spiritual enlightenment. That is a Buddhist concept, not a Christian one. The world is not a shadow that masks true reality. We are not souls imprisoned in flesh. The world is real, created by God for human enjoyment.

Pleasure heightens our senses. It increases our awareness. It lifts us above the routine.

We can certainly understand this when we consider sexual intercourse, perhaps the most sensual and pleasurable of all human experiences. Sexual intimacy arouses all the human senses. Sounds, smells, taste, sight, and of course touch all come into play in lovemaking. The Song of Songs, a biblical book that describes the intense lovemaking of a man and a woman, confirms our view as it uses metaphors to describe the experience. Throughout the Song, the description of the woman focuses on her physical beauty. It uses images of taste, reflecting the deep kisses the man places all over her body (Song 4:3, 11; 5:1). The man describes her breasts as twin fawns, an image of softness, anticipating his touch. Every conceivable sweet-smelling spice describes the garden, which is her body (Song 4:13-15). Their conversation is the ecstatic sound that arouses them to climax.

The Bible is a sensuous book. It recognizes that God made us to enjoy bodily pleasure. But if that is so, why do we find so little real pleasure in life? Why is it that the things we enjoy doing often seem to lead to our harm?

Pleasure Does Not Satisfy

God created Adam and Eve with a capacity to relish life. He created a world that provided the opportunity for intense and satisfying sensual pleasures. God's blessing (Gen. 1:28) included the rich land of Eden, where they lived. Genesis 2:9-12 informs us that "God planted all sorts of trees in the garden—beautiful trees that produced delicious fruit. At the center of the garden he placed the tree of life and the tree of the knowledge of good and evil. A river flowed from the land of Eden, watering the garden and then dividing into four branches. One of these branches is the Pishon, which flows around the entire land of Havilah, where gold is found. The gold of that land is exceptionally pure; aromatic resin and onyx stone are also found there." Clearly, this land was built for pleasure.

Adam and Eve lived in the Garden completely fulfilled as they communed intimately with God and as they feasted on the good bounty that he provided for them. God did, however, place in the Garden a tree from which they were forbidden to eat. Under Satan's prodding, Adam and Eve became absorbed in its beauty, fascinated at what was being withheld from them, and then rebellious. They weren't satisfied with the blessing that God had generously given them. They gave in to the temptation and ate the fruit.

The result? They were thrown out of the Garden. As we have seen in previous chapters, this meant not only that they would now struggle for control over the chaos, harmony in relationships, and satisfying rewards for their work, but also that they would search in vain for deeply fulfilling pleasure.

Adam and Eve left the Garden of Eden and entered a desolate and harsh environment, the world in which we now live. Like them, we desire to return to the pleasures of Eden, but there is no possibility of return (Gen. 3:24).

Or is there? Is it possible for pleasure not only to nourish and momentarily satisfy but also to increase our hunger for what lies beyond the moment of satisfaction?

We believe it is. It is our premise that pleasure works simultaneously to satisfy and to increase hunger. The real danger is when pleasure satisfies without increasing a hunger for the God who made all pleasure and loves sensuality.

Finding an Escape from a Hard Existence

Honest people will admit that life is a struggle. The Teacher in the book of Ecclesiastes was hard nosed in his honesty. After coming to the conclusion that people live most of their lives "frustrated, discouraged, and angry" (Eccles. 5:17), he goes on to encourage them to pursue some measure of relief through pleasurable experience: "It is good and proper for a man to eat and drink, and to find satisfaction in his toilsome labor under the sun during the few days of life God has given him—for this is his lot. Moreover, when God gives any man wealth and possessions, and enables him to enjoy them, to accept his lot and be happy in his work—this is a gift of God. He seldom reflects on the days of his life, because God keeps him occupied with gladness of heart" (Eccles. 5:18-20, NIV).

This passage is extremely subtle. Once again, remember that the Teacher is giving this advice after he has concluded that life has no meaning: "'Meaningless! Meaningless! . . . Utterly meaningless. Everything is meaningless" (Eccles. 1:2 and throughout the book). This passage, and the others like it (Eccles. 2:24-26; 3:12-13; 8:15; 9:7), are commonly referred to as carpe diem passages; that is, they are encouragement to "seize the day." In contemporary phraseology, these passages say, grab all the gusto you can.

The passage also recognizes that just because someone has money does not mean that person can actually derive enjoyment from it. Indeed, in Ecclesiastes 6:1-2 the Teacher points out that it is more often the case that those who have money don't have any more enjoyment than those who do.

However, a few people are blissfully happy. They have wealth, and they enjoy it. Ecclesiastes 5:20 is key to understanding this. "He seldom reflects on the days of his life, because God keeps him occupied with gladness of heart" (NIV).

We need to pay close attention to what the Teacher is saying here. What is the purpose of pleasure? To keep us from thinking about our troubles. In a word, pleasure serves as an anesthetic to our soul. Life is a mess, but we can divert our attention from it with a few pleasures. We can watch TV all evening and not give a thought to the fact that we have a horrible relationship with our children. We can take a vacation and sit on the beach to forget about our demeaning job back home.

The Teacher would say that pleasure anesthetizes the heart. In the light of a world without meaning—without ultimate purpose—that's the best we can hope for, he says.

As I read the book of Ecclesiastes, I can't help but think that the Teacher himself was not one of the privileged few who could divert himself through simple pleasure. His frustration and disappointment with the setbacks of life speak too loudly for me to think he includes himself among those who can drown their disappointment with a few drinks. Rather, I hear him speaking these words with a certain wistfulness but also a measure of disdain in his voice.

How can someone live from party to party as if everything is fine in the world? And even if the world is just peachy keen, there is a little problem called death that is going to take all the fun away.

With this latter point in mind, the Teacher gives his listeners some morbid advice: "It is better to spend your time at funerals than at festivals. For you are going to die, and you should think about it while there is still time. Sorrow is better than laughter, for sadness has a refining influence on us. A wise person thinks much about death, while the fool thinks only about having a good time now" (Eccles. 7:2-4).

If this advice seems contradictory to his earlier advice about grabbing all the enjoyment we can, that's because it is! The Teacher is struggling under the sun, apart from God's revelation. On one level, he would love to melt into the oblivion of pleasure, but he knows that to do so is to ignore reality. Apart from God, pleasure is just a momentary diversion before death.

Why then doesn't pleasure satisfy? Pleasure was not intended to fill our deepest desires and needs. It is a temporary and false substitute for God.

The Idolatry of Pleasure

I (Tremper) love barbecue potato chips. If they are done just right with the proper amount of flavoring, they taste so good going down. However, I am never satisfied with one chip or even a lunch-sized bag; I always want more. In my mind, I know that if I eat too many, it will make me feel slightly ill and certainly make me feel guilty about my weight. But I am amazed how rarely that stops me from eating one after another. The pleasure of each chip leads to a desire for the next.

The problem with pleasure is that it never leads to complete satisfaction. It always leaves us wanting more. Usually, we do not give up on pleasure even when we recognize its transience; we rather pursue it more intensely. This is particularly true when we feel empty.

When life is hard, pleasure can be a diversion. We often move from a properly moderate enjoyment of pleasure to a consuming need for sensuous experiences.

Noah put in long, long hours as an analyst. His work on the Pearson project led him to challenge the conventional wisdom of the firm; it put him into a make-or-break struggle with the top leadership, even the owners of the company. Noah faced a little more deeply than ever before that he was up against huge forces, including the national pride fueled by a holocaust that had occurred nearly sixty years before the meeting. His reputation, his livelihood were on the line.

When he finished the meeting, he needed to be the team player by joining the group for dinner. His attempt at connecting with his wife by phone only made him feel worse, especially after not having told her about the trip. Noah was in hot water at work and home.

On the one hand he went out to dinner with his associates to avoid offending them and to gather information that would direct his strategy for the next day. On the other hand he went to dinner to escape the pressures the day had brought. The glorious meal, the free-flowing wine, and the convivial conversation lifted him out of the battle; it transported him to the Novocain numbness that the Teacher recommends in the "carpe diem" passages.

Was Noah wrong? Yes. He used legitimate pleasures to escape facing his anger at Joan for her conversation in the car. His failure to tell her about the trip was likely a punishment for her confronting him in Jack and Marcia's presence. He then compounded his failure by posturing in front of his associates, by being more concerned about their response than connecting with his wife.

Add to this the tension and fear about the next day's meeting, and it should be clear that Noah used pleasure to flee reality. He not only fled from the pressure of the meeting and the possibility of being fired, but he was also running from his failure of Joan. Pleasure at that point was an anesthetic rather than a stimulus that drew Noah to consider God's goodness. Pleasure is meant to prompt us to praise God. Whenever we use pleasure to flee, we usually indulge to the point of oblivion. We overdo the pleasure to accomplish the desired end: escape. But pleasure that is full of praise has a boundary, an acknowledged limit that allows the heart to taste pleasure while also whetting the appetite for more.

True enjoyment of pleasure always causes the heart to hunger, to ache for what no pleasure can provide: direct, consuming encounter with God. Paradoxically, godly sensuality and pleasure enriches the heart and body while also deepening a soul ache and a physical hunger for the day of consummation. Sadly, few people embrace pleasure for this purpose. Instead, the pleasure of sensuality more often than not leads to idolatry.

Consider the typical American couple. Both work hard all day, spend the evening getting their kids to do their homework and finish their chores. At bedtime, they tuck in the kids, read them a short Bible passage, hear them say their prayers, and kiss them good night. Then, exhausted, the parents flop into bed, whip out the remote, and watch TV until they fall asleep—only to wake up in the morning and begin the routine again, hanging on until the weekend.

My point is not that TV is inherently evil. My point is not that it is always wrong to escape the pain of a difficult world with some pleasant diversion, which TV can provide. My point is that we can slowly, unintentionally, mindlessly become addicted to those things that take us away from our problems and give us a shot of Novocain in the soul. We may soon find that what our soul yearns for more than anything else is not God or our family but *Seinfeld, Frasier,* and *ER.*

It may not be the television that attracts us. It may be other innocuous things like video games, reading, playing tennis, or sleeping. It may be seriously damaging and dangerous like promiscuous sex, heavy drinking, drugs, or the like. The tragedy, though, is that ultimately all of these things will let us down.

They will let us down because we have to turn off the TV to go to work. We have to deceive and steal to get drugs, and even if that is not an issue, eventually we have to come down from our high. The orgasm ends, followed by exhaustion and then ultimately the need for another sexual fix.

And then there is death. Death takes away all pleasure, evil and benign. If we live our lives for pleasure, we know that it will end once and for all with death. As the Teacher says, "The dead know nothing. They have no further reward, nor are they remembered. Whatever they did in their lifetime—loving, hating, envying—is all long gone. They no longer have a part in anything here on earth" (Eccles. 9:5-6).

The bottom line is that pleasure will let us down because it is a false god. If we pursue pleasure as our reason for existence, it will always disappoint. If we live our lives for those things that give us joy, we will become entrapped in our devotion to them. They not only will deny us the joy that we want, but they also will ultimately bring us pain.

LAUREN passed by the casino every day as she traveled from her home in Santa Fe to her work in the northern part of Albuquerque. Her work was pure drudgery, and she really had nothing at home. Her two children had grown up and had moved to the East Coast. Her husband had died two years earlier of a heart attack, and she had to continue working as a receptionist. One day she could not resist stopping in at the casino. It was right off the highway, and the flashing lights and the expensive-looking building had intrigued her with its glittery promise of excitement. What could it hurt to check it out?

She parked her car and walked in, nervously looking about to see if anyone she knew would spot her there. She reasoned that if someone from her church saw her, at least they would be implicated by their presence as well. She walked apprehensively to the slot machines. She was awed by the furnishings, the tuxedo-clad employees, and the music. By the time she got to the slots, she had forgotten her concerns and reached for a quarter. She put the quarter in the machine and gave the arm a tug. She stood back and watched the machine whirl. Suddenly alarms and a buzzer went off. At first she was frightened, but then she saw the stream of quarters flow from the mouth of the machine. She couldn't believe it. She had won!

Once she had a handful of quarters, she saw no reason to stop. An hour later, she left with her profits. They had dwindled to five dollars, but she didn't care. She had had a great time and had made a little money.

Work the next day seemed even more dreary than before. She had not intended it, but when she reached the exit ramp for the casino, she found herself driving toward the parking lot. This time she lost five dollars before she could pull herself away. *No problem,* she thought. *I was able to forget myself for an hour and a half, and I'm still even.*

A month later Lauren began to get worried. She was able to keep herself limited to two trips a week to the casino, but her money losses were significant for her relatively low income. In spite of her worries, she found it hard not to go. Very little else in her life gave her any excitement or interest. It was a temptation too hard to resist.

Lauren's idol is amazingly similar to the idols that tempted the people of God in the Old Testament. We learn from the prophets that many of God's children were seduced to worship the god Baal and the many other deities of the Canaanites, whom they had neglected to remove from the Promised Land. We know from the Old Testament and archaeological texts that much of the appeal of Baal worship came from its promise of pleasure.

Baal was the god of fertility. He was the one who blessed the land with crops and a woman's womb with children. In a part of the world where rainfall was never certain and lives depended on harvest, Baal played a major role. Baal's wives, who were also his sisters, were important goddesses of love and war.

Worship of Baal and other false gods thus involved sensuous pleasures that were not allowed in the lives of the Israelites. We see this at the time Aaron and the people turned against God in the wilderness and worshiped the golden calf. Remember the conversation between Moses and Joshua as they returned to the camp after receiving the Ten Commandments. "When Joshua heard the noise of the people shouting below them, he exclaimed to Moses, 'It sounds as if there is a war in the camp!' But Moses replied, 'No, it's neither a cry of victory nor a cry of defeat. It is the sound of a celebration'" (Exod. 32:17-18). What they were hearing was the aftermath of the construction of the idol. The people "celebrated with feasting and drinking, and indulged themselves in pagan revelry" (Exod. 32:6). The "pagan revelry" likely included illicit sexual relations among the worshipers. These we know were a part of the worship of fertility gods like Baal in the ancient Near East.

The point is that Lauren, the Israelites, and all of us are tempted by what takes us out of our everyday existence. We are lured by things that give our hectic world a shot of pleasure. The alternative appears to be the boredom of the routine.

Coping with Boredom

We seek pleasure to fill the void in our lives. In other words, pleasure is a remedy to boredom. Boredom arises in the context of a lack of stimulation, an absence of desire and passion.

If we desire nothing, we are empty. We may desire to fill the void, but if we do not know what would satisfy our emptiness, then we still experience boredom.

Boredom is the younger sibling of sadness and depression. It can grow to the proportions of despair, if felt intensely enough and for a long period of time. We can say it so flippantly, "I'm bored," but those simple words can mask a much deeper problem.

Boredom can propel us into desperate attempts at pleasure. According to University of Virginia professor Patricia Spacks's intriguing study of boredom as a literary and psychological category, boredom can mask an underlying aggression and can even lead to murder. She recounts the report of a young person who committed a random murder, justifying his act with the casual comment, "I was bored."[1]

Boredom may not lead to such a desperate act, but even less dangerous attempts at alleviating emptiness can be harmful to a well-rounded and enjoyable life.

I (Tremper) remember a long period during which I battled with loneliness. I had just moved to Columbus, Ohio, from New Jersey. I had no real friends to speak of, but I found solace in reading books. My mother would beg me to go out and play with the neighbor children. I really wanted to do that, but I was too frightened at the possibility of rejection.

Since the avenue to relational pleasure was blocked to me, I found other ways to make the time pass. I remember going out the door as if to play and then sneaking back into the house through another door. I would quietly go upstairs into my rather spacious closet. Closing the door and turning on a flashlight, I would spend the morning reading.

I read the entire Tom Swift series and more in that closet. Books were, and still are, my "drug of choice." Through a good book (or movie), I can escape the present tedium of routine and enter a much more exciting world.

Ultimately, however, boredom will land us in a downward cycle of depression. Eventually I tired of the Tom Swift books, and I couldn't make the time pass so quickly. I remember looking at the clock and feeling disappointment that it was only midafternoon. I had nothing to do. Those minutes and hours before a decent TV show came on (another escape from the routine) seemed an eternity to me.

Boredom accompanies a lack of activity, but we can be bored just as easily when we are busy. Many, many people hate their work because they find it boring. This is just as true of people who work in high-powered professional jobs as it is of those who work routine manual jobs. Boredom arises when people feel no passion or desire, no interest in the activity with which they are involved.

Why is boredom a relatively common part of our experience?

The sad truth is that our world is a boring place. At least that's the view of the Teacher. The book of Ecclesiastes opens with a depressing picture of life in a fallen world:

What do people get for all their hard work? Generations come and go, but nothing really changes. The sun rises and sets and hurries around to rise again. The wind blows south and north, here and there, twisting back and forth, getting nowhere. The rivers run into the sea, but the sea is never full. Then the water returns again to the rivers and flows again to the sea. Everything is so weary and tiresome! No matter how much we see, we are never satisfied. No matter how much we hear, we are not content.

History merely repeats itself. It has all been done before. Nothing under the sun is truly new. What can you point to that is new? How do you know it didn't already exist long ago? We don't remember what happened in those former times. And in future generations, no one will remember what we are doing now. Ecclesiastes 1:3-11

THE TEACHER paints a dreary picture from nature and history. Nothing is really new.

Today I am writing on my back porch, where I can take a moment to look up at the beautiful fall foliage in my backyard. While the colors are striking, I am not surprised by them. I have seen the same scene every fall for the past sixteen years that I have lived here. I drive on the same roads most days, back and forth from the seminary, and when I go on a trip to a new location, the planes, hotels, and scenery are pretty much the same everywhere. The longer we live, the more calloused we become because these "new" experiences are really not so new.

Even our actions are not new. It is a ploy of ministers and politicians who want to get elected to tell us that our society has never sunk so low. As a student of history, I can only say along with the Teacher: "Do not say, 'Why were the old days better than these?' For it is not wise to ask such questions" (Eccles. 7:10, NIV). Why isn't this question a wise one? Because everyone but the greatest fool knows that the past is as bad as the present and the future. There is "nothing new under the sun."

Boredom is an inescapable experience in a fallen world. Is there any hope to escape the routine of a humdrum existence?

15

Restoring Pleasure through Joy in Suffering

WE HAVE SEEN enough to realize that we are not going to find the purpose of life in pleasure. Not only is pleasure transitory, it also is not always available. And when we find something enjoyable, it will sooner consume us than help us. Pleasure may give us momentary respite from the monotony or pain of life, but it doesn't give us much more.

Let's explore the reasons for that a bit more deeply. It may help us overcome the impasse.

In the study of boredom cited in the previous chapter, Patricia Meyer Spacks points out that, though people have been bored through history, it is experienced at a new level of intensity in the present. She refers to studies by other scholars, sociologists, and psychologists and offers an intriguing reason why. It is not wealth or increased leisure that has led to heightened boredom. It is a "metaphysical void," a lack of ultimate meaning.[1]

People pursue pleasure in harmful and destructive ways to fill the void. They don't know God; they think this life is all there is. It thus becomes important to try to enjoy every second of it. However, since pleasure is a false god, tantalizing us but never fulfilling us, we find ourselves sucked into an obsessive, even addictive pursuit of the rush of a good feeling. Soon, however, we become numb to feeling anything at all.

The movie *The People versus Larry Flint,* a commentary on the decadence in our society, focuses on the life of the pornographer who founded *Hustler* magazine. But it also portrays the sad life of his wife, who allowed nothing to stand in the way of a good feeling. As the movie progresses, she moves from being a shocking woman to a pathetic creature, a slave to her pursuit of pleasure. To achieve her end, she engages in bizarre sexual behavior and also becomes a serious drug addict. Sex becomes so common that she no longer derives any satisfaction from her behavior. She changes from a young and vibrant woman to a haggard person sadly obsessed with pursuing her next high. She eventually contracts AIDS, and her body and mind slowly follow her soul in its deterioration.

It is hard for many people to identify with someone like Flynt's wife. She is an extreme case, but even God-fearing people can find themselves caught up with the allure of illegitimate pleasure. Why? They come to God with a false understanding. Jesus promises us life, abundant life now and an eternity with him. Paul says that the Christian life is filled with joy. But often, after the first wave of our conversion is over, we find that we continue to struggle. We suffer as a result of our own sin and the sin of others. Where is the joy? Where is the abundant life?

Soon we are attracted by the pleasures of the world. Slowly our efforts to relieve our suffering and depression take over the place of prime importance is our lives.

In this way, we are very similar to the ancient Israelite man. He grew up in the community of faith, hearing about Yahweh, the great God who gives every good gift. But one year, his crops are not good, and his wife gets sick. He sees his neighbor thriving and enjoying life. His neighbor, who worships Baal, is wealthy and enjoys having sexual intercourse with that beautiful temple prostitute. He finds his heart attracted away from God and toward the idol of pleasure.

Solomon is a prime example of this dynamic in the Bible. Solomon had it all, but apparently it wasn't enough. He was the wealthiest man in Israel. He had power beyond all others in his country. Through Solomon's wealth and power, he had access to unimaginable pleasures. He was also the wisest man on the face of the earth.

Solomon, though, wanted pleasures that were forbidden to him. "King Solomon loved many foreign women. Besides Pharaoh's daughter, he married women from Moab, Ammon, Edom, Sidon, and from among the Hittites. The Lord had clearly instructed his people not to intermarry with those nations, because the women they married would lead them to worship their gods" (1 Kings 11:1-2). When Solomon gave in to the temptation and married foreign wives, he also found himself worshiping their gods and goddesses. As a result, God judged this wealthy, powerful, and wise king.

Just as Solomon provides a negative example, the poet of Psalm 73 serves as a positive example. He too was tempted by what he described as a dichotomy between his faith and his experience. He was a godly man who lived around wicked people. He, however, was suffering, while they were rich and happy. Because of this contrast, he "came so close to the edge of the cliff!" (Ps. 73:2). He almost said, "My faith is bringing me no enjoyment. What's the use of it all?" But before he made that fatal plunge, he saw something that drew him back, "Then one day I went into your sanctuary, O God" (Ps. 73:17). He went into God's presence, and as he once again put God first in his life, he found his thinking transformed. He realized anew that "God is good to Israel" (Ps. 73:1). In a word, he recognized that a child of God finds pleasure in the midst of suffering in a chaotic world.

Joy in the Midst of Suffering

We are made for Eden, but we live in a fallen world. We yearn to experience the pleasures of the Garden and find it difficult to live in a world of trouble and pain. We desire not only the sensuous pleasures of God's creation but also the foundation of all enjoyment: life in the intimate presence of God.

Is there any joy outside the Garden? Our experience confirms that the Teacher was right when he said that joy under the sun is fleeting and does not fulfill us. Christians who believe that the life of faith is a life of unending success and happiness mislead themselves. Life is a struggle; it is a time of suffering. Honest people will admit that to themselves; Scripture teaches it. According to Paul, we "suffer now" because "everything on earth was subjected to God's curse" (Rom. 8:18, 20).

This passage may not have been in Joan's mind when she went to pick up dinner, but when she listened to the wistful, sorrowful Irish song, she sang along quietly. Her heart rose from the specific pain of her day with Erin, of Jessie's hard life, and the turmoil of her phone call with Noah. Joan did not flee sorrow. She sang along with it. But she also decided to enjoy a good meal and an escape from the normal routine of making a meal for her kids.

Her plan for a nice bath, a new magazine, and a video seems less of a flight from reality than an acknowledgment that she could do little about her situation except strengthen herself to stay in the battle. Was this a conscious, well-thought-through plan? No. She had spent the day doing errands. Her world was shattered by the phone call with Noah, and she was hurt, angry, and confused.

Notice what Joan did *not* do. She did not succumb to the old pattern of bingeing and purging. She did not watch more TV. She chose healthy food, a magazine, and a well-loved movie. But God had other plans for her night. Her memory of old patterns of finding relief in the midst of pain compelled her to turn on Christian radio. The show she turned to infuriated her. It was so untrue to her life. The arousal of her passionate anger and the horror of her situation turned her to a fight rather than to a moment of oasis-like rest. But it was her fight that opened her heart to sorrow, to the tears that had pushed against her all day.

Oddly for Christians, it is surrendering our emptiness to our Father in the *midst* of our struggle that opens our heart to the sorrow and unwept tears that we so desperately want him to touch. Joan stepped into the river of tears that have been wept before her. She tasted the wet, salty anguish of Jesus and his brothers and sisters who have cried: "My God, my God, why have you forsaken me?"

For Joan the pursuit of legitimate pleasure brought comfort. Comfort brought relief, but it brought even deeper desire. Her desire for more brought back memories of how she used to kill her heart's desire when it unnerved her; in turn, God used that memory to send her fleeing to the radio. That flight brought a fight, and the fight brought her back to the only One who can offer comfort and pleasure: Jesus, the One who suffered ultimate pain for our pleasure.

To live confident, happy lives, we must understand the paradox that our joy comes in the midst of suffering. We find pleasure not by denying the pain of life but in the face of it:

> Therefore, since we have been made right in God's sight by faith, we have peace with God because of what Jesus Christ our Lord has done for us. Because of our faith, Christ has brought us into this place of highest privilege where we now stand, and we confidently and joyfully look forward to sharing God's glory.
>
> We can rejoice, too, when we run into problems and trials, for we know that they are good for us—they help us learn to endure. Romans 5:1-3

Our hearts ache, but we always have joy. 2 Corinthians 6:10

JOY in the midst of suffering! It sounds wonderful, but what does it really mean? Does it mean that we feel happy, not sad, when we discover we have terminal cancer? Does it mean that when our child is arrested we "praise the Lord anyway"? Nothing could be further from the truth.

Our Joy Is Based on Future Realities

We can rejoice in the midst of our present sufferings because we know with an absolute certainty that this life is not the end of our story. The author of the book of Hebrews encourages his fellow Christians when he says to them, "You suffered along with those who were thrown into jail. When all you owned was taken from you, you accepted it with joy. You knew you had better things waiting for you in eternity" (Heb. 10:34).

We know, after all, that we will once again return to the Garden (Rev. 22), indeed something even better than the Garden, where we will live in the presence of God forever and where every tear will be wiped away (Rev. 21:4). Like the psalmist in Psalm 73, we know that though the ungodly seem happier on the surface than we are now, God will lead us "to a glorious destiny" (Ps. 73:24).

Jesus himself is our model. We follow in his glorious path. Peter makes this clear when he states: "Dear friends, don't be surprised at the fiery trials you are going through, as if something strange were happening to you. Instead, be very glad—because these trials will make you partners with Christ in his suffering, and afterward you will have the wonderful joy of sharing his glory when it is displayed to all the world" (1 Pet. 4:12-13; see also Col. 1:24).

Jesus suffered here on earth. He experienced abuse, neglect, and execution. We share in Christ's sufferings as we experience disappointment and trouble.

But Jesus' death was not the end of his story. No, he was brought into his Father's presence, where he rules over the universe. In the same way, our complete fulfillment will take place in the future, and that can sustain us in the present.

Joy in the Present

Does that mean that Christianity is really a faith that is "pie in the sky by and by"? Does that mean that joy is reserved only for the future?

Complete fulfillment will come only in heaven, that is true. But God in his grace gives us glimpses of what is to come. Once again Jesus is our example. He suffered on earth, but he also had moments of celebration. He attended a happy wedding ceremony; he banqueted at the home of the rich; he received a foot wash with expensive perfume. Indeed, in contrast to the ministry of John the Baptist, Jesus himself characterized his life as a time of feasting and drinking (Matt. 11:16-19).

We also get a taste of the pleasures of heaven now, and that taste often comes through sensual pleasure. The enjoyment of a delicious meal, the hearing of a powerful symphony, the smell of flowers, the caresses of a loved one—these and other experiences have the power to release us from the grip of our present turmoil and cause us consider the incomprehensible joys that lie ahead of us. They sustain us as we live in a trouble-filled world.

These pleasures are God-given gifts for our enjoyment in the present world. While we cannot find our ultimate meaning here, we must not feel guilt as we enjoy these divine pleasures. We must remember that when we delight in pleasure, God is pleased. He has, after all, built our bodies with intense nerve endings suited to the stimulation of the senses. Sitting down to a sumptuous meal or experiencing the ecstasy of sexual intercourse with our spouse should cause us to praise our Creator and look forward to the heavenly joys to which they point us.

Pleasure: Above the Sun

Under the sun, pleasure frustrates. It titillates, but ultimately it lets us down. It may be enjoyable as long as it lasts, but it doesn't last long. As long as we think that all we have is the present life, the transience of pleasure can lead to obsessive grasping for the feeling again. Under the sun we are also driven to illicit desire and fulfillment. We will seek only pleasure and avoid pain at all costs.

If we fear God, we will recognize that true pleasure is that which anticipates the glory to come. It will drive us away from illegitimate desire. However—and this is an important distinction—that does not mean that all legitimate pleasure is nonsensual. Indeed, pleasure is at the heart of God. He built us with the dense nerve endings that lead to intense sensual desire. Enjoy a savory meal, not just in itself, but as a gift from God. Be carried away by powerful music as an anticipation of the music of heaven. Be enticed by the smell of the sea, the scent of a flower. Be seduced by the caresses and kisses of your spouse. Enjoy these moments of bliss as God's gift that opens a brief glimpse of the utter ecstasy to come when we live in God's glorious presence.

➤ *How Do We Chase after* **Pleasure***?*

1. Be honest with yourself. What do you enjoy doing more than anything else? If you had a completely free day and all the money in the world, how would you spend that day?

2. Does the search for pleasure consume you? Do you avoid pleasure? Would you consider yourself an addictive person? How would others characterize you?

3. Imagine your most enjoyable day, doing exactly what you want to do for fun and relaxation. After that day, do you see yourself thanking God? trying to forget that God knows what you've done? not even giving God a thought? Why or why not?

4. What sensual pleasures do you enjoy in life?

5. Would you characterize the pleasure you experience as a gift from God or an idol that enslaves? If the latter, how do you break the bondage?

6. How can you enjoy life in the midst of disappointment and even pain?

7. What do the feelings of joy you experience in the present teach you about heaven?

8. What Scripture passages help you understand God's joy when we feel pleasure?

PART FIVE

Chasing after
WISDOM

16
The Coup

NOAH woke up to the sound of a phone ringing somewhere in the room. He knew he heard a phone, but he couldn't locate the sound or move his body. He felt pinned to the bed.

The first thing Noah became aware of was his mouth: it was dry, thick. He had a hard time swallowing without tasting a gluelike texture that felt as if someone had left a can of Spam in his mouth. Noah's forehead thumped with every heartbeat. It kept rhythm, but it was a pulse that made him want to turn over and cover his head with a pillow.

The phone kept ringing. He then recalled where he was and what he had to do. He had to get up and prepare either to be fired or to be pardoned for his report on the Pearson stock.

Noah felt sick, and his steps were faltering and slow. He plodded to the shower without looking at the mirror. He knew if he looked, it would only sicken him more. *Why did I drink so much? I don't think I drank that much, but maybe the combination of the food, the cigars, and the wine— actually a lot of wine—probably took me way of out of my normal zone. I hope I didn't say anything I shouldn't have said.* His mind began to race to the conversation at the Blue Note. He could not even recall the taxi ride home. No matter. Nothing he said last night could influence the decision of the Brothers.

The two Andrajian brothers would have returned to their comfortable hotel, had a bowl of soup, and perhaps shared a dessert at a table in an inexpensive restaurant and made the decision regarding the Pearson stock. It was a decision that would affect Noah's life for many years.

He finally began to press himself toward the task. He had an hour to dress, eat breakfast, and make it to the meeting on the thirty-eighth floor of the Moody Building on 54th Street. He knew he would not be able to keep breakfast down, so he had a few more minutes to consider the weight of the day.

Noah's head throbbed, but fear began to push the physical effects of a hangover to the side. He felt as if he could easily let his spinning head and churning stomach win the day, but instead, he concentrated and made a few mental notes to underscore his conviction that he had made the right analysis of the Pearson portfolio.

Brothers Consolidated had a long history of selling stocks short and had made a great deal of money through the formula they used to determine when to buy and sell. In one major stock evaluation report Noah had effectively thrown the set of criteria for selling short into the Dumpster and challenged the way the firm did business. Noah's superiors were far less concerned about the threat of losing millions on the Pearson deal than they were about having their business philosophy challenged the way Noah had. No one believed the Brothers would permit a relative newcomer to the firm to take the family in an utterly different path.

Conventional wisdom could not have been more wrong.

When Noah reached the thirty-eighth floor, drips of sweat already trickled down his starched white shirt. Noah came into the conference room, and only a few people even noted his arrival. He was clearly marked as the sacrificial offering, and no one wanted to be mistaken as his confidant for fear of being taken outside the city gates with him to pay for the sins of the group.

The Brothers entered the room, and the meeting began. "Gentlemen, we have run a tight and competitive organization for many years. We have nothing to be ashamed of, and we are proud of the work you have all done. But the market is changing. Business is changing. We must change. We have reviewed the work of Mr. Noah Adamson, and we consider his insight and knowledge of the Pearson account to be a paradigm for evaluating and decision making on all our accounts."

Sam Andrajian, the older brother, looked at Noah and smiled. "Noah, I know that many people in this room doubted your work. They probably also assumed that your employment in this firm would soon be finished. Nothing could be further from the truth. We would like you to consider taking the position of senior vice president of analysis, working from Chicago, of course, advising and monitoring all the other analysts. We would like to know in several days if this would be acceptable to you. Of course, we plan to increase your income proportionately to the weight of the position."

James, the chief analyst in the New York office, and his staff of six paled and barely breathed as Sam spoke. It was a clear palace coup, and the senior analyst could feel the blade perilously suspended over his neck. He did not know whether to speak or remain inert and perhaps avoid losing his head. The Brothers did not wait for anyone to speak. They stood and walked out. Sam Andrajian walked by Noah, put his hand on his shoulder, and squeezed it. "Good job, Son." The Brothers departed.

The room seemed to lose air. The cabin had become depressurized, and no oxygen masks dropped. The men stared straight ahead, and no one said a word. Finally, Noah rose. He gathered up his briefcase and walked to the door. No one moved. Before Noah walked out, one of the junior men said, "Nice Hail Mary pass, Noah. I'll look forward to working with you."

Noah walked out of the room with his head lost in the clouds of success. He simply could not fathom what just happened. He walked to the elevator and didn't know whether to dance or to maintain his professional cool. He quickly calculated that his salary would triple and that his power would grow well beyond even his bosses in the Chicago office. In fact, it slowly dawned on Noah that he had just become their boss, at least in matters that affected their lives on the most basic level: what they bought and sold, and therefore how much they earned each year. He could barely contain himself with the thought of managing their most sacred commodity: money.

The air hit him squarely in the face when he walked out the door and onto 54th Street. His senses were alive, and the air was abrasive. Checking his watch, he noticed that he had three hours before his flight to Chicago would leave. He decided to walk. Carrying his head upright, he affected the swagger of a financial Brahmin.

Noah walked briskly as the wind whipped around the concrete canyons. Even though he had not remembered to take along his trench coat, he barely noticed the deepening chill. Time passed quickly, and in thirty minutes he had covered twenty blocks.

He stopped at the window of a three-story bookstore. One of the books in the window promised financial security in a matter of one year. He muttered to no one in particular, "Funny, I just achieved that in about ten minutes."

Noah thought back to the years and years of reading, the fine professors he had had in graduate school, the lengthy conversations with the few men who had encouraged him to pursue the risky world of stocks, and he chuckled, "No, it has been more like fifteen years that allowed that ten minutes to come to pass." He shuddered as he thought of the many hours he had spent in apparently purposeless study, review, and conversation. The chill of the wind drove him into the bookstore.

As soon as Noah walked into the warmth of the bookstore, he felt the first tinge of nausea. He dismissed it as the lingering effect of an indulgent night. He walked to the section that best fit his interests: Business. The gurus of hope beckoned to him as soon as he walked to their aisle. The glossy covers of the business books often pictured their authors: tan, confident, relaxed, and unashamedly rich. Noah lifted a few books from the shelf and settled into a comfortable chair to skim their contents.

The first book promised to lead readers into grand sums of money through a real estate deal. The second book promised a calamity that would make gold necessary for backing up near-useless paper. The third promised an investment strategy that would net readers a guaranteed 22 percent return. Noah laughed out loud and dumped all three books on the floor. The bookstore hired people to put the books away; he didn't want them to lose their job.

As he left his chair, Noah walked past the psychology section. He picked up a few books and noticed the same claims—just different focus. Depressed? This book will make you well in ten weeks. Divorced? You can find the love you deserve without all the hassle, disappointment, or loneliness you have felt so often. Dependent? Even if you have been a weak wimp or a spineless pushover, you can learn verbal combat techniques that will send people running for cover.

Noah felt even more sick. He seldom checked out the religion section of a bookstore, but he felt the tug to explore what was on the shelf. He moved past the books that taught New Age chanting and channeling and the empowerment spirituality that offered the opportunity to become a god or goddess. He finally found a few books that seemed to be based on the Bible. He walked back to his comfortable seat and began to read the dust jacket and the first few pages of a book.

He felt a tinge of irritation. It was obvious, at first glance, that he was looking at a well-used common formula. In some ways the book looked just like the business books or the psychology books. Each book made promises he knew it could not fulfill—if it did, it went further than claims found in the Bible. Each book was dressed in dignified tones but sounded the same shrill message: 4 Steps, 7 Steps, 12 Steps—easily understood, somewhat demanding, but really quite simple to fulfill—and you, too, can have a big, big taste of heaven now. He felt a growing degree of repulsion.

These books are no different from the others. What a game. It's the same sales job, no different from selling soap, fast cars, or even soft-porn magazines. Noah thought about the men sitting around the conference table. They had made the same mistake. They went for the conventional. They did what the herd had dictated, and they died in their stolid predictability.

Noah could feel his hands tighten around the book. He felt giddy and indignant. It hit him again that he had just won. He had won because he had dared to break the mold and challenge the system. He had stepped outside the rut, and though he could have crashed and burned in one fiery moment, he had not bailed out. He had won.

Noah looked at the wisdom touted in the books that lined the shelves around him and felt superior and irritated. He did not need the babble of the experts. He did not need the gurus of finance, the psyche, or even the spirit. He had made it without them. He knew enough to know that he didn't need to know what they knew: he either already knew it or would learn it by the hard work of working well.

Noah's brief detour into the bookstore had eaten up only another half hour. He had to return to the hotel, check out, and take a cab back to La Guardia. He had plenty of time, but he knew it was time to return to the real world.

He headed back to 54th Street. It was nearly 10:30. The streets were relatively empty. He walked deliberately. He would not stop again until he got to the hotel. His pace quickened as a cold shiver ran over his back. His suit coat was not a sufficient buffer to keep the chill at bay. As much as the bookstore had irritated and confirmed in him the strength of his will and the uniqueness of his perspective, it had still been a warm place, even if filled with the vapid wisdom of the day.

Noah felt like a gunslinger who had finished off the bad guys and was walking to collect his well-deserved reward. If asked if he felt pride, Noah would have been surprised by the question and uncertain how to answer. He did not feel pride at his storehouse of knowledge or bravado. He was far more confused at the refusal of intelligent people to see what he had seen. He was curious about why they had chosen to remain ensconced in the well-worn rut that had worked once but would not serve the good of the corporation or themselves in the future. He walked on, baffled, happy, and still strangely out of sorts with his body.

His eyes fell on an older couple walking a half block ahead of him. They were walking deliberately, but age and something else he could not describe made their pace much slower than his. The woman appeared to be about seventy. Her hair was wrapped in a rain bonnet, and her feet were clad in galoshes that reminded him of boots girls had worn when he was in fifth grade. Noah chuckled at her preparations for rain: it had been the driest fall in New York in years. There was no prospect of rain in the forecast.

As odd as the couple appeared, they were endearing even from forty yards behind. The woman's arm was linked around the man's left arm. His right hand gently touched her arm. It was clear she was the slower of the two. Apparently, he paced himself to her stride. He appeared to mirror her stature; his white hair and Winston hat were bent at about the same degree as her shoulders.

Noah sped up to get closer to them. Once he was about ten feet away, he slowed down to be able to observe them at a respectful distance. Close enough to hear them talk, he noticed their accents, which he guessed were Eastern European. On closer observation, Noah could see prayer-shawl cords hanging underneath the man's coat. Noah was intrigued by their lively chatter, which lightly cloaked their obviously tender regard for each other. Noah loved New York for moments like this.

He was enchanted by the couple, but he felt a surge of acidity in his mouth and deeper in his throat. His whole chest felt the seismic presence of heartburn.

Noah was irritated that he had no antacid in his briefcase. He remarked out loud: "If I had talked to Joan before I left, she would have reminded me to—"

He stopped midsentence and said loudly, "Joan! I can't believe I haven't called her." He looked to heaven. "What was I thinking? I'm a mess."

Noah picked up his pace. He had to call Joan before he got on the plane—in part to let her know the great news; mostly to apologize for not having told her he was leaving and for not having called her since arriving in New York.

He looked at the dark figures in front of him. They were approaching the corner to cross the street. Others were streaming against the light, dodging traffic; the older couple was wisely waiting for the light to turn green. Noah almost ran to the light. He looked at their hold on each other and thought, *I have never touched Joan with such poise. These two argue, but they are in love.* Noah's heart was beating wildly, but his legs felt weak and rubbery.

Noah stood directly to the left of the old woman. Traffic was zipping by at staggering speeds. While Noah pretended to stare at the light, he focused his eyes on the couple. The veins on the man's hands bulged and were bluish brown; the woman's face showed the marks of recent surgery, probably skin cancer. Her eyes were wet from the breeze, but they sparkled like lights over water. Her red lipstick seemed thick and too bright for her age, but her face was quiet and thoughtful from a lifetime of living.

Noah wanted to tell the woman he was sorry for the way he had treated Joan. He wanted to ask the man how he had loved this woman for a lifetime. Noah would no more have talked to them than pour his heart out on national TV, but the impulse served to bring him back to his senses. It had been a long morning, an exhausting several days, and he could be forgiven for a few moments of sentimentality given his physical state.

The light changed, and Noah stepped into the street. He never saw the streaking yellow cab that was trying to make it through the intersection just after the light had turned. It was a blur of a moment. He simultaneously felt a sharp jolt on his hip and a hand wrench his body back from the street. He crashed on the curb, but his fall was blunted by what felt like a soft pillow. In a timeless flutter of light and darkness cascading around him, Noah was startled to find the woman under him. A muscular hand from the crowd reached down and lifted Noah off the woman. She barely moved, and her husband reached down to help her sit up.

Noah was stretched out on the sidewalk. Countless people walked by, barely noticing the two bodies sitting and lying on the ground and an older man kneeling between them. Noah leaned forward and said, "Are you all right?" He could feel his head throb and his heart sink with fear that she was terribly hurt.

The older man put his hand on Noah's arm and said, "My Rosie has suffered too much in this life to be too troubled being the landing pad for an airborne goyim." A small smile crossed his lips, and Noah could see the woman smack her husband on the leg.

"Don't make the boy feel bad, Jakob, he is a tourist." Noah winced at the word He was not a tourist; he was a businessman, a juggler of multimillion-dollar deals.

"Ask the boy, Jakob, if he is hurt."

Jakob turned to Noah, and his eyes laughed: "Rosie, he is far more fit than you, so why don't you tend to yourself, and we will let him call his chiropractor on his own."

"Jakob, you are more rude than that Arab who almost split that young boy's head."

Noah broke their repartee. "Ma'am, I am fine. I think the cab mirror grazed my hip, but there are no broken bones, thanks to you. If you had not pulled me out of the way, I would be dead."

"Oh, you are daft. I probably hurt you worse by yanking on your shoulder. I probably caused you to tear your suit."

Noah felt so startled by her words he began to cry. "No, no, no. If you hadn't stopped me, ma'am, I would be dead, simple as that. You saved my life. I am here because of you."

Jakob put his arm around his wife's shoulders. "The boy is true, Rosie. Now sit still until we can find out what to do next."

Noah crawled to face Rosie eye to eye. Tears streamed down his cheeks. "I can't thank you enough." Rosie knew Noah was sincere. She said nothing. Noah saw her quiet eyes, and for the first lucid moment out of the shock, he felt the fear that raced through him. He had almost died, and some old woman had yanked him out of the grave.

He put his shaking head into his hands and sobbed, "What have I done to my wife?"

17

"Wisdom Ought to Put Me on Top"

IN OUR AGE of easy access to information and education, we place a high priority on knowledge. Sometimes we even deify knowledge, assuming that if we know enough and use our knowledge to make the right decisions, life will always work out for us.

Do any of these scenarios sound familiar to you?

"HOW dumb! I couldn't believe I had left out the igniter. I should have paid the additional twenty dollars to have the store assemble the grill. But I thought I was smart enough. The guy at the hardware store told me it would take only twenty minutes to put together. I believed them. After all, I can follow instructions. I read ten languages and have a Ph.D. from

an Ivy League school. How could I fail to put a grill together, right?
Wrong. I just wasted four hours, and the stupid grill still doesn't work."

- *"I was so embarrassed last night at dinner. I could hardly say a sentence
  without stumbling over my own words. And Rachel is so articulate.
  I know she didn't try to show me up or anything, but I just felt so stupid.
  Why can't I be a better conversationalist?"*

- *"And I thought that programming a VCR was hard! Navigating the Web
  is driving me crazy. I do a search for a specific homepage, and I come
  up with 22,343 possibilities. How do you narrow it down? I guess that's
  why the book The Internet for Dummies is such a big seller."*

DO YOU ever say that to yourself—"If only I were smarter. . ."? You may
be able to put a grill together in twenty minutes, but what about the
plumbing? Do you understand enough about the financial markets to
take care of your finances competently? Can you fly a plane? How many
languages do you know? Wouldn't you just love to know Spanish? As
you look into the sky and see the stars, do you feel intrigued about how
far they are and what wonders are out there? How about quarks and lep-
tons, the very stuff of matter? The list of things to know, some necessary
for everyday life and others that simply tug at our curiosity, is simply
endless. You would like to know more, but, in the final analysis, gaining
wisdom is as difficult as trying to chase the wind. . . .

Knowledge Means Power

Yes, knowledge means power. The smarter we are, the easier it is to navigate life. We stand in awe of the thirteen-year-old who graduates from
MIT, the high school or college valedictorian, the molecular scientist. We
look with joy and envy at our favorite television or movie heroes as they
get themselves out of life-threatening jams through the power of their
intellect and ingenuity. We marvel when James Bond or Mr. Spock over-
comes adversity with his wide range of knowledge about the world and
how it works.

We want to be smarter because we want an edge in a world driven by
information. Information is gold, and access to it is like having a pirate's
map. Noah is the buccaneer that surfs the Internet and has access to
information that even a decade ago would have been unobtainable. But

Noah is more than "connected"; he is savvy and shrewd. He is willing to take risks with the information he possesses.

But knowledge truly "puffs up" unless it is used to serve others. And most learning comes at such cost and time that we often hoard our information and stand aloof, feeling superior to those who are not "in the know." Noah's superior knowledge brought him success because he was willing to stand outside the stream of conventional wisdom/knowledge.

His knowledge of the ways of the world also caused him to look at the self-help wisdom with appropriate suspicion. What is marketed as wisdom is often an illusion of mastery that disappears in thin air when reality dawns. The stacks of self-help books that promised Noah control and power did not allure him; they sickened him. But his disgust at their superficial solutions and hollow promises did not compel him to challenge the basis of his own knowledge or what he did with it. It allowed him only to stand aside from the marketing pitches and feel superior. It would take another of God's intrusions into his life to compel him to reconsider what he "knew."

What happens when we pursue knowledge? What becomes of the knowledge? Does it really lead to power? to life?

Listen to someone who pursued knowledge with a passion: "I devoted myself to search for understanding and to explore by wisdom everything being done in the world. . . . I said to myself, 'Look, I am wiser than any of the kings who ruled in Jerusalem before me. I have greater wisdom and knowledge than any of them.' So I worked hard to distinguish wisdom from foolishness. But now I realize that even this was like chasing the wind. For the greater my wisdom, the greater my grief. To increase knowledge only increases sorrow" (Eccles. 1:13, 16-18).

What can the Teacher mean? Surely being intelligent contributes to happiness, not to sorrow and grief.

Let me share with you Richard's story. Richard was incredibly bright. He graduated from high school early. His small community extolled him, and most adults wished that their children had his abilities. He was accepted into one of the country's most prestigious schools. He excelled in college, completed a doctoral program, and soon began a teaching career.

Richard, though brilliant, was an utter failure as a teacher. He had no social skills and could not form a lasting relationship with anyone. He had little ability to communicate with students, so he was an unpopular teacher. He thrived at writing learned papers that only a handful could understand, but that is what gave him his only sense of success, so he spent most of his time doing research. His academic reputation encouraged the university to give Richard tenure, but he was miserable inside.

Contrary to popular expectation, Richard's great intelligence did not lead to happiness. He is a living illustration of the Teacher's denial of the connection between intelligence and success in life. Richard's realization is not uncommon.

In a recent best-selling book, *Emotional Intelligence,* Daniel Goleman counters the popular idea that people's high IQ will place the world at their fingertips. Goleman's study led to the conclusion that "a high IQ is no guarantee of prosperity, prestige, or happiness in life." He goes on to cite a study of college graduates with varying IQs; the study shows no correlation between the graduates' IQ and their "salary, productivity, or status" or their "happiness with friendships, family, and romantic relationships." His conclusion is "at best, IQ contributes about 20 percent to the factors that determine life success, which leaves 80 percent to other forces."[1]

In this way, Goleman simply stumbles across a truth stated long ago by the Bible. Once again it is the Teacher who pierces our preconceptions to tell us that life is not won by the pursuit of intelligence. We can be the smartest person in the world but still bumble through life.

Knowledge in the Garden

But the Teacher was not the first to burst the balloon. We should have learned the lesson from the Garden of Eden.

Humanity's fall from an intimate relationship with God took place by eating the fruit of the tree. We all know that, but we often forget what kind of tree it was. Adam and Eve rebelled against God by eating from the tree of the knowledge of good and evil.

When the serpent tempted Eve, he cast his spell over her by telling her that the fruit of that tree would give her further knowledge: "You will become just like God, knowing everything, both good and evil" (Gen. 3:5).

And when Adam and Eve ate, their knowledge increased, or in the words of the biblical text, "their eyes were opened" (Gen. 3:7). They then knew they were naked. They fled from each other, and they hid from God.

We can hear the Teacher say again, "The greater my wisdom, the greater my grief. To increase knowledge only increases sorrow" (Eccles. 1:18).

Think of the tremendous strides humankind has made in just the past hundred years! We have gone from riding horses to driving cars to launching space shuttles. We have progressed from pencils to computers, from Pony Express to E-mail and faxes.

But have these unquestionable and marvelous advances brought happiness and success to the world? Has the world grown in harmony and community? The answer is obvious. Pursuing intelligence under the sun is meaningless.

If Not Intelligence, Then Wisdom

People who know the Bible well know that it is not intelligence that is prized, but wisdom. Hear the book of Proverbs:

Happy is the person who finds wisdom and gains understanding. For the profit of wisdom is better than silver, and her wages are better than gold. Wisdom is more precious than rubies; nothing you desire can compare with her. She offers you life in her right hand, and riches and honor in her left. She will guide you down delightful paths; all her ways are satisfying. Wisdom is a tree of life to those who embrace her; happy are those who hold her tightly. Proverbs 3:13-18

WHAT is the difference between intelligence and wisdom? To be smart, a person has to know a lot of facts. Remember back to your school days as you prepared for tests. The teachers gave you large amounts of material that you had to memorize in order to succeed on the test. Early on, it might be a list of spelling words. Later it was the battles of the Civil War. If you took a foreign language, then you had lists of vocabulary and grammatical rules to memorize.

As you progressed through the grades, learning became more than rote memorization. You needed to synthesize facts, requiring the ability to take principles and apply them to previously unseen problems. Nonetheless, even then, everything had its basis in knowing facts.

Biblical wisdom, on the other hand, is more like a skill. It is more a "knowing how" than a "knowing that." At its height, wisdom is an ability to have insight as to the best way to live life.

Indeed, in many ways biblical wisdom is similar to Goleman's concept of emotional intelligence. Emotional intelligence goes well beyond facts; it "includes self-control, zeal and persistence and the ability to motivate oneself."[2] He expands on this concept later in his book, when he says that emotional intelligence includes "abilities such as being able to motivate oneself and persist in the face of frustration; to control impulse and delay gratification; to regulate one's moods and keep distress from swamping the ability to think; to empathize and to hope."[3]

Biblically wise people can navigate life successfully not only because they know many facts but also because they know the right time to express their emotions and make decisions. They do not get buried in disappointment when they experience a setback. Rather, they look at the situation and have hope that things will get better.

At the heart of wisdom, as we saw in the first chapter about control, is the ability to know the right time for a thought, an action, or an emotion.

Daniel: Wise beyond His Years

Daniel is a biblical example of a wise person. In the year 605 B.C. his hometown was overrun by the Babylonians, and he was carted off to Babylon as an exile. Babylon was the richest, most powerful country in that part of the world. Imagine Daniel and his friends as they were brought into the capital city. At that time, Daniel was a young man. Most people would be shaking in their boots, ready to do whatever was necessary to survive.

But Daniel was calm as he was brought into the precincts of Nebuchadnezzar's palace and placed under the direction of Ashpenaz, the palace chief. Daniel remained calm even when he had to make a life-and-death decision. Daniel had a committed relationship to the God of Israel, and he could not in good conscience eat the pagan food that he was commanded to eat (Dan. 1:8-10). He tactfully asked Ashpenaz whether he and his friends could be allowed to eat food other than the food required by the king. Ashpenaz was afraid to give Daniel permission, fearing not only for Daniel's skin but also for his own.

Daniel hit an apparent dead end, but he did not panic. He did not grow depressed. He came up with another plan. He convinced the food-serving attendant to allow Daniel and his friends to eat other food. The attendant agreed to Daniel's plan.

The result was that Daniel and his three friends remained faithful to their God and actually became stronger and wiser than all the others. Indeed, we are told that "in all matters requiring wisdom and balanced judgment, the king found the advice of these young men to be ten times better than that of all the magicians and enchanters in his entire kingdom" (Dan. 1:20). Through insight and planning, Daniel achieved his goal.

We cannot read the book of Daniel or the book of Proverbs without having a deep desire to obtain the kind of wisdom that leads to success and happiness. We want to be able to navigate life no matter what troubles or setbacks we encounter.

The Limits of Wisdom
Wisdom Goes Only So Far

But even wisdom is insufficient. Wisdom is limited because it depends on our ability to know the right time and place for a word or an action. As the Teacher perceptively observed, "God has made everything beautiful for its own time. He has planted eternity in the human heart, but even so, people cannot see the whole scope of God's work from beginning to end" (Eccles. 3:11).

The book of Job tells a story that illustrates the limits of human wisdom. Though the reader knows that Job's suffering is the result of debate between Satan and God, none of the human participants in the drama have a clue. Job's life is thrown into chaos, and he is left to ponder why. Job loses his family, his wealth, and his health, and he wonders what he should do next. After all, he knew that his relationship with God had been good, so what could he have done to deserve his fate?

His three friends, however, thought that they had the wisdom to determine both the cause of Job's suffering and its cure. They declared that Job was obviously a sinner; he needed to repent. It was as simple as that. The problem was that Job knew that his suffering was not the result of something he had done.

Job's wisdom as well as his friends' wisdom left them in the dark. They could only complain and argue. We will come back to this story in the next chapter.

Wisdom Has No Sure Rewards

The lure of wisdom is that it can bring us a successful life. It provides a way for us to survive and thrive in an uncertain world. The Teacher at one point says as much: "Being wise is as good as being rich; in fact, it is better. Wisdom or money can get you almost anything, but it's important to know that only wisdom can save your life" (Eccles. 7:11-12).

But elsewhere he acknowledges that you can't always depend on wisdom. Sometimes it lets you down: "In this meaningless life, I have seen everything, including the fact that some good people die young and some wicked people live on and on. So don't be too good or too wise! Why destroy yourself? On the other hand, don't be too wicked either—don't be a fool! Why should you die before your time? So try to walk a middle course" (Eccles. 7:15-18).

This passage is staggering when we pause to consider it. Did you ever imagine that the Bible would caution you to beware of being too good or too wise? Now we must remember that the Teacher restricted his observations to truth as it is under the sun, apart from spiritual realities. And in that light, his observation strikes us as quite true. We know not only godly and wise people who suffer deeply but also godless and selfish people who live blindly blissful lives.

Two people I know, Charles and Mark, illustrate this point quite well. Charles sacrificed dearly for the Lord. He had gifts and energy to create a wonderfully meaningful and prosperous life for himself in the United States, but he and his wife felt called into ministry overseas. They ministered for years in Asia, and as a result of their self-denying labors, many people came to the Lord. Today Charles is still relatively young and continues to sacrificially serve the Lord. How has the Lord rewarded his wise and good servant? Charles suffers from a host of diseases that may eventually take his life. His wife's health also suffers. Charles, a wise servant of God, sacrificed dearly for his Lord.

On the other hand is Mark. Mark is the father of a close friend who recently died. Mark's son served the Lord devotedly during his short life. Cancer took him, leaving his wife and children desolate. Mark, however, lives and prospers, although he has abused his body for years through various addictions, living the life of the fool. He seems happy enough, even though his drunken driving without a license has put him in jail a number of times and has put a few other people in the hospital. Mark acts as if he does not have a care in the world.

Wisdom is no guarantee of the good life. Again, the Teacher says: "I have observed something else in this world of ours. . . . The wise are often poor, and the skillful are not necessarily wealthy. And those who are educated don't always lead successful lives. It is all decided by chance, by being at the right place at the right time" (Eccles. 9:11).

But even if the godly wise lived wonderful lives, the Teacher tells us that it still is not worth it.

The End of Wisdom

The Teacher was not a fool; indeed, he was recognized by many as a professional wise man (Eccles. 12:9). And he pointed out the advantages of wisdom over foolishness: "So I decided to compare wisdom and folly, and anyone else would come to the same conclusions I did. Wisdom is of more value than foolishness, just as light is better than darkness. For the wise person sees, while the fool is blind" (Eccles. 2:12-14).

So it appears that the Teacher acknowledged that in some sense wisdom can be a guide to life. He gives us the vivid metaphor of sight and blindness. A fool is someone who tries to live life with a blindfold, and the result has to be knocking into the furniture and sore shins. On the other hand, the wise can walk confidently and safely through life because their eyes are wide open, seeing all the obstacles before they run into them.

Many people are wise, but only in their own estimation. Therefore, they end up running into obstacles that are as dangerous as a fast-moving cab. Many people believe that they see things that other people—people less intelligent, less educated, less sophisticated—fail to notice. One of the saddest sights is great intelligence and learning that has made people even more blind. That kind of blindness leads to moral, spiritual, and relational stupidity.

Noah is brilliant in his own field, but he is a fool with regard to life. He is bright enough to keep an intellectual force field around his heart, and he uses his well-groomed contempt to wound anyone who might get too close. But people with even a dime's worth of sense know when something is wrong with their inner world and their relationships. Noah was blind and walked into danger, but the Spirit of God had aroused Noah to take notice of an older couple who clearly loved each other. Their lives were a wake-up call that made it clear to Noah that something was terribly wrong with his life, even though on the surface his life appeared to be wildly successful. Wisdom warns and alerts the heart that one of the greatest obstacles in navigating life is pride and defensiveness.

But the Teacher does not stop with these observations. He continues:

"Yet I saw that wise and foolish people share the same fate. Both of them die. Just as the fool will die, so will I. So of what value is all my wisdom? Then I said to myself, 'This is all so meaningless!' For the wise person and the fool both die, and in the days to come, both will be forgotten" (Eccles. 2:14b-16).

Death brings wisdom to an end. Even if wisdom brought wonderful rewards, it will not forestall death or make it any easier. Death is the great equalizer that puts all people on the same plane. Often God uses death or its near presence to awaken people to the small, insignificant part they play in the universe. It is this sober wisdom that Rosie offers Noah in plucking him from death.

Someone might respond, though, that wisdom and kindness will live on in memory; their deeds and accomplishments will bless the following generations. The Teacher told a story to crush that hope:

> There was a small town with only a few people living it, and a great king came with his army and besieged it. There was a poor, wise man living there who knew how to save the town, and so it was rescued. But afterward no one thought any more about him. Then I realized that though wisdom is better than strength, those who are wise will be despised if they are poor. What they say will not be appreciated for long. Ecclesiastes 9:14-16

WISE people not only will not be appreciated for long; they won't even be remembered! All the accomplishments of our wisdom don't last very long, and they are then buried in the sands of time.

The Corruption of Wisdom

People can be wise but use their wisdom for evil purposes. People can have insight into the best way to navigate life but use it to personal advantage at the expense of other people.

In 2 Samuel 13:3, Jonadab is called "shrewd" (NIV) or "crafty" (NLT). These are acceptable translations of the original Hebrew word, which meant "wise." This is appropriate for its context because craftiness and shrewdness are essentially wisdom gone bad.

Jonadab could look at a situation and see how to achieve its successful conclusion. His friend, Prince Amnon, had a problem. He was in love with his half sister Tamar, but "it seemed impossible that he could ever fulfill his love for her" (2 Sam. 13:2). Amnon called Jonadab for his advice. Jonadab casually and quickly responded by telling Amnon to feign sickness and ask Tamar to be his nurse. Amnon did what Jonadab suggested. When Tamar came to Amnon's house to care for him, Amnon raped her. Jonadab, the crafty friend, is the incarnation of wisdom gone bad.

We can see the actual transition from good to evil wisdom in Solomon. He was the paragon of godly wisdom at the beginning of his reign. He ruled selflessly, caring less about money and power than about his people's relationship with God. But he fell in love with foreign women, women who worshiped other gods and from whom he should have kept his distance. Solomon's wisdom turned to folly toward the end of his life, and the result was the eventual division of Israel into two parts (1 Kings 12).

WE HAVE seen enough to conclude that wisdom is not the ultimate answer. Pursuing it does not lead to lasting significance. But is it as meaningless as the Teacher would have us believe?

18
Another Awakening

THE RIDE to the airport was eerie. The cab smelled like sweat and garlic. The Middle Eastern driver, head swathed in a turquoise cloth, drove with the same kind of abandon that less than an hour before could have cost Noah his life.

Noah slumped against the door, leaning his head against the cool window. He tried to sort out images swirling through his mind. Soon after Noah was hurt, a policeman who saw the cab hit Noah reported the driver. Noah was told that the driver would be arrested and likely made a scapegoat for all the murderous driving in the city. Noah was also told he would have to return as a witness. If he refused, he would be charged with some crime. It did not matter what he did or didn't do, he would have to return in a few weeks to help the city make this hapless driver hang from the yardarm to warn other cabbies to drive with a little less zeal.

Noah did not mind. He had to return soon anyway. He had to look into the eyes of the woman who had yanked him out of the grave. At the time he was hit, he had been so stunned that he wasn't able articulate his feelings to Jakob and Rosie. He had had enough sense to get their address and phone number. But as he thought about what had happened, he realized that a call would never do. He wanted to look into their aged faces and somehow do what he never had done with any human being: thank them for existing, thank them for saving him.

When he arrived at the airport, he had no time to call Joan. He dashed down the congested aisle to reach the plane door moments before it closed. He slumped in his first-class seat and let the flight attendant serve him a plastic glass of Scotch to calm the adrenaline that marched through his blood. Then and only then did he feel the pulsing bruise on his leg and pelvis. He went to the rest room, unbuckled his pants, and saw the blue web of broken vessels and the reddish cast of coagulating blood just below the surface of his skin. He felt faint.

A flight attendant knocked on the door to tell him he was holding up the plane's departure. He didn't care. She could have screamed in his face, and it would not have hurried him a second faster.

Slowly he dressed himself and looked one last time in the mirror. He had to know what he looked like. It was not the desire to regain composure; it was to discover what he had lost and never knew he possessed. He looked into his aging face. He was tired and lonely, but for what felt like the first time in his life, he saw beyond his skin, the surface of his existence. He saw a strange flame in his eyes. It was a flame different from the spark that he often felt before he made a big presentation or when he took on a peer in a debate. It was different from when he jumped into the waters of the unknown to wrest clarity from chaos. He looked like a man who had a soul. It was something he had never noticed before. He liked the eyes that peered back at him.

The trip home was uneventful. He checked his calendar before landing and was stunned to see that the Bible study was scheduled to be at his home that night. He was thrilled. He had forgotten about the evening in the wash of the last few days, but even if the study had been held at the shrine of Elvis and even if his car were to be towed for the second time, he would not have missed the evening. He was not surprised by his excitement, but he would not have been able to say why.

When Noah got off the plane, he could barely walk. Each step was labored, and he noticed his pants were torn and streaked with dirt. He chuckled and smiled at the passing glances that indicated he was a spectacle. It didn't matter.

The Bible Study

As each person arrived at the Bible study, Joan made an apology about Noah's absence. She was clearly distraught and could not hide her irritation and fear. She had not talked with Janet, Noah's secretary, all day, but she had dialed the number at least twenty times. She wondered if she would see him that night or if he would call.

She had asked God for wisdom and knew he was willing to give to all who asked without finding fault, but she had no more idea what to say or do than when she had first begun to pray.

The group was edgy. Jack directed everyone to sit rather than letting the tension increase. "Joan, it is obvious you are in pain, and we don't want to intrude. But we also don't want to ignore what you have been going through. Do you want to talk? We were going to look at Ecclesiastes' view of knowledge, wisdom, and skill in living, but I must confess I have no idea how to proceed tonight. We can just pray for you tonight. We can proceed. If you wish, we can cancel and give you space. Joan, what do you need from us?"

Jessie slid closer to Joan and put her arm around her shoulder. Mimi got off the floor and sat near Joan's feet and put her hand on her leg. Joan could feel the attentive care of each person in the group. She hated being on the spot, but she felt the warmth of their love. Before she could speak, everyone froze when the garage door began to open.

It seemed like an interminable period of time before Noah opened the door, walked into the kitchen, and then into the family room where the Bible study group waited. He stood in the opening between the kitchen and family room, his coat in one hand and his briefcase in the other. His pants were disheveled; his face was tired. He clearly walked with a limp. No one had ever seen Noah so soiled by life—or more radiant.

Joan gasped. She did not know whether to run to him or sit as quietly as she could. Instead, she stood up, her hands to her mouth and eyes wide in disbelief. No one spoke, but Joan slowly approached Noah as if she were being drawn to him by a tow rope pulling her up a steep incline. She did not fight the inevitable movement up the mountain, but without the pull, she would never have approached him. Noah hobbled to her, dropped both his coat and briefcase, and put his arms around her and began to shake. No words came. No tears flowed. But the weight of thousands of days of determined distance and well-groomed independence fell from him like the scales from a blind man's eyes.

He could not stop shaking. He could not let go of Joan. Joan slid her arms around him, sensing he could not move or stand. She guided him to the nearest chair. Noah again felt for the second time that day the concentrated power of a woman's hands and arms as she led him to safety. He followed her with obedient gratitude.

Mark spoke first: "Noah, we will leave if that's what you want. It's apparent that something has happened, and maybe it's better for you to talk with your wife first without us here."

Suzi leaned against her husband and put her hand on his leg, "We're newlyweds, but we know enough to know when it's time to leave. Noah, would you like us to leave the two of you alone so that you can talk?"

Noah looked at Suzi and Mark with kindness. "I suspect you are right. You already have a far better foundation in your marriage than we do in ours. The last few days—actually the last six hours—have made that painfully clear. I want you to stay for a few minutes and let me tell you what I have gone through—no, what I have taken in today. Then, you are right, I have so many things to say to Joan, and at least for now, it's better for me to say them just to her."

Jack sat forward and asked, "Are you in pain, Noah?"

"I am. I actually could use some Advil if anyone has some."

Joan jumped up and within a minute was back with water and three pills.

"Thanks, honey." Joan flinched. It was the second time in several days he used a word she had never heard; this time it sounded authentic.

"On the way home, I got a Bible from the back of the plane and looked at the first chapter of Ecclesiastes again. I read something that I will paraphrase. It said: 'I worked hard to see the difference between wisdom and foolishness. But it is no different from any other endeavor: it's chasing after wind. For the more I know, the more I'm in pain. The more wisdom I gain, the more sorrow I feel.' I don't know if I get it yet, but even though I didn't quote it exactly, this single point stands out: Knowledge and wisdom lead not to greater control but to more pain and sorrow.

"I don't know how to tell you what I have been through the last few weeks. For one, I have been in a furious battle to change the direction of the company I work for. And today I won that war. Not the battle, but the war. I was promoted to senior vice president of analysis for the entire firm. It is an incredible honor. I have been so consumed with this war that I have neglected my wife, my boys. You too." Noah looked at the group, and most of the faces were intent and expectant. Joan's eyes were riveted to the floor.

"But the success I achieved today was almost lost today forever. Far more, I was almost lost for this life." Joan's face frantically turned toward him.

"I almost died today." Noah's body began to shake again. For the first time, he covered his face with his hands and let the tears stream down his cheeks. Joan had never seen Noah weep. She quickly came out of her chair and put her arms around him. He wept and did not once attempt to hinder the flow.

Jack instinctively bowed his head. Marcia followed, and soon the whole group began to pray silently. Noah's tears began to subside after many minutes, and Jack asked if he could pray for Noah and Joan. Noah looked straight at Jack and said, "Please, Jack. I have never needed someone to pray for me more than I do now." Jack rose, and without a word the group stood and surrounded the red-eyed Noah and silent Joan.

"Father, we are privileged beyond words to be part of this moment with two people we love. Beyond all words, we thank you for preserving Noah's life. We don't know the details. We know only that you were directly and intimately involved in plucking him from death. Whatever your purpose in this event, we ask that you use it to further save his heart and win it for you. I ask that you would take his gratitude and deepen his love for you, for his wife, for the path you have set for him from eternity. Don't let the evil one take away the good fruit that we trust will come from this great rescue. Our great God, we pray that Noah will not try to figure out too soon what you are doing in his life. Keep him from his tendency to try to manage his life and figure out the principles you want him to learn. Give him a profound taste of your love." Jack stopped. A few others prayed, and after a few moments, they returned to their seats.

Noah looked at each person, and it was as if he had awakened from a dream. He saw tears in the eyes of many. He could not discount their love. He finally looked at Joan and said, "I don't know what to say. I know you know that I have not put a lot of energy into our relationship. I have never really wanted to know you or the kids. I didn't know it before, but I know now that if I had been wiser about you and the kids, I would have known you were suffering, and I would have done something to change the direction of our world. I didn't. And I have no excuse. I have spent my life learning and knowing more than anyone else in my field. And today it took me to both the height of my career and almost the end of my life. What's it worth—all my work, my reading, my knowledge?

"In a blink of an eye, lost in my thoughts, reeling from pride and the thrill of victory, I nearly walked into the path of a cab. And an angel—or what I saw later, a plump Jewish woman with a thick Eastern accent—plucked me from death. I can't tell you why, but for a couple blocks I followed her and her husband and found myself saying, 'They are in love.' They had more sensual contact and passion in their hobbled walk and their touch than I have ever known with you, Joan. It's not your fault. It is . . ." Noah closed his eyes, and from their hidden spring tears poured out and wet the ground for the harvest that was to come.

This time no one moved. They waited for Noah to resume. Shortly, he did. "It is my fault. I can barely say more. I have not wanted to see what kind of man I was to my family, to you, Joan. The knowledge I have chosen to live for was designed to get me ahead, to keep me out of the fray of life. It is clear to me now I have not wanted to know you or for anyone to know me. More knowledge means more pain. I don't know why, but I can't bear myself or my direction, but I don't know what is ahead."

Joan put her hands on his leg. Noah looked down at her as she sat near his feet. It seemed to him as if the position ought to be reversed. He ought to be sitting at the feet of the woman who had spoken so boldly in a car, who had suffered the loneliness of his detachment and contempt. Instead, he towered above her, and she soared above him. Her eyes were rich in hope, gentle in forgiveness. He felt the inexorable exhaustion that comes when a soul moves.

19

Restoring Wisdom
through Relationship

THE TEACHER has eradicated any naive trust we may have in intelligence and wisdom. Pursuing wisdom as a way of living in a troubled world does not work in the end. We are left bewildered as we face unexpected tragedy. We are confused by evil, not only in the world, but also in our own hearts. We will never be smart enough or insightful enough to live life effortlessly and without being hurt.

But are we reduced to "chasing the wind"? The Bible suggests that we are not. Ecclesiastes encourages us to gain an above-the-sun perspective by pursuing God.

Noah had more than a mere "near death" experience. To trivialize his awakening by saying, "It often happens" is to miss what Noah came to see. He almost died, but worse, he almost lived like a successful, arrogant, self-possessed fool. It was not "near death" that changed him; it was seeing that he had not come near to life, especially near to his wife.

What do people gain if they possess the world but lose their soul? Worse than nothing, because all they possess will come to mock and haunt them for giving up the only "reality" that will last for eternity: Their soul and their relationships.

Noah came to face one simple truth: All our knowledge or gain that takes us to greater self-sufficiency is, in fact, rubbish. It is the basis of our self-righteousness, therefore, that causes our blindness. Most of us must be plucked from the fire, as Noah was, before we begin to see the light.

Let's return to the story of Job to see how God plucked him from his blindness. We have seen how Job and his friends tried to grapple with his predicament through the power of their wisdom, their understanding of how life worked. To these friends, Job's suffering was a result of his sin. The solution was obvious to them: repent and act faithfully. The problem was that Job knew that losing his family, wealth, and health was not due to disobedience.

On the other hand, Job, though he did not know the reason why he suffered, also had his own idea of the right course of action. He would confront God with the injustice God had perpetrated against him! That is how he would navigate the huge obstacles that loomed in his life.

In one sense, Job got what he wanted, a meeting with God. But Job was ill prepared for what that signified. Job wanted to place God on trial, challenging what Job perceived God had done to him. Instead, God put Job on trial, and the trial was precisely in this area of wisdom: "Then the Lord answered Job from the whirlwind: 'Who is this that questions my wisdom with such ignorant words? Brace yourself, because I have some questions for you, and you must answer them'" (Job 38:1-3).

In chapters 38 through 41, God questions Job's wisdom, and he presents his own. He asks Job a series of questions about the making and running of the universe. God also describes how he is the One who endows some creatures with wisdom while withholding it from others (e.g., the ostrich in Job 39:13-18).

What is God really telling Job? What is he asking Job to do? We get our answer when we observe Job's response to God. Job responds twice, and the first response (Job 40:3-5) has the tenor of the second:

"I know that you can do anything, and no one can stop you. You ask, 'Who is this that questions my wisdom with such ignorance?' It is I. And I was talking about things I did not understand, things far too wonderful for me.

"You said, 'Listen and I will speak! I have some questions for you, and you must answer them.'

"I had heard about you before, but now I have seen you with my own eyes. I take back everything I said, and I sit in dust and ashes to show my repentance." Job 42:2-6

THROUGH his suffering, Job learned a lesson that the book that bears his name intends us to hear: Wisdom is not learning certain things; wisdom is a *relationship*. Job's response to God's challenge is to surrender to Wisdom himself. In the words of C. S. Lewis: "I know now, Lord, why you utter no answer. You are yourself the answer. Before your face questions die away."[1]

Embracing Lady Wisdom

As Job bends his knee, our attention is brought back to the book of Proverbs and the motto that begins the book: "Fear of the Lord is the beginning of knowledge" (Prov. 1:7). We often misunderstand the book of Proverbs as a book about learning or knowing certain things; but it is a book about a relationship. The book is structured in a way that forces us to remember that the pithy principles in chapters 10 through 31 should never be read outside of the context of the lesson of the first nine chapters and its banner headline: The source of true wisdom is a relationship to God.

The book of Proverbs was addressed to men in its ancient context. Its application extends to both sexes, but the language of Lady Wisdom is particularly appealing to men. The underlying metaphor of the chapter is that the reader is on the path of life when he sees this attractive woman who calls to him to join her in her house. A complication is introduced by the fact that the chapter describes a second woman; a woman we will call Dame Folly. Hear the text describe her and her words:

The woman named Folly is loud and brash. She is ignorant and doesn't even know it. She sits in her doorway on the heights overlooking the city. She calls out to men going by who are minding their own business. "Come home with me," she urges the simple. To those without good judgment, she

says, "Stolen water is refreshing; food eaten in secret tastes the best!" But
the men don't realize that her former guests are now in the grave.
Proverbs 9:13-18

Two women, Wisdom and Folly, invite the men to enter into an intimate
relationship with them. Who are these women?

Our answer comes from the fact that their houses are located on the
high point of the city. In the ancient Near East, only one building could
stand on the highest point of the city, namely, the temple. Wisdom clearly
represents God's wisdom; indeed, Lady Wisdom stands for God himself.
On the other hand, Folly represents all the false gods and goddesses, the
idols, that try to seduce God's people away from their true Master.

For our purposes, the most important insight that these chapters of
Proverbs give us is that wisdom is a relationship. As we embrace Lady
Wisdom, we enter into a deep and abiding relationship with God himself.

Christ, the Wisdom of God

As Christians, we should read Proverbs 1–9 from the perspective of the
New Testament, which tells us that if we want to see God's wisdom, look
at Christ. If we want to be wise, then have a relationship with Jesus
Christ.

The apostle Paul understood this: "In [Christ] lie hidden all the trea-
sures of wisdom and knowledge" (Col. 2:3). Jesus Christ is the wisdom
of God: He is a wisdom that the world finds to be foolishness.

In the New Testament, Paul tells us that "God in his wisdom saw to it
that the world would never find him through human wisdom" (1 Cor.
1:21). But where does he say true wisdom is found? In Christ, and "we
can understand these things, for we have the mind of Christ" (1 Cor.
2:16).

Christ is the wisdom of God. We find wisdom only when we turn to
him. But what does this mean in practical terms?

How to Live Wisely

We want to know it all. We desire to live life in a way that escapes harm.
When threatened with trouble, we want to know the way to get out of it.
But pursuing this kind of wisdom is a dead end. Hope is found only
where Job found it: by surrendering to God.

We can't know it all. Indeed, we can know only a very little about

God's vast and rich creation. Awareness of our limitations should breed humility and dependence.

Intellectual arrogance is the product of a narrow mind. Certainly it is possible for some people to surpass other people in their specific areas of human knowledge. Brain surgeons know much more about that complex organ than most lawyers do, for example. Bible scholars have a better grasp of the content of God's Word than most other Christians do. Astronomers and mathematicians can amaze us with their discussions of quarks and black holes. But there is so much in the world that these people do not know.

Streetwise people know how to get information to live successfully in the city, but they may not know much about farming. Putting a farmer in the middle of New York City or putting an urban dweller in charge of a dairy farm is the stuff of comedies.

Only God knows it all. Only he knows everything about everything, and that is why we bow before him. We need to remain humble toward and dependent on God and other people. That we do not have all the skills for living should engender a sense of community in us, both in the church and in the world.

Paul beautifully expresses this truth in regard to the church. No one has all the gifts! Rather, "all of you together are Christ's body, and each one of you is a separate and necessary part of it" (1 Cor. 12:27). And here the church is a mirror of the world. We are dependent on each other's gifts to work together to live wisely. And these gifts are divinely bestowed, which means that we are ultimately dependent on God himself.

This picture—a world of people, each gifted by God with wisdom in a diversity of areas, working together in harmony and helping each other to navigate life—is an attractive one. But as beautiful as this picture seems, we all know that the picture is far from the reality, not only in the world, but even in the church.

Life is more like a war. People hoard their knowledge and their gifts for their own selfish ends. Many are as apt to use it to harm others as to help them.

How should we react to this reality? Hear what Jesus told his disciples as he sent them out into the world: "I am sending you out like sheep among wolves. Therefore be as shrewd as snakes and as innocent as doves" (Matt. 10:16, NIV). First, we should not become like the self-centered hoarders of knowledge. As we go out among the wolves, we need to remain sheep. We need to retain our innocence, our humility, and our dependence on one another.

But in another sense we need to be as shrewd as snakes. To be shrewd is to be wise with a wary eye on the other person. To be shrewd is to expect the other person to try to harm you and to be prepared to defend yourself. And the snake metaphor suggests that in our interaction with others, we should not be so predictable but, rather, get people to consider the truth in unexpected ways.

Christians need to hear this message as it relates to our intelligence. To be humble and dependent does not mean to sacrifice our intelligence to our faith. If we do, we betray our faith, which claims not only our hearts but also our minds.

Evangelical Christianity has a reputation as being anti-intellectual, and sometimes we are. But the Bible suggests that things should be otherwise. Two passages have always motivated me in this regard. The apostle Peter encourages us to "always be prepared to give an answer to everyone who asks you to give the reason for the hope that you have" (1 Peter 3:15, NIV). And Paul, describing the life of the mind as a battle, commands us to "take captive every thought to make it obedient to Christ" (2 Cor. 10:5, NIV).

Christians are blessed with the mind of Christ. We have a responsibility to reflect that mind to the rest of the world.

Wisdom: Above the Sun

We cannot find a more powerful and eloquent exposition of the difference between wisdom under the sun and wisdom above the sun than that which Paul gives us in 1 Corinthians 1:18–2:16. The contrast is severe. The wisdom of the cross is "foolishness" to the wisdom of the world. In the same measure, God has made the wisdom of the world's philosophers, scholars, and debaters foolish and has "shown their wisdom to be useless nonsense."

God has chosen not to provide a system of thought that proves his existence. To know God does not depend on our IQ. The Bible does not evaluate intelligence in the same way that the world does. God reveals himself not through logic but through paradox, insight, and metaphor. A genius may not recognize God, but a young child may know God intimately. A brilliant physicist may discover things about the constitution of matter that no other mortal can see or even understand, but a mentally impaired person can know the God who created all matter.

Fear of God, the openmouthed awe that puts God first in our lives, compels us to recognize that all true wisdom comes from God. Getting along in life does not depend on our native intelligence or our degrees. It depends on our relationship to God, a willingness to embrace God's wisdom, even though that willingness may lead us to appear foolish to others.

Above the sun, we find insight in the Word. The Word is first of all a person, Jesus Christ. Wisdom above the sun, in other words, is a relationship. And that person who is Wisdom has spoken to us wise words. Fear of God drives us to those words, which we find in the Bible. The whole Bible then becomes a divinely inspired guide as we navigate life. But the Bible not only gives us guidelines and principles but also engenders in us a mind-set or worldview that lifts us above our own limited perspective to enable us to see ourselves, others, and our world from the viewpoint of God himself.

In this light, our fear of God energizes our attempts to learn about God's world in the light of his Word. God's people, far from being anti-intellectual, should be the world's most passionate learners as we explore the wonders of his creation, contemplate the complexities of life, and marvel at the majesty of our Creator.

➤ *How Do We Chase* **Wisdom?**

1. Who is the wisest human being you know? What makes him or her so wise?
2. What can you do to gain wisdom?
3. What benefits are derived from education, from learning new skills?
4. What is of most value to you for practical day-to-day living?
5. In what way does God give his children wisdom to live life successfully?
6. What does it mean to live a successful life?
7. What Scripture passages help ground you in God's wisdom?

PART SIX

Chasing after
SPIRITUALITY

20
The Revelation

THE ALARM CLOCK clattered, and Noah reached over and silenced it with his usual early-morning swat. He lay in bed and fought the urge to stay there forever. He sat up slightly to make sure that the uncomfortableness of his posture would override the bed's seduction.

Noah remembered he was going to have breakfast with Jack. He checked his emotional gauge to see how much he was dreading the time, and he was surprised to note he was looking forward to their talk. Noah remembered that he had asked Jack to meet with him. He had even set the agenda: "I need to talk about my life with God. This accident is a wake-up call, and I don't like the sound. But I think it's crucial for me to rethink where I'm heading." Noah felt a tinge of fear as he thought about what this conversation might mean for his life.

Noah had begun to talk about subjects that for him had been viewed as out of the realm of polite conversation. For the first time in his marriage to Joan, Noah had initiated meaningful conversation with her. At first, he was stiff and abrupt, but over several days it was clear to Joan that Noah was a different man. He cried. He didn't leave the room when conflict started. He even came back to talk with her about things that they had discussed days earlier, indicating that he continued to mull things over.

At first Joan was thrilled, but it then dawned on her that Noah's changes were requiring something of her, too, and that made her uncomfortable. When Noah shared his fears with her, she felt warmed by his honesty but afraid of her inability to say anything that would matter. It was as if both of them were thawing from the bitter cold, and her hope of a warm, intimate engagement with Noah now included the agony of frozen parts coming back to life. She was unnerved by the tension and rest, the fear and the hope all mixed together. She hoped the conversation with Jack would help Noah sort through things in a way that she felt unable to offer.

Noah arrived at the restaurant before Jack did. Noah had never been late to any event in his life. Jack was prompt and considerate of time, but he rarely arrived anywhere twenty minutes ahead of time. Noah liked to be the one to greet his companion. He liked to have marked his space before the "guest" arrived.

Noah liked this diner. It was a throwback to the fifties and the happy days of leisurely breakfasts, carefree orders not restricted by cholesterol, and women with hair that could hold a small hammer, let alone a No. 2 pencil. For a proper man, Noah had some strange quirks. He rose from his chair as he saw Jack enter the front door. "Jack. Good to see you. Thanks for meeting me this early."

"My privilege, Noah. I see you have already started without me."

"Just warming up the table, Jack. Do you want coffee?"

"Are you kidding? It's one addiction I see no reason to break, or even worry about. Couldn't start another day in this world without it."

Small talk continued until the waitress slapped down the plastic menus and waited for them to hurry. She popped her gum, and the sound grated on Jack; Noah was amused by her surly inattention. He had always wanted a mother who would snarl and snap gum. Instead, his mother parroted upbeat aphorisms that took him over the edge. Noah hoped that Jack would not be upbeat.

"Jack, I don't know yet how to explain what happened to me in New York or even how to explain what has happened since I got back. All I know is I want something more with God, in my marriage, and—I think—in life."

Jack smiled, and his eyes seemed thrilled with Noah's words. Noah winced, but he was not going to let Jack's potential joy derail him from talking.

"Jack, I think you know I have been a Christian who believed all the truths without really taking them seriously. I don't think I was a hypocrite, but I certainly did not give God and my spiritual life much priority."

Noah went on to tell Jack how he had come to know Christ and his fears in college that God would make him go to seminary or be a pastor. He shared with Jack enough about his spiritual life that it was apparent that he did not have a regular quiet time, a prayer life, or many other spiritual disciplines. Noah had not approached his spiritual life the way he would evaluate or pick a stock. And he felt both exposed and needy. He had to go the next step to living life to the full.

Jack asked, "Do you want to talk about what happened in New York or about where you are with God now? I'm confused about what you want to think through this morning."

"Me too," Noah said softly. "I know I am at the beginning of a major change in my life. Jack, I'm not comfortable feeling out of control, and I have to head in a different direction with Joan, with God. I know that, but I just don't know what that means or what it looks like. If you asked me to give an analysis of a stock, I could tell you about its profit margin, what its competition is doing, and what tough issues it faces in this quarter. But put me in a position to reevaluate my life, and I'm lost. Where do I begin?"

Jack sat forward, and his well-starched shirt crinkled as he put his elbows on the table. "Noah, if you had asked me this question six months ago, I would have laid out a Bible study plan, told you about a prayer seminar that is coming to town in a few weeks, and helped you map out a time, place, and procedure to develop spiritual discipline. There are some great books I still can put in your hands to get you thinking in these areas. No doubt—really, no doubt—I want you to do all that.

"And six months ago I would have left this breakfast and felt as if great things are going to happen because you are finally on track. I used to believe there was a clear, relatively simple process to growing spiritually. I still think there are some crucial things you need to know and do—and do regularly in a disciplined way. That's how I have lived my Christian life, and I would have told you it was not only the right way, but the way to 'be right' with God."

Noah looked at Jack. He had always felt that Jack was sophisticated, a bit too suave. He had never really liked Jack because Jack seemed either to know all the answers or at least to know where to find them.

Jack looked away. He seemed momentarily distracted. He did not continue, and the silence was uncomfortable. Normally Noah would fill the gap with a change of conversation. Noah remained silent and did not disrupt the growing tension.

Jack looked back at Noah and said, "I'm not sure, Noah, that what I'm about to say is fair to you. You are just rethinking the direction of your life, and I am about to throw a possible roadblock in your way. I've been going through a significant struggle too. And the truths I would have offered to you with utter confidence six months ago—the ones I want to talk about now—seem a tad hollow and more like noise than real substance and truth. Noah, let me put you on the spot. Do you want me to talk about what I have been through the last six months? I want to answer your question about what to do to find God's purposes for you, but it's nearly impossible to do that in the same way I would have done several months ago."

Noah was both intrigued and drawn to Jack. Jack seemed at a loss, almost helpless. But he also seemed more at rest than Noah had ever seen him. "Jack, I didn't think a matter this big would be finished by the time both of us have to go to work. So, yes, absolutely. Tell me what has happened to you."

Jack sat back and said, "Crap. Lots and lots of crap has sort of fallen on my well-groomed garden. I know plants need fertilizer, but when the pile is four feet tall and six feet wide and the wind is blowing the wrong way and your air conditioner . . . Well, you get my point. What happened is actually simple to describe, but what it has done to me is hard to explain. I don't want to compare it to your accident, but I do see some similarities. Six months ago, the man who was my spiritual mentor, a pastor who befriended me when I joined my first law practice, left his wife. Yes, you can already predict it. He is having an affair with a woman who was on the staff of his church. He called me recently to ask if I knew anyone who might offer him a job.

"I listened to him, and I could not believe my ears. This man has a doctorate in theology from one of the most conservative seminaries in the country. He has taught in Christian schools, has been part of the board of a major mission, and has been a pastor for twenty-five years. What can I say? He is, or was, a man I have patterned my life after since I was in my midtwenties. He has written books about prayer and reading the Bible. Six months ago I would have suggested that you read one of his books. I still recommend it, but I have lots of questions. What happened? What took a strong, articulate, conservative theologian, pastor, man of God to such an end? And then for him to call me and ask me to help him get a job so he could live with this woman—I just have not been the same."

Noah did not look away. Several weeks earlier he would have been angry that Jack had not answered his own questions. Now he felt as if Jack's questions were important.

Jack continued, "Noah, I can't tell you how many times I have heard this warning: 'Don't let your faith rest on any human, only on the finished work of Christ.' I know that. I really do, but somehow I assumed that if I simply did all the things that my mentor did and followed him on his path, I would grow and accumulate godliness in the same way we hope our portfolios will grow in value year by year. I was wrong. Or at least I think I was wrong."

Noah stopped Jack. "But he simply wasn't consistent with what he taught you? If he had been consistent, he wouldn't have fallen away from the Lord, right?"

"Perhaps. I suspect, though I didn't ask him, that he was having his quiet times and his prayer time and was in the Word even when he was well ensconced in the affair. Don't for a minute think, Noah, that I'm questioning the value of spiritual discipline. I think something else was going on. I still don't know how to say it, but I think it boils down to what I know about your life, and mine too. We are more committed to a system, to a way of working the chaos into some order than we are to entering the world around us with trust or faith."

Noah's attention perked up even more when Jack included him. "What do you mean?"

"I mean that you are a man who can't bear losing control. Frankly, any intimate relationship requires more humility, more openness, pain, and trust than either of us is capable of giving. Right?"

Noah felt a frown growing from his brow to his eyes. But he knew Jack was right. "Well, I feel irritated at you enough to indicate maybe you are right, or right enough that I want to dispute you."

Jack laughed. It was a warm, guileless laugh. It was the laughter of recognition. "No question you are irritated. Noah, do you know how often you get irritated with me? If I had a ten-dollar bill for each time I have seen that look, I could retire and send your kids through college." Noah had always like Jack's playful banter.

"So what do you think happened?"

Jack exhaled quickly and shrugged his shoulders. "I don't know, but what I have noticed after being a Christian for a little over thirty years is that Christians are not a lot different from their so-called secular counterparts. Oh, we believe. We are going to heaven. But we have just as many, if not more, egotists, arrogant know-it-alls, and thin-skinned surface rules that cover over the fact that most of us don't have the slightest idea how to deal with our teenage daughters or our money or our lonely wives than the proverbial man in the moon.

"Don't worry, I will calm down, but I'm sick, truly sick, of what I have done to so many friends. When they struggled, I gave them a book or a series of steps to help them resolve the problem. I rarely ever listened to them. I rarely suffered with them. I answered their questions and held them accountable to manage life the way I assumed was right. I remembered a man whose daughter wanted to go to a movie. Well, I told him exactly what to do. I told him he simply had to be a man and hold the limits of morality and just say no. Well, what I didn't know was that he was a mean man who never took time to hear out his kids or his wife. And so all I was doing was giving him a moral stick to beat his family more effectively. I blessed his self-righteousness and encouraged him to stand apart from the hard questions with renewed moral vigor. It kills me."

Noah flinched. The waitress towered above them with a pot of coffee in each hand. If she had not overheard the conversation, she had at least caught the mood of intensity, anger, and sorrow. She seemed not only unusually quiet but also respectful.

"Youse guys want any more java?"

"No, I'll take the check," Jack replied softly.

The waitress turned quickly to escape the unexpected, unmanly honesty she sensed surrounded their conversation.

"Jack, I'm not a dumb man. Usually I am fairly quick in getting the gist of a conversation, but I'm still missing what you are saying to me."

Jack scratched his starchy shirtsleeve. "Someday I'm going to wear a jeans shirt to work and see if anyone has a heart attack." Jack paused and pushed the latticed edges of his fried eggs into the untouched portion of his hash browns. He seemed distracted, and Noah did not know whether to be quiet or to ask his question again. Jack looked up. "Noah, we both know that Joan has been very lonely and afraid to ask for much or tell you how unhappy she has been. True?"

Noah was not surprised by his question, but he had no idea where Jack was going. "Well, yes. I don't know how afraid Joan is or has been, but I can tell you I think she is having more trouble with me this last week than she has had in a long time. So what's your point?"

"Simple. You and I usually dictate the agenda. We are men who are used to getting our way. We know how to intimidate, obligate, ingratiate. We are men of words, and we know our own field well enough to command good salaries and respect, or at least healthy fear. But I'm no better at relating to my wife than you are at relating to Joan. If you really asked Marcia what it is like to be married to me, I think if she were honest, she would say, 'He loves me, up to a point.' And when that point is reached, I draw the line and either evade the issue or somehow make her feel that it is her problem.

"I wonder if that's what my mentor did. I wonder if he used spiritual techniques to corral life and box God, but he must have been as distant with his wife and with God as we are. I don't think he had a sexual problem. I don't think he simply gave in to sexual desire and fell. I think it was his devilish commitment to wrap a nice system around the chaos and then throw away all the other data that indicated he was still a mess. His system didn't take away the mess. It didn't take away his need to be forgiven daily. But I think he used the system not only to hide the mess but also to feel pride, or at least a thrill, in the power that he did what so many others do not have the discipline to accomplish. I'm convinced that he was lying to himself long before he had the affair. What makes me sick is that I never asked him the hard questions, fearing that he would patronize me or lecture me with a reminder of how to pursue God like a good Christian.

"Do you see my reluctance, Noah, to graft you into that vine? Yet, I know you need to start doing what you probably have never done—opening your heart and revamping your time commitments so you can pray and be in the Word."

Noah looked at Jack, and he felt warmth for a man who had been his senior, a distant guide he never took seriously enough to ask for help. Noah realized they would be friends. It felt good. He thought he would have a direction to pursue after meeting with Jack; instead, he had the faint hope that they had become friends.

Noah realized that the same might be true for his relationship with God.

21

"Spirituality Ought to Save Me"

MANY people today are turning their attention to spiritual matters. Books with words like *angels* or *God* in their titles have become best-sellers. More people than ever are willing to admit that there is more to life than what we can see and touch. Many churches have record attendance.

Do any of these scenarios sound familiar to you?

"LIFE is so busy. I spend all of my time running here and there for myself, my husband, and the kids. I have to work to help make ends meet, manage the household, and take care of the family. I hardly ever get a moment to think about anything but the next task. There's got to be something more to life!"

- *"Sure, I believe God exists. Who can explain life otherwise? But you don't really think he has anything to do with our everyday life, do you? I think all the talk about heaven and hell is nothing more than wishful thinking."*

- *"Jen at work says that Christianity explains it all. But when I ask her questions, all I get are pat answers. 'Praise the Lord' this and 'praise the Lord' that. She's always saying the Lord told her this and that. Imagine the Lord telling her to leave work early to get her hair done! I'm not sure I want a God who tells me when my hair needs to be done. I don't want a prepackaged God; I want to believe in something greater, grander, more wonderful than that."*

WHAT do you think about God? We assume that most readers of this book are Christians. If you are, take a moment and ask yourself how you understand God. Who is he? What's he like? How do you know? Do you think you understand him? Does he ever surprise you?

But perhaps you don't believe in God. Do you want to know God, the true God of the universe? Have you tried? Perhaps you have, and to your amazement, he is as hard to hold on to as the wind.

The Pull to Religion

It is not unusual for people to turn to religion in order to find meaning in their lives, especially as people get older or when tragedy intrudes. As men and women approach middle age, they have lived long enough to have failed to find significance in some of the areas we have already explored.

Control over life seems beyond their grasp. Relationships have let them down. Work is tiring and unfulfilling. Life continues to confuse and overwhelm. Religion seems like the logical refuge from the mess of everyday living.

Life must have something more, something that infuses the rest of our existence with significance. Noah's brush with tragedy stirred in him an awakening. In fact, the couple he followed for a few blocks stirred in him the faint reminder that he was a lonely man, devoid of intimacy and the kind of meaning that comes from a deeper pursuit of something other than mere success and control.

Noah was enamored, elated with his success. He soared on the winds of his achievement. It is not only age and tragedy that awakens us to "the more." Often it is a dream fulfilled. Once we achieve the long-awaited goal that has organized our life and provided the energy for our daily labor, we come face-to-face with an even greater emptiness that was hidden as long as the pursuit of the dream provided a reason to keep on striving.

Noah was "set up" by God. He was given success and then a vision of an older couple whose touch and care for one another mocked his empty marriage. Few people experience such intense interactions, but no one escapes the daily call to consider life in light of tragedy and success.

The morning paper records the daily presence of death, crime, political victories, and the uncertainties that affect each of our lives. We may see those events at a distance, but somewhere inside us we know that tomorrow, the tragedy could be ours. If we had eyes to see, we would recognize how God orchestrates life to call us to "consider our ways."

For many people, religion becomes a way to cope with life without coming to grips with God. My own story runs along these lines but begins much earlier in life. For as far back as I remember, life worried me. I have no idea why I felt as I did. I had loving parents and lived in a safe community, but I grew up with a sense that other people—and certainly God—found me inadequate. From the time I was in elementary school, I struggled with feelings of guilt and a fear of dying.

I sought refuge in the church. What could make better sense? I knew that "good" people went to church and followed its rules, and so that's where I went to find meaning. I met other good kids there and found myself feeling quite comfortable with the direction of my life—at least on the surface. Even so, an empty feeling in the pit of my stomach would simply not go away.

I had school friends who did not go to my church. I remember how upset I would get with them when they did something that I found morally objectionable. My three closest friends were Dan and two Daves. It was the late sixties, and two of them began experimenting with drugs during our junior year in high school. I took comfort in the one friend who didn't succumb to the prevalent temptation of our day! Or so I thought. I remember how distraught and depressed I was when I found out that the last of the three smoked marijuana. I felt I was all alone, except in the warmth and comfort of my church. But even that feeling began to fade over time.

Before the end of my high school career I began to experience a new kind of emptiness. My faithful attendance of worship services and youth group activities should have made me close to God, but I realized that it didn't. As I honestly reflected on my real feelings toward God, I recognized that even after many years of church attendance I had no idea who God was.

Little did I know that God was preparing something wonderful for me.

Smug Religion

Looking back, I now understand that I was not a Christian during this time, even though I was a model church member, especially for a teenager! I did everything "right." I wasn't sneaking off with my friends for a beer or causing trouble at home for my parents. I was very moral, very religious—and very smug.

Smugness is the result of a religion of externals. It is a complacency that can develop only when we understand our connection with God to be the result of a "to do" list.

Actually, my list, in conformity with many other people, included more "don'ts" than "do's." Sure, I needed to do my chores, go to church, be nice to people, pray occasionally, and perhaps read the Bible. But I was also careful not to do many other things: I wasn't supposed to swear, drink, lie, masturbate, or engage in any kind of sexual activity whatsoever. Nasty thoughts were harder to control, but I rationalized that nasty thoughts weren't as bad as nasty deeds.

Now I wasn't completely smug, because I was not perfect in my obedience to my understanding of what religion required of me in order to be rewarded with acceptance. But I could get close. And don't most of those of us who operate with this concept of religion operate with a "justice scale" idea of our worth? In other words, it's not that we are always good and right, but rather that we do more good things than bad things. Our good actions far outweigh our bad actions, and, we think, a reasonable God will certainly take that into account. Who, after all, can be perfect?

It amazed me, however, how quickly my smugness turned to emptiness. I had a gnawing sense that there was more to life than going to church and behaving myself, though I was too afraid to explore too deeply.

Narrow Spirituality

Let me share with you the stories of two people, each of whom felt he had found the pathway to intimacy with God.

John's eyes grew serious as he spoke to his fellow church leaders. "I thought I had become a Christian when I was a child. I loved Christ and tried my best to obey him. I prayed and read my Bible and felt that God loved me. I even went to seminary at an evangelical school. But when I took the course on "Love Discipleship," I finally understood what the grace of God is all about. I'm not even sure if I was a Christian before now. I learned that we don't have to do anything; we depend on our heavenly Father. We are not orphans; we are children of the heavenly Father. We should not feel any guilt about what we do or don't do. I guess I wasn't really a Christian as I thought. I strongly suggest that you take this course to find out what Christianity is really about."

Peter just returned from seminary, where he had been studying the "doctrines of grace." He realized that his unenlightened friends were still laboring under the horrible misconception that human beings had free will and that evangelism meant persuading troubled people to choose Jesus. Such views Peter now understood were quite unorthodox. Over the summer break he would organize a Bible study where he would show his friends how to truly understand the Bible. He knew this would make him unpopular, but it was for their own spiritual good. God is a God of truth and will brook no error.

Both John and Peter felt that they found the route to God by means of a particular method or approach, what I am calling spirituality. Indeed, Peter's attitude and actions are very similar to mine right after I finished my first year of seminary and returned to do a summer internship in my home city of Columbus, Ohio. My feeling was that most Christians simply misunderstood the teaching of the Bible concerning the nature of God and their own hearts and that they needed to learn the truth or they would languish. The way to spiritual growth was through teaching and learning the true nature of God.

I was resisting another form of Christian spirituality that was more experiential, that is focused on people's emotions. I still felt the pain of being rebuked by a Christian friend, Mary, for not speaking in tongues. She questioned my leadership role in the campus fellowship. She felt that if I had not experienced the second baptism, then I was not adequate to lead others.

Such a subjective, experiential, emotional approach to God seemed dangerous to me then. I believed we needed to base our relationship to God on our understanding, not on our shifting feelings.

Now, please do not misunderstand me. I still believe that the Bible's
teaching is best reflected by talking about God as sovereign and human
beings as utterly dependent on him for our salvation. But I am less smug
about the idea that I had captured the one and only route to intimacy
with God.

So many times during my Christian life, I have been told that if only I
would do this thing or that thing, I would experience fresh intimacy with
God. If only I would go to a small group meeting or exercise spiritual
discipline or have a morning quiet time . . . If only I would learn these
doctrines or speak in tongues or take communion more often . . . If only
I would experience healing or deal with my past or confess my sins more
often or pray more often . . . If only, if only, then I would have a better
relationship with Jesus.

When Externals Take Over

John, Peter, Mary, and I had all come to believe that we had a corner on
how to approach God. My point is not that we were wrong to think that
what we believed was right and biblical, but we were wrong to think that
there was only one right way to grow in faith. Along with that belief
comes the conviction that if my way is right and true, then all other
means of growth are wrong. The logic of this argument then forces me to
think that not only can I not learn from other means, but I must whole-
heartedly resist them. Further, I must force everyone else to fit into my
mold.

My first clear lesson about this reality came in the context of a college
fellowship. Dan and I went to college in the early seventies, at the beginning of the "Jesus Movement." Those were exciting times. We regularly
saw our friends come to faith in Christ. During our freshman year at
Ohio Wesleyan University, five of us started a weekly fellowship at the
beginning of the fall semester, and by the end of the school year, the
group had grown to about a hundred students. Most of the new people
were recently converted, including my old friend and roommate Dan.

We began the second year with great enthusiasm. We had no adult
leadership, but many of us had been Christians for over two years. With
our new maturity, we fully expected God to do great things.

Soon, however, we found that our maturing took us in surprising, different directions. Some of us had come under the influence of a well-
known Reformed theologian who lived in the area at the time; to us wor-

ship had to be orderly and intellectual. Others had discovered the Holy Spirit and wanted to baptize everyone else in the Spirit; to these brothers and sisters worship should be exciting and emotional. Others came under the influence of a Bible teacher who understood God's history of salvation as divided into discrete dispensations; to them speaking in tongues was of the devil.

The bickering began. How would worship be conducted? How would we encourage others to seek a relationship with God? Bickering turned into fighting, and soon separate groups were formed. Amazingly, God overruled our pitiful theological infighting, and many people still came to know him, but the example of Christian love we were demonstrating was disastrous.

Please do not hear us as saying that anything goes in our approach to God. Please do not understand us as saying that these three views of the Bible and faith are unequivocally or even equally legitimate. What is at issue here is the complete disdain we felt for each other and the incredible confidence that we had in our own approach to God. We were chasing after God through our own constructs of spirituality, and at times it devolved to little more than being a fan of a particular sports team. We wanted our team to win and crush all the opponents. In this we found security and peace. We had it right, and everyone else had it wrong. In a word, we had God in a box of our own making.

Despite the obvious problems, however, at least John, Peter, Mary, and I knew that spirituality involves an internal change. True, our views were myopic in understanding internal change as simply a change in intellectual understanding or a change in attitude or a change in feelings.

Even more dangerous, however, is seeking spiritual fulfillment through our behavior only; that is, doing religious acts that are based on fear or the false assumption that life may finally work if we do what God wants. Neither motive flows from a desire to thank God for what he has done in our lives. The trap here is legalism. And while we don't like to admit it, none of us has escaped the tentacles of self-righteousness and legalism.

Most likely, Jack was a reasonable but true-blue legalist. He believed that a daily quiet time, a regular prayer list, and tithing were among the spiritual disciplines that were not only necessary but sufficient for spiritual growth. The assumption that Jack and others seem to make is that spiritual discipline is enough to bring about substantial and near com-

plete change. People from other traditions seem to believe that real
maturity is reached only after we are delivered from satanic presence or
can speak in tongues or get out of denial or propagate the theories of
Christian leader X.

The assumption underlying every form of legalism is threefold: (1)
Maturity involves a distinct event, level of knowledge, or act(s); (2) once
the person has experienced the event, reached the level of knowledge, or
done the act, he or she has reached maturity; and (3) when a person
reaches maturity, he or she no longer struggles with the internal conflict
of the spirit and flesh.

Jack was brilliant at offering systems to people. He set up a plan of
prayer, study, and service. And, of course, people changed. But seldom
did he ask hard questions about their relationships or their lives. He seldom made any connection between their past and their current struggles.
He seldom helped people see how their past related to their current
struggles or how their current struggles involved a failure to trust God
for their future. Jack gave people a false sense of control in the present
rather than open to them a vision of their past and future. He offered a
system. He offered a system and did not care to know the individual's
heart.

Whether it be in personal contacts with others or in our relationship
with God, we want a system that enables us to do right and avoid wrong.
In my own denomination is a running controversy over the form of worship. At the heart of the issue is a theological doctrine called the "regulative principle." The principle, in short, means that God, not people,
regulates worship. We can worship God only in ways that God himself
directs in his Word; we cannot add anything or take anything away from
that.

Now on the surface this sounds appealing and easy to apply. It is
appealing because it protects against leaders' adding nonbiblical requirements to worship: "You must kneel when you pray." "You must publicly
confess your private sins." The Scriptures do not require this, so you
don't *have* do it. Unfortunately some advocates of the regulative principle
go much further. They say that if the Bible doesn't command a certain
action for worship, then we don't do it. And if we do, then we are sin-
ning. This perspective—combined with a strong sense of tradition and a
belief that Old Testament worship is now completely obsolete—leads to
a very stern and circumscribed idea of worship in some quarters.

Several years ago I attended an ordination service for one of my students. I settled myself comfortably in the pew, and the presiding minister strode in with robes flowing. He gazed at the room, noticed the presence of several people who worshiped in "looser congregations," and began a tirade on the evils of worshiping God in chairs rather than pews and praying with hands lifted to heaven rather than quietly folded in front of our closed eyes and bowed heads.

By my tone, you have probably picked up that my sentiments are on the other side of the debate, arguing for a much broader understanding of biblical worship and more diversity in worship styles. My church meets in a school auditorium. We dress casually, sing Scripture songs, and raise our hands in prayer.

Once again, it is not that I am against pews, quiet prayer, robes, or even incense for that matter. The problem is promoting one's narrow view of spirituality, especially one focused on the externals rather than on the heart, at the expense of other legitimate forms of spiritual expression. Such restrictions ultimately emanate from a narrow view of God and lead to a smugness that believes we have God under our control.

God: Revealed and Unchanging

Narrow views of spirituality depend on the idea that God has revealed himself to us completely, or at least extensively, and acts toward us in a totally predictable manner. We know the right way to God because God has clearly shown it to us. And there is more than a kernel of truth here, to be sure.

After all, the Bible clearly teaches that God has revealed himself to men and women. Indeed, the whole Bible is such a revelation. If we are to know anything about God, it must come from his own revelation. God is so far above us (Isa. 55:8-9), he is so unlike anything we know (Ps. 89:6), that, unless he comes to us and shows himself to us, we will not know him. We may have a general sense that there is a Creator God, but unless he rips through our sin and finiteness with his revelation, we will not truly know him in a personal way.

God has revealed himself to us. We can know him.

It is also true that God is unchanging. He is not fickle, changing his mind on a whim. After all, the Lord himself proclaimed, "I the Lord do not change" (Mal. 3:6, NIV). Hebrews 6:17 similarly speaks of "the unchanging nature of [God's] purpose" (NIV).

God reveals himself, and he is unchanging. Can we not then expect that God is predictable? Can we not assume then that he will be utterly clear about the proper way to approach him in order to know him intimately? Should we not expect him to tell us what he wants from us?

If we believe this, then we will expect finally to find meaning and contentment in one area of our lives. We believe that it is reasonable to think that once we find God and learn what pleases him, all our problems will go away.

Once again, the Teacher has some disturbing things to say. He will not let us rest with merely knowing we need God. He will not allow us to be content to please God by making our relationship with him a series of checklists or a rote, remote, smug practice of righteousness.

22

*Restoring Spirituality
through Passion*

NOAH AND JACK joined their hearts in facing the mystery of spirituality. True spirituality involves the dynamics of relationship. Knowing any person involves engaging our hearts in mystery, in the essential presence of another. We cannot know ourselves without knowing another person.

Knowing God is not a matter of "doing" religion right. It is not a matter of merely mapping out the necessary tasks and then conforming to the list with consistency and conscientiousness. Spirituality involves the development of a relationship that engages all that we are with the totality of who God has revealed himself to be in the Bible.

It means struggling with him and surrendering to him, loving him, and worshiping him. It means facing the places in which we worship and love other gods. True spirituality invites us to a relationship in which we experience our most profound confusion and rest, disappointment and joy.

Do we find our ultimate significance in spirituality? Is religion the refuge in which we find rest? To answer these questions, we begin in the Old Testament with the story of Israel. After all, as Paul told us, "These events [that are recorded in the Old Testament] happened as a warning to us, so that we would not crave evil things as they did or worship idols as some of them did" (1 Cor. 10:6-7).

God chose the Israelites to be his special people. They did nothing to deserve their status as God's people (Deut. 7:7-11). God wanted their hearts, so he revealed himself to them. He made promises to them, promises that he would never break.

The Israelites often thought they knew the way to God's heart, but they were wrong. They worshiped God with their bodies but not with their hearts. They found a kind of false contentment in their "spirituality," which was based on their presuming upon God's revelation and unchangeable nature.

God put certain demands on them. He asked them to offer sacrifices, to pay their vows, to pray. God assured them of his loving presence in their midst by having his house, the temple, constructed in the most prominent place in their major city, Jerusalem. The Israelites could look to that building and say confidently, "God is here; we have nothing to fear. He will never allow anything to happen to us because of the temple."

According to Jeremiah 7, the people of God came to worship at the temple and said, "We are safe!" (Jer. 7:10). They became a smug and falsely confident people because they felt that God was unchangeable and that they were doing what he demanded: offering sacrifices and coming to the temple.

But a short time after Jeremiah's speech concerning the temple, God used the Babylonian army to destroy Jerusalem and carry off its people. The temple, his home, was plundered, and the cry of God's people went up to heaven (Lamentations).

How could this happen to a people to whom God revealed himself? How could this happen in the light of the unchangeable promises of God?

Making Religion an Idol

It seems like a bizarre idea, doesn't it? How can I get too much of religion? How can I go wrong by putting my energy and time into the things of God?

We have just seen that Israel was chosen as God's special people; he drew them into an intimate relationship. Too frequently, however, they did not return the love that he showed them. They were too interested in immediate gratification. They were attracted to the forms of worship practiced by their neighbors, who worshiped concrete deities in charge of agricultural fertility and sexual enjoyment. They were gods who, represented by statues of gold and silver, could be seen and touched.

While some Israelites abandoned their God (Yahweh) to worship Baal, Chemosh, or Dagon, most continued to participate in the worship of Yahweh—or at least to go through the motions. They were circumcised, and they had their children circumcised. They went to the temple and participated in the festivals. They even offered expensive sacrifices. They did everything a good "Yahweh worshiper" should do!

But, perhaps subtly at first, their zeal for Yahweh was perverted into a zeal for "religious appearances." The sacrifices they offered were intended not to express remorse over sin and love to Yahweh but to put on a show of piety and perhaps wealth for neighbors ("I offered a bull; you can afford only a bird"). The temple itself, which Solomon said could not contain God, became a prison for God in the minds of the Israelites. They believed they were invincible as long as they were connected to the temple because God wouldn't let his own glory be diminished.

The history of the Israelite people in the Old Testament reveals a twisted desire in the hearts of all religious people. It is a desire to control God so we can manipulate him to serve us.

That, after all, is the heart of idolatry. Sinful, selfish people do not like the idea of a God who is more powerful than they are. Through idolatry we pare God down to our size.

The Folly of Religion

As we have seen, the Teacher desperately looked for meaning to life on earth. His desperation, however, did not allow him easy answers, and as a result, he did not find rest in the superficiality of life.

The Teacher looked to religion in the hope that meaning could be found there, but as with the other potential avenues of significance, he was soon disappointed. He quickly recognized the idolatry of "religious" people. Let's listen to his observations and advice, because they expose the folly of religion.

> As you enter the house of God, keep your ears open and your mouth shut! Don't be a fool who doesn't realize that mindless offerings to God are evil. And don't make rash promises to God, for he is in heaven, and you are only here on earth. So let your words be few.
>
> Just as being too busy gives you nightmares, being a fool makes you a blabbermouth.
>
> So when you make a promise to God, don't delay in following through, for God takes no pleasure in fools. Keep all the promises you make to him. It is better to say nothing than to promise something that you don't follow through on. In such cases, your mouth is making you sin. And don't defend yourself by telling the Temple messenger that the promise you made was a mistake. That would make God angry, and he might wipe out everything you have achieved. Ecclesiastes 5:1-6

THE Teacher blasts those smug Israelites who would make religion a matter of "do's" and "don'ts." He condemns the public display that merely went through the motions of religion. They offered the required sacrifices. They paid for the animals, took them up to the temple, and with great ostentation offered them to God. They also took vows and promised impressive gifts. They also prayed long and fancy prayers. They did all these things and received the blessing of the community. They were good, Yahweh-worshiping people. After all, hadn't God asked for sacrifices, vows, and prayers? Indeed, he had.

So what was the Teacher's problem? He saw through people's intentions and motives. He realized that the sacrifices were not from the heart; they were "mindless." The prayers of the people were flowery, but they revealed no real passion for God.

The Teacher gives such superficial religious people a reminder: God "is in heaven, and you are only here on earth" (Eccles. 5:2). In other words, you don't have God under control by your superficial spirituality. You cannot manipulate God by your religious actions, and as a result your religion will not bring you satisfaction and peace.

Centuries later, when he was on earth, Jesus ran into people with a similar mind-set. Jesus had some very hard things to tell these people:

*How terrible it will be for you teachers of religious law and you Phari-
sees. Hypocrites! You are so careful to clean the outside of the cup and
the dish, but inside you are filthy—full of greed and self-indulgence!
Blind Pharisees! . . .*

*How terrible it will be for you teachers of the religious law and you
Pharisees. Hypocrites! You are like whitewashed tombs—beautiful on the
outside but filled on the inside with dead people's bones and all sorts of
impurity.* Matt. 23:25-27

THE Pharisees, according to the New Testament, were a highly religious
group who tended to all the minute details of religion. They did everything that the law and their customs required of them. But Jesus judges
them, not of falling short of their ideal, but of acting only on the surface
and not from a heart of devotion.

Passion Turning Sour

Of course, the Teacher and Jesus both speak of a religion of externals; that
is, a religion that requires only actions and not a heart of passion. This is a
religion that seeks to control God; it says, "If I am 'good,' then God will
bless me. If I am not good, then something bad will happen to me."

Once again, such beliefs assume that God is utterly transparent and predictable. We often labor to make the Christian life into a formula: obedience = blessing and disobedience = curse. But is this the way life really
works? The Teacher points out what our experience teaches us daily: Good
people often suffer, and bad people often prosper. "In this meaningless life,
I have seen everything, including the fact that some good people die young
and some wicked people live on and on" (Eccles. 7:15).

Superficial religion is a danger today as well. Today we can find countless approaches to God and the spiritual life, each approach promising
success and happiness if a series of steps are performed or principles are
understood. The self-help industry has infringed on true spirituality by
offering the secrets to a happy, satisfied, mostly problem-free faith. Everywhere about us is the implicit promise that God is in the business of
securing our earthly well-being if we merely know and do "God" right.

Take Jack for instance. He became a Christian when he was in law
school. He worked hard and had a good future ahead of him, but he felt a
gnawing emptiness that prompted him to return to church. He met a pastor who sincerely and consistently pursued God. He offered Jack the gos-

pel. Jack was drawn to the simple message that his sins would be erased and judgment passed from him for eternity by simply receiving Christ as his Savior and Lord. He accepted Jesus.

The first five years were an incredible time. His whole attitude toward life changed. He had his vitality back and entered into a steady process of learning to follow Christ through prayer, Bible study, and consistent church work.

During these wonderful days, he got involved in countless ministries at church. The worship exhilarated him. The leadership of the church recognized his wisdom and his commitment to God and elected him to the elder board.

Jack felt that life was finally under control. There was nothing that could bring him down. He knew God, and he knew what God expected from him.

But even before Jack learned about his mentor's affair, he felt an acute lack of excitement and joy. He hated to admit it, but he was worn down by years of working with Christians. At first, he felt he needed to work harder and to reemploy the techniques he had learned to keep his spiritual life fresh and alive. Renewed attention to the "basics" initially increased his spiritual vigor, but the news of the affair cut deeply and seemed to sap much of his enthusiasm.

When Jack started the Ecclesiastes Bible study, he was aware that life was not working. The Teacher disturbed him, but deep down he found solace, strange comfort in the radical message that life, including his spiritual life, was not as predictable as he thought it was supposed to be. He regretted the years of offering others advice and direction based on the implicit assumption that we can somehow control God.

Jack's meeting with Noah prompted him to see that walking in uncertainty and struggling with God might actually take both of them further than merely offering his old standard lines for following God. Jack is a case study in the movement from the first flames of spiritual passion to smugness to emptiness and back to a deeper burning ember of hope.

From Smugness to Emptiness

Smugness results from thinking we have God figured out. We know what he wants, and we do it. The "how-to" list may differ from person to person, but it could include going to church, reading the Bible, praying, fast-ing, regular repentance, attendance at small groups, memorizing a confession of faith, and on and on.

As difficult as some of these demands are, they are controllable things from a predictable God. For that reason, smugness leads to a false sense of security because these are things I can do if I put my mind to it.

But, as we have already seen, smugness can be achieved only if we are committed to living superficially. It is the reward for just going through the motions. Smug people can't think too deeply about the true state of their hearts. That would lead to disaster.

However, maintaining the pretense is hard to do in a fallen world. Too often events unsettle our all-too-complacent view of ourselves. Whether it is illness, family trouble, financial difficulties, or some other near disaster, we get periodic lessons that, no matter how hard we try, we cannot control life, even through our chosen mode of spirituality.

Psalm 30 suggests that these troubling intrusions are not arbitrary but are the wise intervention of God himself. Psalm 30 is a thanksgiving psalm. It is a song sung by a person who once suffered but afterward experienced the gracious restoration of God.

> I will praise you, Lord, for you have rescued me.
> You refused to let my enemies triumph over me.
> O Lord my God, I cried out to you for help,
> and you restored my health.
> You brought me up from the grave, O Lord.
> You kept me from falling into the pit of death.
> Sing to the Lord, all you godly ones!
> Praise his holy name.
> His anger lasts for a moment,
> but his favor lasts a lifetime!
> Weeping may go on all night,
> but joy comes with the morning.
> When I was prosperous I said,
> "Nothing can stop me now!"
> Your favor, O Lord, made me as secure as a mountain.
> Then you turned away from me, and I was shattered.
> I cried out to you, O Lord.
> I begged the Lord for mercy, saying,
> "What will you gain if I die,

if I sink down into the grave?
Can my dust praise you from the grave?
Can it tell the world of your faithfulness?
Hear me, Lord, and have mercy on me.
Help me, O Lord."
You have turned my mourning into joyful dancing.
You have taken away my clothes of mourning and clothed me with joy,
that I might sing praises to you and not be silent.
O Lord my God, I will give you thanks forever!

IT IS clear from allusions in the text that the psalmist's trouble was a physical illness that threatened to kill him. But, in the light of his experience, he understood that God had allowed the illness in order to get his attention. You see, the psalmist had grown complacent, but God would not let him remain smug. God withdrew his protecting hand and let the psalmist experience what life was like without him. God will never leave us or forsake us, but at times he will hide and let us experience life as it would be if he did not exist or had abandoned us. His silence is not a turning of his back on us in anger or disgust; it is a gift that awakens us from the slumber of complacency through a revelation of our utter emptiness without him. The psalmist remembered his previous affliction with the following words: "When I was prosperous I said, 'Nothing can stop me now!' Your favor, O Lord, made me as secure as a mountain. Then you turned away from me, and I was shattered" (Ps. 30:6-7).

The psalmist's smugness quickly turned to emptiness. He was without God. Complacency is the result of a superficial relationship with God, and it will not last.

ALLOW me to return to my own story, which I began in the previous chapter. I sought meaning and refuge in the church while I was in high school. I did everything a good Christian was expected to do. I went to church; I was moral; I attended youth group; I didn't smoke weed.

God blessed me. I had good friends in the fellowship. I won a starting position my senior year on our state championship football team. I had an attractive girlfriend, Dianne, from the church.

In the spring, however, the relationship broke off. Dianne informed me that she did not want a serious relationship with a man who wanted to be a minister because it was not a lifestyle she wanted.

My smugness soon led to emptiness. I remember losing interest in church. Life just did not seem worth it any longer. I was no longer a Christian who felt that life was under control. I was unaware that God was engendering in my heart a divine fear that would catapult me above the sun.

A God of Passion

The simple truth is that God will not let himself be boxed in. He will not allow us to think that we can control him. God has indeed revealed himself to us so that we can truly know him, but he has not revealed himself exhaustively. He has preserved a sense of mystery. God does not change, but he also is not predictable.

This latter point needs further exploration. At the end of the last chapter we cited a number of texts that asserted God's unchangeableness. But we also need to present another strand of biblical teaching best represented by Hosea 11.

Hosea 11 recounts the original passion that God had for his people, the Israelites. However, Israel became complacent and turned against their Lord. Similar to the experience of the psalmist above, God then determined to abandon them and punish them. But God then utters these incredible words:

> "Oh, how can I give you up, Israel? How can I let you go? How can I destroy you like Admah and Zeboiim? My heart is torn within me, and my compassion overflows. No, I will not punish you as much as my burning anger tells me to. I will not completely destroy Israel, for I am God and not a mere mortal. I am the Holy One living among you, and I will not come to destroy." Hos. 11:8-9

THE passage describes the churning of decision that moves God from a purpose of destroying his smug people to a more redemptive punishment, one that will lead to a restoration of relationship. "'For someday the people will follow the Lord. I will roar like a lion, and my people will return trembling from the west. Like a flock of birds, they will come from Egypt. Flying like doves, they will return from Assyria. And I will bring them home again,' says the Lord" (Hos. 11:10-11).

Often theologians worry about a passage like this because it seems to describe a fickle God who can get carried away with his emotions. They thus describe the passions of God as a metaphor, not something real, and they explain away God's change of mind as simply "apparent." They worry because if God can change his mind, how can we be sure that he will always be for us?

This worry is poorly founded. Where the Bible says God changes his mind is always in contexts like this one, in which he changes his mind for our good, for our redemption. He could have destroyed, and indeed announced that he would destroy, his people for the types of sins they had committed, but after his internal struggle, he announces that he will not. There will be a restoration after a purifying exile.

The most fascinating aspect of this passage is the motivation God gives for his change of mind. We often say that God can't change his mind. God says he will change his mind because he is God and not a human being. What does he mean?

He means that, unlike offended people, he has the capacity for grace. It is not in human nature to be merciful; it is a divine trait. God here chooses to exercise it.

Passionate Surrender

The bottom line is that God does not want our superficial worship. He does not tolerate our complacency. He will take our smugness and turn it to emptiness. By doing this, he will show us that he does not want our "proper actions." He wants our hearts.

The prophets and poets made this clear in terms of Old Testament worship. Psalm 51, for instance, is the prayer of a formerly smug David. After his initial, intimate relationship with God, David had grown complacent and was serving God just on the surface, as the sin with Bathsheba indicated. God revealed David's hidden rebellion. This psalm is a testimony to his rekindled passion and to his return to a heartfelt devotion to God:

> *You would not be pleased with sacrifices,*
> *or I would bring them.*
> *If I brought you a burnt offering,*
> *you would not accept it.*
> *The sacrifice you want is a broken spirit.*
> *A broken and repentant heart, O God,*
> *you will not despise.*
> Psalm 51:16-17

I LEARNED this lesson myself as I moved from the smugness of my connection with the church to the emptiness of life having gone awry. Little did I realize that God was setting the stage for an earth-moving transformation in my life. After a few months of listlessness, a friend explained to me that Christianity was not an institution or a lifestyle; it was a relationship with a person, Jesus Christ. It was not a matter of doing things to please him, but it was a matter of surrender, a sacrifice of one's being to the one who invites us to "love the Lord your God with all your heart, all your soul, all your strength, and all your mind" (Luke 10:27). In response, I turned my life over to Christ.

Focus on Jesus

Of course, my conversion was not the end of the story of my pursuit of God; it was just the beginning. While my relationship to Christ has grown over the years, I have also experienced troubling and lonely times in which I have tried to find new answers to my spiritual dilemma. I have argued that perhaps something was wrong in my life because I didn't pray enough. . . . Then I find myself back in the cycle. Praying, in other words, becomes a form of legalism. Legalism, in one sense, feels burdensome, but its attraction is that it is controllable; it is something I can do.

But God keeps us unsettled. He will not allow us to get complacent. Hebrews 12:5-13 talks about our God as a God who injects difficulties into our lives and reminds us that "No discipline is enjoyable while it is happening—it is painful! But afterward there will be a quiet harvest of right living for those who are trained in this way" (Heb. 12:11).

When God does break through our smugness in this way, he prods us to remember it is not the *form* but rather the *encounter* that is important. It is not how much we pray, how well we know the Bible, but it is how these things lead us into a more intimate relationship with him.

God himself reveals and conceals himself to us in a variety of ways. By doing so, he leaves us with a sense of wonder tinged with mystery. When we lose a sense of mystery, our wonder turns cynical. When we lose a sense of wonder, we can become confused in the mystery.

Our approach to God must be open for surprises. This does not mean that we have no direction at all. God does tell us pretty clearly what we should do. A life with no prayer or Scripture reading or fellowship with believers is a paltry existence at best. But to say that you need to have a quiet time at the beginning of the day to get right with God or that you must speak in tongues to really experience the Holy Spirit are oppressive requirements imposed by legalistic standards, not by God himself.

On the other hand, God does forbid certain things in his worship. A notable instance of this is the prohibition to make and worship an image, even of the true God (Exod. 20:4-6). We must know the Scriptures well enough to know what God desires and what he doesn't.

Within these parameters, however, we have tremendous freedom in our approach to God. We need to be careful where we put requirements on ourselves and especially on others. This is an important warning because we have such a tendency to require others to do what we find spiritually rewarding, partly out of concern for others, but more often because it confirms our own "rightness."

I will conclude by recounting a recent phone call I had from a man named Travis. Travis landscapes a large retreat center. He has a passionate heart for God, but he contacted me because he was deeply concerned that he might have to give up a practice that had nourished him for years. Once a week, Travis would get up and go to a secluded part of the retreat center. He would pray and read Scripture, and then at the end of his time of intimacy with God, he would take a bit of wine and bread, remember the death of Christ for his sins, and give thanks.

He did not consider this communion, a sacrament that he took regularly at our church. He did not tell many people about his private time of worship, and he never insisted that other people do this to get close to God. But one of the church leaders heard about this practice and told him he had to stop it. Travis was told that only a pastor could oversee this ritual and that he was in serious spiritual trouble over it.

For a month, Travis was emotionally torn, not able to draw close to the Lord. Finally, however, he realized that he was giving in to the expectations of other people, not the Bible. Travis, through his story, becomes an encouragement and example of surrender to God and a willingness to be open to meet God wherever and whenever he chooses to meet us.

Spirituality: Above the Sun

Above the sun, we get a sense of God's mystery and unpredictability. We know God, to be sure, but we do not know him exhaustively. His unpredictability does not mean he is arbitrary, but we cannot ever reduce his goodness to us to a trite formula.

Our above-the-sun perspective means that we cannot presume that we can manipulate God through our rituals. We will encounter him not only in the expected places, but he will surprise us where we would least expect him.

Under the sun our predictable view of God will lead eventually to smugness, then emptiness. God wants better for us. He will smash the idol that we have made for him and reveal himself to us in ever richer tones. Our worship then moves from smugness to passion as we look for him not only in the "religious" corners of our lives but in every aspect of ← our existence. Our passion for God is not something we work up, but it is ignited by his passionate pursuit of us.

Our present spirituality is a mere prelude to heaven. We really know little about heaven, but one thing we know is that our worship continues. We will see him face-to-face, but the surprise and wonder and mystery will never stop: "No longer will anything be cursed. For the throne of God and of the Lamb will be there, and his servants will worship him. And they will see his face, and his name will be written on their foreheads. And there will be no night there—no need for lamps or sun—for the Lord God will shine on them. And they will reign forever and ever" (Rev. 22:3-5).

➤ How Do We Chase after **Spirituality?**

1. When is religion harmful? Can Christianity be harmful?
2. One philosopher accused religion of being the "opiate of the people," and another said that religion was "spiritual alcohol." What did they mean, and do they have any basis at all for their statements?
3. What is the difference between a superficial religion and a religion of the heart?
4. How can you tell true religion from false religion?
5. What does it mean to "put God in a box"?
6. What is the difference between contentment and smugness in religion?
7. How has your spiritual life become out of balance?
8. What Scripture passages give you direction as you seek a more meaningful relationship with Christ?

23
The Hospital Visit

THE CONVERSATION with Jack at breakfast played in Noah's mind for the whole ride to work. He did not even notice he had not turned on the radio until he drove into the parking lot. The young executive who had parked in his spot a few weeks ago had taken the space next to his and had parked over the line, so getting in and out of the space would be impossible. Noah's hands clenched the steering wheel, but he was surprised by the smile that crossed his lips. He was irritated, but he felt no energy to make the young man pay. He pictured himself teasing his associate rather than piercing him with his terse commentary and abrupt silence.

Noah's heart was burdened by other matters. He had taken the reins of the organization. He was not only the head of analysis for the whole Andrajian empire, but he was the de facto boss of the Chicago office. He was in a strange position. He set the philosophy for what would be bought and sold through the whole firm, and daily he had the ear of both Andrajian brothers. He did not run the day-to-day operations of the Chicago group, but if he made a two-minute phone call to one of the Brothers, a head would roll. He had the power to do whatever he wanted to the careers of people who a month ago would have subtly ridiculed him in their weekly analysis meetings.

Jonathan had been Noah's daily nemesis. Noah had endured Jonathan's barely concealed disdain and patronizing remarks for years. Jonathan had been a favorite of his Chicago boss, and the change in Noah's promotion had rocked both of them. The boss in particular did not know how to measure his new role with Noah. He had control over operations, but in a single memo Noah could change the direction he set without the slightest possibility it would be questioned or thwarted.

Jonathan made himself invisible whenever Noah was present. He seemed to fade into his papers, staring at his well-ordered sheaf of reports as if he were looking for a holy grail to discern the proper way to survive the new plague that had infected the office. No one knew what to do with Noah.

Noah, at first, had fantasized taking Jonathan apart limb by nasty limb. He saw the well-heeled smile and confidence and wanted to watch Jonathan suffer as he took away his corner office and then set him to tasks that men twenty years his junior would have found humiliating.

But Noah's conversations with Joan had changed his heart. For the first time he shared with her the hatred he felt and had endured at work for years. Joan had never understood why some days Noah's starched shirts came back with the odor of the jungle. Those were the days he suffered the polished slurs of Jonathan and his henchmen with quiet, distant rage. Noah was an angry man who sweated when he wanted to scream.

Joan asked Noah if he wanted to make Jonathan and others pay. When Noah looked into his wife's eyes, he could see the years of hurt he had subjected her to, and without a word he knew she hurt more for him than she did for herself. It killed the pleasure of fantasizing about vengeance.

Noah knew the office grapevine was filled with gossip of what he had done to gain his new position and what he was going to do to consolidate his power. Noah felt that office politics often degenerated to gossip, invective, and power grabbing. The limited resources of the company, including who parked in which spot and who got the most prestigious office, seemed more important to his peers than how the company progressed. Each day when Noah entered the building and greeted the receptionist and the other secretaries, he could see fear in their faces, uncertainty about whether or not they would have jobs the next week.

He saw the same look in the eyes of all his other associates. The only one who avoided his eyes was Jonathan. It was another odd gift of God that Jonathan turned the corner just as Noah walked in the door. Both men approached the same elevator. Neither Noah nor Jonathan could choose another course of action: it would be too obvious.

"Good morning, Noah," Jonathan ventured.

"And good morning to you, Jonathan. I'm glad I bumped into you today. I've been summoned to New York to meet with the staff and the Brothers, and I wanted to get an opinion on the MacKenzie deal before I left. Could you meet with me this morning?"

Jonathan knew he could no more say no to Noah than go to work shining shoes. Jonathan replied with jovial irritation: "No problem, Noah. You name the time."

Noah looked squarely into Jonathan's eyes: "Jonathan, you are a valuable and deeply respected associate. I know we have been at odds for years, but your analyses are weighty and more often than not correct. I don't want to put you in a position of moving your schedule for me; I simply want to know if you have time this morning to give me an update that I can take to New York."

Jonathan's cheeks burned. He had chosen a deferential route that allowed him to be the patronizing servant, but Noah had sincerely praised him and had served him rather than accepted Jonathan's snide effort at concession. Jonathan coughed and looked away. "Sure, Noah, I understand. I just meant that I would be glad to meet with you at your convenience."

"Jonathan, I'm going to be scribbling and reading this morning; drop in whenever you have a moment. If you don't, just let me know when you are available. Thanks."

The elevator door opened, and Noah, who was closest to the door, walked out and went to his interior office as Jonathan hesitated and watched him depart. Before the door closed, Jonathan lurched forward and marched indignantly to his corner window office that looked out over the Chicago skyline. He felt a desperate need for something to soothe the radiating heartburn that filled his chest and mouth.

Noah stepped into his office and shook his head. He didn't know whether to laugh or cry. Jonathan hated him. He wanted to tell Jonathan all was forgiven and what God had done in his life over the last several weeks, but Noah knew that would only filter back through the office grapevine and invite more misunderstanding.

It was time to let gossip run its course. He had found over the years that gossip eventually must escalate for it to keep its flavor. The first draft is never enough to sate the dark pleasure associated with drinking from the grapevine of invective. One taste turns flat and bitter unless it is followed up with even more speculative and mean-spirited news. And then a second and third cup only invite a drunken immersion into more information that is so ridiculous that eventually a few brave souls realize the foolishness of the party. Noah wisely decided to add nothing to Jonathan's cup.

As soon as Noah sat down, he checked his voice mail. The first five messages were routine and required little more than a brief note to himself to get the information needed to answer the questions. The sixth message was from Jakob, Rosie's husband. It was a halting voice that seemed unfamiliar with the prospect of leaving a message on voice mail. Jakob said, "Mr. Adamson, I'm Jakob. You gave me your number, and I do not want to disturb you; but Rosie is in the hospital, and she asked that I call you. If you will be in New York any time soon, she hoped you might give her a call. Her number is 212-930-4500, room 1415. Thank you. Again, I hope I have not disturbed you."

Noah immediately picked the phone up and called the number. Jakob answered.

"Hello, this is Jakob."

"Jakob, this is Noah Adamson. The man your wife pulled from the street a few weeks ago."

"Noah, yes. I called you at your office. I'm so glad you called me back."

"How are you? How is Rosie? Did she recover from the fall?"

"Well, Noah, that is the reason I called you. Rosie insisted I call you. She wanted to see you. You see, when she fell, she hurt herself. And I told her she had to see a doctor. But she is a stubborn woman. How else do you think she could live with me all these years? But after a week the pain got worse, much worse. She cried. She never cries. I took her finally to a doctor. He had to take those X rays, and he found spots, a lot of spots all over her leg, and then in her chest. Noah, she has cancer. She is not well, Noah, and she wants to see you. We have never talked, and I don't know what to say to you. I know you are a very important man and busy, but Rosie felt that she had to see you, before . . ."

Noah could not control his tears. They streamed down his face. He could barely talk. His voice faltered when he tried to speak. All he could say at first was, "Jakob, Jakob, Jakob, I'm so sorry." Noah felt an ache that could be nothing less than the Spirit groaning inside of him with words that he could barely hear but were loud enough to prompt him to say, "I will be there this evening."

It was not even eight o'clock in the morning, and Noah's head spun in circles. He had begun to feel solid and alive. His recent conversations with Joan had been the best of his marriage, and his talk with Jack that morning had opened up a new vista of friendship he had never even considered, let alone thought of as possible. The drive to work had been one of the most pleasant in years, with a breeze blowing through the car window. He liked being awake and alive.

Now he thought of bed. The cool wind had been replaced by the nearly silent drone of the air being driven through the ventilation system. The airy hope that had invaded the car had vanished in the artificial enclosure of his office. Noah sat back in his chair, put his hands behind his head, closed his eyes, and his bedroom flashed in his mind. He felt the draw to rest, and the fury that drove him to that desire seemed to fill the crannies of his soul.

He drifted and relaxed in his anger, but the more he tilted back in his swivel chair, the more dangerous and precarious his position. He stretched his legs out and moved his chair further back to avoid hitting his knees under the desk. The movement was sure and slow, but the momentum carried him past the point of balance. Gravity took over, and Noah landed abruptly on his back. It was as if the room had tilted ninety degrees; Noah's arms were still behind his head, his legs dangled over the chair as if they were still resting on the floor. Nothing had changed in his position other than that he was inelegantly resting on the floor.

He started to laugh. No one could see him, and yet he felt open to the eyes of the world. And it seemed right. He almost wanted to call in his secretary to see him in this position. He did not feel proud; he felt caught in the arms of a great, good cosmic joke. And he wanted someone to laugh with him, at him, for him. Noah felt alive. His heart was sick for Rosie and Jakob, but he felt a pulse in his body and soul, a pulse that signaled he was alive.

Noah's heart filled with gratitude to God as he shifted to the left to begin the process of righting himself. His anger was gone. The sense of God's betrayal in allowing so much to be served on his plate seemed like a distant memory. Noah knew he had the opportunity to join God in whatever he had for him in the new day.

Later That Day

The cab ride to the hospital was not out of the ordinary; it was simply frightening. Noah bumped along and braced himself at each reckless stop and held his ground with every swerve. He spent the early part of the ride talking on a cellular phone to Joan. He knew he could not go to the hospital to honor the couple who had opened his eyes, and particularly the woman who had pulled him into life, without having talked with Joan.

Noah had only recently realized that his wife was a woman of keen spiritual sensitivity, almost uncanny depth. He had ignored her for years and would not have been interested in her prayer life if it had slapped him in the face. He would have thought it good that she prayed, but he would have no more given thought about her heart with God than he had about how she spent her day.

But all that had changed. He cared, and he felt desperate for her assuring voice and the kindness that touched a growing, barely comprehended hunger in his heart.

"Joan. Hi. I don't know how to tell you about the day. I'm off right now to meet Rosie and Jakob. I got a phone call at the office from Jakob. I tried to call you before I left Chicago, but you weren't home. Here is the news. Rosie is in the hospital. I talked to Jakob. He doesn't sound good. I don't know what to expect, and I wanted you to pray for me."

"Honey, slow down. You're going to the hospital? Let's think about what you need to take. I think you should stop at a florist before you see them."

The phone sputtered and crackled. Noah could hear Joan's voice as part of the cacophony, but he could not make out a word she said after she suggested going to a florist. It was an idea that would not have come to him if he had thought about it for hours. He said good-bye in case she could hear. Then he turned off the phone. It felt good to hear her voice, even her worry for him, but he felt as if it was time to be alone and turn his heart to this strange God who had rescued him.

What should he say to Jakob and Rosie? How was he to speak to people he had thought about and imagined for weeks but had never really talked to longer than a few minutes?

The cab dropped him off at the front of Riverside Hospital in the Bronx. The ride had been quicker than he expected, and he had a few extra minutes. He used the time to walk down the block to a florist. He chose a bouquet of flowers that matched the scarf and dress Rosie had worn the day of the accident. He wanted to make her happy. He felt a deep resolve to do whatever he could do to bring her joy.

Carrying the flowers, he suddenly felt as if he were going to the hospital to ask Rosie to marry him. He recalled having asked Joan to marry him, and he felt a sudden wave of distress. He had asked her to marry him with the passion of an engineer asking for the specs of a building site. It was cool, informal, and he had plucked away any excitement with his recitation that he didn't know if he wanted children and if that was a problem, the relationship could end with no hard feelings.

He felt sick at how little color and fragrance he had brought into Joan's life, even now. Somehow Rosie and her adoring husband had brought more passion to his marriage and more conviction to his soul than all the sermons he had heard, or avoided listening to. He walked to the hospital entrance, found her room number, and proceeded to her room.

The door opened at the fourteenth floor, and before Noah could walk off the elevator, he was pushed against the back wall by the odor. It was unlike any smell he had encountered. It was thick and coated with an antiseptic cleanness, but he knew it was the smell of death. Noah felt a new sickness. He wanted to push the button to descend back into the bright, busy world. He stood in the elevator, and when the doors began to close, he hit the button to open them again. He did this several times until a couple walked to the elevator and clearly intended to get on. Noah knew he had to get off.

He walked to room 1415. Instead of stalling when he got to the door, he smelled the flowers once and walked in as if he were their son. Jakob sat by the window in a metal chair with a green plastic covering. He turned his head when Noah walked into the room and stood with a motion that was rapid and far more fluid than his age would allow. He clearly had been looking for Noah to arrive. Rosie was asleep. Her face looked pale and lifeless. Her thick eyes were closed, and her breathing was labored. Jakob put his finger quickly to his lips, took Noah by the arm, and led him back into the hallway.

"Noah. It's good to see you. Thank you for coming."

Noah looked startled and unsure of himself, "I'm glad to be here, Jakob. How is she?"

"Not good. Not good."

Noah wanted to run, to weep, but Jakob had not loosened his grip. He held Noah like an anchor in the midst of a gale. Noah looked into Jakob's weary face and asked: "How long, Jakob?"

It was the first moment Jakob couldn't look into his eyes. "I'm told soon. But soon is not an answer, is it? I don't suppose anyone knows, do we, when life will pass. But soon means moments must linger longer that we normally allow. She wanted to see you to say thank you for giving her life one last moment of hope."

Noah's eyes filled with tears at the thought that she wanted to thank him. It all seemed so cruel, unexpected. He had come to thank her for being the hand of God; she wanted to bless him for allowing her to give one last time.

Noah spoke quietly. "Jakob, I have much to say to your wife and to you. You know she saved my life. More to the point, you both saved my life—my marriage, my soul. I know this makes no sense, not even to me, but I can't thank you enough. I don't know how to show my gratitude, but what I do have to offer in this strange city is some power that I can put at your disposal to give her the best, and I mean the *finest,* medical care the city has to offer. One phone call and I can have the finest oncologist here in a day. Jakob, will you let me do whatever I can for you both?"

Jakob smiled; his sadness and weariness seemed to dance away with the warmth of the twinkle in his eyes. "Noah, she will be dead within a matter of weeks, at best. That is all I know. I know it would matter to you—I see it in your eyes, your mouth—to help her. So do whatever will bless you in helping us. Don't mention it to Rosie. She will worry it will cost you too much money. Between you and me, all right?"

Noah gripped Jakob's arm and said, "Between you and me. Yes." They walked back into the room.

PART SEVEN

Chasing after
IMMORTALITY

24

The Adoption

NOAH listened to Rosie's gentle laugh. Even more, he kept staring into her quiet, untroubled eyes. As hard as Jakob had worked to keep the knowledge of her impending death from his wife, she knew. She read the grief in his eyes and felt the acrid taste of a foreign, interior enemy that would soon take her life.

She was thrilled to see Noah. As Jakob had said, "She wants to tell you that you have made her life happy." Noah could not fathom the depth of her gratitude.

Jakob and Rosie were childless. They had loved each other for more than fifty years, but Jakob felt that Rosie had a need he could never reach, a void that only a child could fill. It had frustrated Jakob for decades.

But ever since Rosie had rescued Noah from the taxi, she felt as if she had given birth to a child. Her labor to pull him from death to life had released in her an ancient hope that had been locked away many decades earlier.

Finally she felt ready to die.

Rosie treasured her time with Noah much as she would a bar mitzvah, a graduation, a wedding. She had asked Noah if he were a religious man. Noah told her, then, what had happened to him before the accident, what had transpired in his heart when he had seen them walking together. He told her about his lack of love for Joan, his lukewarm devotion to Christ, and what had awakened him in his "new" birth.

Noah's passion for Joan and for Jesus Christ both thrilled and alarmed Jakob. The whole event had unnerved him. It all seemed like passages he had read in Jewish mystical writings: dark, mysterious, and overwhelming. Jakob folded his arms to keep some distance from Noah's story but leaned forward so as not to miss a single word or gesture.

The conversation lasted nearly an hour. It ended only because one of the nurses on the floor finally noticed that Noah had stayed well beyond visiting hours reserved only for family members. When the nurse told Noah he had to leave, Jakob stood and said, "This is Rosie's son. He can stay. He can come and go as he wishes, even if that means that I must go, if you find that necessary." The nurse backed down. Rosie glowed. Noah stood and said he had to make a few phone calls. He told Rosie he would be back that evening.

Noah and Jakob walked out together. Jakob linked his left arm around Noah's right and placed his right hand on Noah's forearm. The gesture reminded Noah of the first time he had seen Rosie and Jakob.

Never before had Noah felt so empowered to carry out a task. Jakob walked Noah to the elevator; neither man spoke until the door opened. Noah looked at the slightly bent man and felt like a little boy who wanted to hold on to his daddy. Noah said, "Jakob, there may be nothing any physician can do, but I want to find the best doctor in this city to see Rosie soon. I promise." Tears welled in his eyes.

Jakob could not look at Noah. He patted the younger man on the arm and turned away. Noah could see Jakob dab his eyes as he walked back to the room.

Noah returned to the office like a man whose mission was commissioned by God. He knew deep in his heart that Rosie would not live, but it did not matter. He had to honor her life even if she could not be healed.

He first went to find Sam Andrajian. When Sam saw the intensity in Noah's face, he knew something serious had happened. Noah poured out the story, telling Sam everything that had happened since that fateful meeting weeks before. Sam felt the stirrings of anguish and desperation in Noah. He felt the same pain he always experienced when someone spoke of losing a mother. He felt the horror of death, the loss of love, and the ringing shots that took his mother's life many decades before.

If Noah had asked for a hundred thousand dollars, Sam would have granted it with little thought. So when Noah asked Sam only to arrange for the finest oncologist to take over the care of Noah's adopted mother, Sam readily agreed. He picked up the phone and called the medical director of New York Mercy Hospital, a prestigious hospital to which the Andrajians donated millions of dollars every year. After several minutes on the phone, Sam Andrajian turned to Noah and declared, "Consider it done."

And it was.

Rosie was transferred by ambulance that evening to the care of Mercy Hospital's finest oncologists. She had a private room, round-the-clock nursing care, and a group of physicians who cared for her as they would have served Sam Andrajian's mother. In fact, several thought they were taking care of Sam's mother.

Noah stayed in New York for several more days. Each day was spent doing a few hours of work and then rushing off to the hospital. Rosie was uncomfortable with the luxurious setting. She had never stayed in a nicer room, even on some of their most expensive vacations. She felt like a queen. She also felt undeserving and out of place. But, like a good son, Noah chastised her and told her that if she kept complaining, he would fill the room with even more flowers.

For hours Noah sat and listened to Rosie talk about her family. It was a new experience for Noah. He had rarely been patient enough before to listen to people talk about their families, their relatives. Rosie told Noah that she had watched her father being dragged away by the SS when she was only ten years old. Her father had been a Jew. She told Noah how she had stayed by her mother's bedside for three days, afraid that her mother would never stop sobbing.

Rosie's voice cracked as she told Noah about the last night she saw her

mother. Her father's brother had arranged for the family's escape to Kra-
kow, but the night they were to flee, her mother would not dress or leave
the bed. The uncle pled with her mother, even threatened her, but nothing would get her to leave. She would wait for her husband to return, or
disappear in her grief. There was no moving her.

Rosie recounted how she held on to the bedpost as her uncle pulled
her from her mother, trying to save Rosie and her three brothers. Rosie's
uncle put his hand across her mouth and pulled her from the bed. As he
slung her over his shoulder, she watched as her mother did not turn to
see her only daughter carried away from her. It was Rosie's last glimpse
of her mother.

"Life is over in an instant," Rosie said, "but the memory of that
moment has never left me. In a flash, I was carried away from my
mother, and every other memory of her is framed by the sounds of her
muffled cries and her arms twisted over her head. Never have I been able
to erase that night. I realized that life is always a heartbeat away from
death.

"Noah, it has been my curse and my salvation. I can't tell you how I
hate death. I don't want to die. I don't want to leave Jakob. I'm afraid. I
would be a fool not to be afraid. But on the other hand, to know that
each moment is but an instant from death has given me such a joy in living. I think I knew even when I was only ten years old that people decide
whether they will live, really live, or simply go through the motions of
life.

"Death comes. It stalks. But it does not have the final power to win.
You see, when Jakob would go off to his store, I knew each day he left
that it might be the last time I saw the light in his eyes or the furrow of
his heavy brow. I never resented him for leaving. And I have never hated
my mother for dying before her time. I simply knew I could not die
before my day, and I could not deny that death is ever present.

"Noah, death is like looking at the horizon on the ocean. You know
that it is the horizon and that it limits what you can see, but you also
know that if you could get nearer, you would see further. But the line,
that horrible line, will keep you from seeing what is way on the other
side. It is like that for me with death, Noah. The horizon is all I can see,
but I know there is more on the other side. Death has been the one daily
reality that makes my life not only small but also grand. I'm but a small,
small breathing being, and I'm not the Creator. But I'm grateful for each

breath I've been granted. Each breath seemed more remarkable to me than any failure or any pain. When my friends would complain or when they remarked behind my back about being barren, I always thought, *but I am alive.* I am alive, and I will die. My death may be in a moment, so I will hold lightly the moment now, glory in it. It may not be mine in another moment.

"How grand, Noah, to be alive, to know that I had a son—a son I had not been granted until my womb was dried up. It is true what you have told me, Noah—about your Savior, Jesus, a resurrection, a coming to life only because death appears to have won. I have a son, Noah, a *son*. Death does not seem as cruel. I know resurrection too. I thank you that you were sent so that I could die knowing that my heart could feel this full."

Noah felt his eyes widen and pulse with tears. He could not save her. He knew he was meant only to drink her in as a gift. He also knew that he would never be the same.

Rosie knew hope because she had a dream come true in this life; her hope of life beyond death was limited by the horizon that continually moved beyond her sight, no matter how close she came to it. Noah wanted her to see beyond the sun's limit, to see what Jack would call "above the sun." Noah wanted Rosie to know the same thrill of a dream realized in meeting a God who had canceled her debt and restored her through the suffering servant Messiah.

But instead of lecturing Rosie and denying her under-the-sun perspective, he joined her. Her anguish became his. Her muffled cries at being torn from her mother became his own wound; her resolve not to succumb to death before her time was as much now his calling as it was hers.

Noah sensed that Rosie's stories would lead the way to the path he would walk. Her grip on him was more sure than when she pulled him from death. He felt as if she had birthed him, raised him, and sent him to live—all in a matter of days.

Noah felt the call to live, to live fully, abundantly. He knew it was time to be a husband, a father. It was time to understand the stories of his mother and father and to see God's movement in the places he had not even thought God to exist. It was time to look deeply into the horizon, the limits and the losses of dreams unfulfilled. Noah had never been a man who wanted to look to the past or too far into the future. It was too painful to remember and to dream, but if Rosie had the courage to bring the past and the future into the present, then a man who knew the Resurrection could do so with even greater courage and hope.

As Noah prepared to leave Rosie's room that night, he somehow knew he would not see her alive again. He saw her lips quiver, but her eyes were kind and strong. As he turned the corner and walked into the hallway, her face lingered in his heart like a full moon in the dark woods. His pain was too deep for tears, his hope too great for words.

It was time to go home.

25

"Living a Good Life Ought to Be Enough"

IF YOU are reading this book, you are alive—or are you? On a basic level, life is breathing, eating, and sleeping. But on another level, being "alive" is being excited about life, attuned to all the wonders of God's creation. On this level most of us go up and down, sometimes finding life worthwhile and at other times feeling as if we can barely drag ourselves from morning to night. And then, over all of us looms the shadow of death.

Do any of these scenarios sound familiar to you?

"MY annual checkup is next week. That ruins this week and the week after as I wait for the results of the tests. I can't believe that my neighbor was diagnosed with melanoma. He's only five years older than I am. I'm sure that mole on my stomach has changed color slightly, but how much does it need to change before I get concerned?"

- *"I've been doing sit-ups every day for three weeks, and I still have a flabby stomach. I used to have one of those incredible 'six-pack' stomachs. My son is in incredible shape. I should tell him to enjoy it before he has trouble getting up out of a chair."*

- *"I can't believe it! She thought I was that old! I am that old, but usually people think I look so much younger than I am. This was the first time someone thought I was actually older than my real age. I wonder if it's the five pounds I've put on. Maybe I'm acting older now. Could I be getting some gray hairs or even a wrinkle? I better check next time I'm near a mirror. This really is too much. Well, I really shouldn't let it get to me. There is always hair coloring, and I'm going to schedule in an additional workout each week to get that five pounds off. In no time, I will be back to my old form, looking younger than I really am."*

Do you think much about death? What's your reaction? Do you repress the thought? Do you fight it?

We can't stop the clock. Sooner or later our time runs out. Try as we might, holding on to our vitality, our strength, our enjoyment—even our very life—is as futile as trying to catch the wind. . . .

IF you have ever walked into a hospital room to see a loved one dying, then you understand Noah's agony and helplessness. Noah has power to change Rosie's hospital and physicians, but he can't keep death at bay. Our helplessness in the face of aging, decay, and death continually reminds us of impotence and loneliness. We are willing to do almost anything to avoid facing this wall.

Enjoying Life

The Teacher has taken us on a frustrating journey. He has taken a long, hard look at life under the sun. He has looked into a number of different areas—control, relationships, work, pleasure, wisdom, and spirituality—to find significance and has come up with a depressing conclusion: *It's all meaningless.* He has stamped all of life with this motto.

Or has he? So far he has looked at the issues of power/control, relationships, work/money, pleasure, wisdom, culture, and spirituality, and each time he has come up empty.

Five times through the book, however, he has gone a bit further and spoken of a joy that can be found in life itself. After pronouncing something meaningless, he has immediately gone on to say:

So I decided there is nothing better than to enjoy food and drink and to find satisfaction in work. Ecclesiastes 2:24

So I saw that there is nothing better for people than to be happy in their work. Ecclesiastes 3:22

It is good for people to eat well, drink a good glass of wine, and enjoy their work—whatever they do under the sun—for however long God lets them live. And it is a good thing to receive wealth from God and the good health to enjoy it. To enjoy your work and accept your lot in life—that is indeed a gift from God. People who do this rarely look with sorrow on the past, for God has given them reasons for joy. Ecclesiastes 5:18-20

So I recommend having fun, because there is nothing better for people to do in this world than to eat, drink, and enjoy life. That way they will experience some happiness along with all the hard work God gives them. Ecclesiastes 8:15

Young man, it's wonderful to be young! Enjoy every minute of it. Do everything you want to do; take it all in. But remember that you must give an account to God for everything you do. So banish grief and pain. Ecclesiastes 11:9-10

CARPE diem! Seize the day! The Latin phrase and its English translation capture the Teacher's sentiment in these verses. The Teacher tells us that joy is found in life itself! If there is no abiding meaning to our existence, perhaps we should simply repress the question and grab whatever enjoyment we can out of life today. We shouldn't worry about tomorrow. We shouldn't worry about the long-term benefits of our lives because there are none. We should just live for the day. When you experience satisfaction, don't ask any deep questions, just embrace the feeling.

Affirming Life, Fleeing Death

The Teacher's point seems obvious to the point of absurdity. Is it better to be sick or well? potent or impotent? arthritic or agile? young or old? alive or dead?

Much of our culture echoes the Teacher's attitude: We need to pursue life, health, and vitality. And we need to avoid at all costs the opposites of these: decay, disease, and death.

Examine our concept of male and female beauty. Who graces the covers of our magazines? Those who epitomize the forces of life. They are young and vigorous, tanned and healthy. And inside those magazines are articles announcing that our society pursues vitality, health, and life with a vengeance. A survey of recent magazines yields the following revealing titles: "Why Appearance Matters More Than Ever," "Why Sex Heals," "The Lifestyle Makeover: Take Your Life from Good to Great," "Crash Course: Beautiful, Healthy Nails," "Healthy Eating on the Run."

Once again, how can we deny the value of life? And if life is precious, then we must pursue the qualities that make life the best that it can be for as long as we can. We pursue vitality, not impotence; health, not sickness; strength, not weakness.

Living the Abundant Life

Isn't that the appeal of the gospel, after all—life? One of Jesus' most well-known statements is about life: "For God so loved the world that he gave his only Son, so that everyone who believes in him will not perish but have eternal life" (John 3:16). A similar passage promises that Jesus has come to bring a superabundance to life: "I have come that they may have life, and have it to the full" (John 10:10, NIV).

Life is at the core of the Good News, and, as many evangelists point out, you don't have to wait until the afterlife to experience the joy of Jesus. You can have abundant life right now! All you have to do is accept Jesus, and your life will change from the drab, problem-filled disaster it is now to one that is vital and wonderful.

And those of us who, through God's grace, took that step of faith know this truth. Our lives have been filled with new light. At the heart of the gospel is the promise of life.

I can see this wonderful cycle repeat itself in my sons' generation. Right now, my middle son, Tim, hosts a Bible study for his high school friends. The Bible study is run by an organization that works with private schools on the East Coast. Over the past two years a number of Tim's friends have embraced the Good News of Jesus Christ. We have seen how their lives are filled with a new level of life and vitality.

Among a number of exciting and inspiring stories, Ned's stands out by the level of excitement he feels toward his newfound faith. After turning to Jesus, he truly "caught fire." He felt a new level of enjoyment in life. His problems seemed to disappear. He no longer dreaded the day but woke up with a passion to experience what God had planned for him and to share with others his new faith. He truly felt that the gift of a joy-filled eternal life began the second he asked Jesus into his heart. It seemed to him, as it seemed to most of us at the beginning of our journey of faith, that he would never again have a problem.

The Erosion of Life

Just last night it was Ned's turn to share at the Bible study. He has been a Christian now for about a year and a half. He told the group that he had much to be thankful for. He loved the Lord, and he had even seen one of his parents become a Christian. But he had been surprised by a new level of loneliness that had come over him. His passion for the Lord had alienated him from a number of his friends at school. They withdrew from him as he pressed them with the claims of Christ, and they were put off that he would no longer go out with them to drink and cause others harm. Some of his Christian friends were less than supportive as well. He was hanging in there, but he was feeling less joy. He wondered if he had lost his "first love" because life did not seem quite as abundant as it had at first.

Those of us who have been Christians for a time can sympathize with Ned. Some of us heard the gospel presented as a way to rid our lives of all problems and hassles. Some presentations of the gospel go so far as to suggest that the acceptance of Christianity will bring dramatic physical healings and even monetary gains.

When Dan and I first conceived of this book, we wanted to name it *The Abundant Life: You Should Have Read the Fine Print!* Though we were wisely advised to change the title, it captures the point we want to make here. The Bible is far from promising a life without care or suffering. If anything, the Bible teaches that becoming a Christian increases our pain.

Paul is the preeminent interpreter of the pain in a Christian's life, perhaps because his life was anything but devoid of it (Eph. 3:13; 2 Cor.

12). In any case, Paul reminds us that our faith in Christ does not exempt us from suffering. He invites his brothers and sisters into a community of sufferers. He urges his fellow Christians not to be ashamed "of me, either, even though I'm in prison for Christ. With the strength God gives you, be ready to suffer with me for the proclamation of the Good News" (2 Tim. 1:8). He not only expects difficulties in life after he becomes a Christian, but he also sees their value for the believer: "We can rejoice, too, when we run into problems and trials, for we know that they are good for us—they help us learn to endure" (Rom. 5:3). Indeed, he clearly sees the Christian life as a path of suffering on the way to glory (Rom. 8:17). We will later explore the nature of that glory.

Death's Intrusion

As a society, we have done an admirable job of promoting life. American culture is upbeat, vibrant, and young. We can keep death at bay—but only temporarily, as a whole generation of baby boomers is discovering.

Both Dan and I were born in 1952, near the beginning of the baby-boomer generation. The first boomers, born in 1945, have now turned fifty. We are beginning to realize that we are on the gradual decline to the grave.

As a result, though we have repressed the thought for a long time, we are beginning to grapple with the reality of death. And once the baby boomers decide to grapple with something, it becomes a major motif of our society. This is because we are not only the largest generation in our country's history, but we are also surely the most self-centered. The generation before us experienced the depression and World War II. They sacrificed and suffered silently. The Generation Xers, our own children, have been silenced by our size and our unwillingness to give up power. No, we boomers grabbed power from our parents in the late sixties and early seventies, and our children will have to rip it out of our hands. We are now facing our demise. Death may not be knocking at the door, but we hear footsteps approaching in the distance.

The Teacher knew of death's intrusion. He realized that the best that a carpe-diem lifestyle could do was temporarily anesthetize one from the inescapable fact that we are going to die. If the Teacher were alive today, he would look at a magazine cover and see beyond the fresh, healthy-looking face to the slow-but-steady process of aging. He would see the encroachment of wrinkles and age spots. He would see the straight back and the flexible joints becoming crooked and painful. Indeed, in perhaps one of the most powerful metaphors of the book, he describes the process of growing old. He paints a picture of the aging process as a time when:

> *the sun and the light*
> *and the moon and the stars grow dark,*
> *and the clouds return after the rain;*
> *when the keepers of the house tremble,*
> *and the strong men stoop,*
> *when the grinders cease because they are few,*
> *and those looking through the windows grow dim;*
> *when the doors to the street are closed*
> *and the sound of grinding fades;*
> *when men rise up at the sound of birds,*
> *but all their songs grow faint;*
> *when men are afraid of heights*
> *and of dangers in the streets;*
> *when the almond tree blossoms*
> *and the grasshopper drags himself along*
> *and desire no longer is stirred.*
> *Then man goes to his eternal home*
> *and mourners go about the streets.*
> *Remember him—before the silver cord is severed,*
> *or the golden bowl is broken;*
> *before the pitcher is shattered at the spring,*
> *or the wheel broken at the well,*
> *and the dust returns to the ground it came from,*
> *and the spirit returns to God who gave it.*
> Ecclesiastes 12:2-7, NIV

THESE are the last words from the Teacher, and they are not encouraging. The book does not conclude with his words. As we know by now, the second wise man comes on the scene and not only affirms the Teacher's understanding of the world under the sun but also points his son and us, his later readers, to something better, something above the sun. But before we turn to that above-the-sun perspective, we must take a hard look at what the Teacher says.

He harshly reminds us in these verses that we will age and we will die. He uses three different metaphors to express this truth.

The first image is found in verse 2 and is a simple one. It sets the mood for what follows. The Teacher, in essence, compares growing old to the darkening gloom of a coming storm. Youth is a time of sunlight and warmth; old age a time of damp darkness.

The focus shifts to a house in the second scene, though we are to imagine the rain clouds outside. Verse 3 describes four classes of people in the house, and they are each languishing. It is clear from the Hebrew words, though this is not carried over into English translations, that there are two groups of women and two groups of men. And then these groups are divided into the aristocrats and the servants of the house. The first group includes the "strong men" and the women of leisure ("those looking through the windows"), both of whom are growing weaker. The same is true for the male servants ("the keepers of the house") and the women who grind the grain. The picture presented in this verse and the next few is that of a neglected house that grows increasingly dilapidated, while life goes on out-side as if nothing is happening. That is, while the house is falling apart, the almond tree is blossoming and the grasshopper keeps going its merry way.

The Teacher wants us to think of that house as our own bodies. We can't neglect it. We may work out every day and take vitamins, but in the end the aging process will catch up with us. Indeed, it has already started!

This is the point of a *San Francisco Chronicle* article entitled "A Time-table of the Ravages of Age: How a Man Ages." It is written with a some-what humorous tone, but the older I get, the less funny it sounds!

> *There are many gruesome things to be said about a man's body as it creeps past the age of 30. At 30 he's not a bad specimen. A little plumper than he used to be, a little slower, a little balder, yet smarter than ever. Still, his body has just passed its peak. It has started dying a little every day, losing about one percent of its functional capacity every year.*
>
> *Cells are disappearing, tissues are stiffening, chemical reactions are slowing down. By age 70 his body temperature will be two degrees lower. He will stand an inch or so shorter and have longer ears. No one under-stands why.*

THIS article sounds remarkably like the Teacher's description. Note that his description of the house and its inhabitants can be read not only as a metaphor of the body as a decaying house but also as an allegory. The New Living Translation indeed translates it in a way that makes this clear: "Your limbs will tremble with age, and your strong legs will grow weak. Your teeth will be too few to do their work, and you will be blind, too" (Eccles. 12:3).

This is not a pretty picture, but it is a true one. The Teacher caps off his final litany of death by describing it as a silver cord that is snapped or a golden bowl that is broken. Life is something precious, and that is why these objects are described by expensive metals. But at death they are rendered useless.

In this concluding speech the Teacher reminds us that death is the end of it all. But he really doesn't focus exclusively on death as much as the painful process leading to death. He laments the increasing difficulty we have interacting with the world as our eyesight gets increasingly worse ("those looking through the windows grow dim" [Eccles. 12:3, NIV]); our ability to chew (and enjoy food) diminishes ("the grinders cease because they are few" [Eccles. 12:3, NIV]); we have difficulty hearing ("all their songs grow faint" [Eccles. 12:4, NIV]); and sexual impotence sets in ("desire no longer is stirred" [Eccles. 12:5, NIV]). Aches and pains lead to debilitating disease and ultimately death. The Teacher describes death as the time when "the dust returns to the ground it came from, and the spirit returns to God who gave it" (Eccles. 12:7, NIV). When properly understood, these are not encouraging words. It is a reversal of the creation of Adam and Eve as described in Genesis 2:7.

Death: The Ultimate Nemesis

No wonder, then, that death threw its long, dark shadow over the Teacher's life. We have hinted at this, but the main reason he could find no meaning in power, relationships, work, pleasure, wisdom, or spirituality was because of death. It did not matter what he achieved in those areas—death brought it all to an end.

The Teacher also challenges the idea that we have an afterlife to put our hope in. At one point, he indicates that though God is in control, we don't know what will happen to us after we die:

This, too, I carefully explored: Even though the actions of godly and wise people are in God's hands, no one knows whether or not God will show them favor in this life. The same destiny ultimately awaits everyone, whether they are righteous or wicked, good or bad, ceremonially clean or unclean, religious or irreligious. Good people receive the same treatment as sinners, and people who take oaths are treated like people who don't. It seems so tragic that one fate comes to all. Ecclesiastes 9:1-3

In another place, he questions whether God treats us any differently from an animal when we die: "For humans and animals both breathe the same air, and both die. So people have no real advantage over the animals. How meaningless! Both go to the same place—the dust from which they came and to which they must return. For who can prove that the human spirit goes upward and the spirit of animals goes downward into the earth?" (Eccles. 3:19-21).

We desire health, strength, vitality, growth, and life. We may have those things, but deep down we know they are only temporary. The road of life always ends in death, and usually death is reached by the path of pain and decay. Many of us who are now active and healthy, surrounded by friends and family, will end up our last months or years incapacitated in an impersonal nursing home, cut off from friends and family. How do we think about our life and achievements in the light of that future reality? The Teacher could only conclude: *It's all meaningless.*

26

Restoring Life
through Death

ON FEBRUARY 13 a car driven by sixteen-year-old Jen Carver was struck
by an ambulance. Ms. Carver was pronounced dead on arrival at the hospital. The driver of the ambulance was admitted to the hospital with
minor cuts to his face and released. No charges would be filed against the
ambulance driver, even though he drove through a red light, because he
had turned on the siren and flashers.

The newspaper ran a short, matter-of-fact article about the accident.
But to the people who knew Jen's family, it was too antiseptic.

Jen had just gotten her license two weeks earlier. She had been so
proud and excited. Her parents were happy, but like most parents of new
drivers, they were worried, especially when Jen went out at night. On the

day of the accident, Jen's family decided to take two cars to church. Jen thought she might take some of her friends out to lunch after youth group, so Mr. and Mrs. Carver left first to go to church, comforted, in part, by the fact that there wasn't much traffic at that time of week.

When Jen didn't show up at the start of church, they were just mildly irritated, thinking that their daughter was taking advantage of her new-found independence to wander in after the singing. But halfway through the sermon their concern bordered on panic.

When they got home, Jen was not there either. Mrs. Carver was the first to notice a message waiting for them on their answering machine. Their minds went numb at the words *There has been an accident.* They completely fell apart when they arrived at the hospital to discover that their baby girl had died.

John, the ambulance driver, didn't feel the pain from the cuts in his face; he was completely devastated. Why hadn't he seen the car before he hit her? He knew that he was technically not at fault. Why hadn't she heard his siren? He would never forget the glimpse he had of her limp body. And then he found out that she was a Christian like himself. How could God let such a thing happen? He would live the rest of his life with the guilt, and Jen Carver . . . John could not stop weeping.

The Horror of Death

The Teacher was absolutely right: Death is horrible. The Bible tells us that we were not made to die; death is unnatural.

All we have to do is go back to the very first chapters of the Bible to learn this lesson. When Adam and Eve were first created, they knew only life; human death was not a part of God's work. But then, in Genesis 3, they sinned. And the result, as they were warned, was death. Human life-spans would now have a limit. Paul explains, "When Adam sinned, sin entered the entire human race. Adam's sin brought death, so death spread to everyone, for everyone sinned" (Rom. 5:12).

Jen's death was not a normal functioning of nature; it was a forceful intrusion of the horrors of sin—not her sin specifically but human sin in general. If sin had never entered the world, Jen would not have died.

Christians should know the horror of death more clearly than anyone else does, but they don't. We repress our fear of death behind pious-sounding platitudes that are true but lack power unless we come to grips with the pain and suffering involved in death and dying.

As hard as it might be for you, contemplate your own death right now. Be bold about it. Imagine slowly slipping out of consciousness. You have a few lucid moments to remember those closest to you. You think of the spouse you are leaving behind. You think of your children and wish you could give them one last bit of advice. You think of your dreams left unfulfilled. You think of unfinished projects, things that you cared about, things that would never come to reality.

Think about death now from the other side. Perhaps someone close to you has died recently. Remember the pain of the sudden separation. Remember how you enjoyed fellowship with that person, how much you respected and loved that person!

Death's horror is in large part separation and the cessation of one's life story. Most stories that we read have a plot that is like a journey. Death is a sudden interruption of that journey; it is an abrupt and early closure of that story. We feel loss as a result.

But even further, we like to imagine death coming softly and sweetly in the night. We think of death as a deep sleep, but study shows that this is often not the case.

A recent study reported on the public radio show "All Things Considered" noted that 40 percent of us die in severe pain (as reported by surviving friends and relatives). Many of the remaining 60 percent felt no pain because they were so highly medicated. Further, a large number of people died without relational support; alone without friends or relatives.[1]

We should not paint a rosy-colored picture: Death is horrible. It is only as we look death in the face and describe it for what it is that we can really understand the truth of what the Teacher is saying. And, even more important, it is only as we understand the horror of death that we can have even an inkling of the significance of Christ's death on the cross. But it is possible to embrace death in a way that humbles us. We are not the owners of time, breath, or life. True humility opens a sense of wonder and pleasure in life itself, thus robbing death of its full power to end and destroy. Even more, a view from above the sun allows us to see that death has lost its sting because, as tragic as it is, death opens the door to our ultimate hope, heaven.

Rosie is a person who has been both unnerved and humanized by the reality of death. Her life was shattered at an early age by her father's death. Then her mother's choice to "die before she was dead" increased Rosie's hatred of death. Her inability to bear children who would carry on her name and her memory added to a life of sorrow. Death did not rob Rosie of her humanity: She continued to hope and dream without bitterness or demand. She had not turned from death but allowed its reality to shape a deep and abiding gratitude for the gift of breath and life. She did not view life as a "given"; instead, she embraced even the tragedies as a gift that increased her passion to dream and wait for God's fulfillment.

Yet Rosie has no final hope of resurrection, no ultimate confidence in the One who has proceeded her and returned from the dead to represent the victory over death. As believers in Jesus Christ, we are to have no less an awareness of death than Rosie and no less a grasp of the utter marvel and glory of every breath. But it is the gospel of Jesus Christ that turns our heart to a different conclusion from the Teacher's conclusion.

Something New under the Sun

Death rendered life impotent in the eyes of the Teacher. He looked to the future and saw his own end, which led him to question the meaning of his life in the present. He looked to the future not with hope but with the oppressive idea that there would never be anything "new under the sun."

The second wise man, who brings the book to a close, is the authoritative voice of Ecclesiastes. We have already seen how this unnamed sage both affirms the Teacher's outlook and takes us further. He affirms the Teacher's view of life under the sun, life apart from God, but he goes on to instruct his son to "fear God," to look above the sun.

It is helpful for us to look at the message of Ecclesiastes, especially what it says about death, in the light of the gospel of Jesus Christ. A key New Testament passage that aids us in understanding the continuing relevance of Ecclesiastes is Romans 8:18-25. This is the only New Testament passage that explicitly picks up the message of Ecclesiastes. We have mentioned parts of this passage before, but it is so important to our understanding of the book of Ecclesiastes and our present struggles that we will quote it now in full.

Yet what we suffer now is nothing compared to the glory he will give us later. For all creation is waiting eagerly for that future day when God will reveal who his children really are. Against its will, everything on earth was subjected to God's curse. All creation anticipates the day when it will join God's children in glorious freedom from death and decay. For we know that all creation has been groaning as in the pains of childbirth right up to the present time. And even we Christians, although we have the Holy Spirit within us as a foretaste of future glory, also groan to be released from pain and suffering. We, too, wait anxiously for that day when God will give us our full rights as his children, including the new bodies he has promised us. Now that we are saved, we eagerly look forward to this freedom. For if you already have something, you don't need to hope for it. But if we look forward to something we don't have yet, we must wait patiently and confidently.

PAUL here describes the world "subjected to God's curse." He looks around him and sees evil, suffering, and injustice. He knows his Old Testament and the pivotal events of Genesis 3. There Adam and Eve take the fateful step of outright rebellion against their loving Creator. They take the side of the serpent, thus causing a breach in their relationship with their true Lord. The result is the curse that has ramifications that reverberate throughout the entire world—under the sun.

Paul would agree, then, with the Teacher. The world is the arena of "death and decay." But where Paul and the Teacher would disagree concerns the future. The Teacher looks to the future with cynicism, despair, and pessimism; he groans, "It's all meaningless." The apostle looks to the future with eagerness, confidence, and patience; he says, "We have a great hope!"

What is the ground of Paul's hope? Jesus Christ. You see, the Teacher was wrong to say "there is nothing new under the sun." From the prophets, he should have known that something new was going to happen in the future and that some*thing* new was a Some*one*—Jesus, the Messiah.

Reflect for a moment on what Christ did. Read the story of the Good News account through the prism of the book of Ecclesiastes. Jesus, who is God, submitted himself to the world under the curse of the covenant. Paul describes Christ in Philippians 2:6-8 in this way: "Though he was God, he did not demand and cling to his rights as God. He made himself nothing; he took the humble position of a slave and appeared in human form. And in human form he obediently humbled himself even further by dying a criminal's death on a cross."

Jesus subjected himself to the under-the-sun realm. The Gospel of John notes this when it states that "the Word became human and lived here on earth among us" (John 1:14), but "the world didn't recognize him when he came" (John 1:10).

Jesus' experience of the world under the curse is amply narrated by the synoptic Gospels. According to Matthew and Luke, Jesus' birth was not a grand welcoming of the long-awaited Messiah to Israel; it took place in an obscure corner of Palestine, in a manger. It was witnessed only by his parents, some shepherds, and animals.

Christ's earthly ministry was mostly a catalog of one frustration after another. It climaxed during the last week, which began on a promising note with his entry into Jerusalem, during which he was greeted by cheering crowds. But soon these crowds were gone, and even the close circle of disciples began to desert him. One intimate associate, Judas, even betrayed him, while another to whom he had given much, Peter, denied him.

Jesus went to the cross alone in the world. But it was not until the eleventh hour on the cross that the worst moment came. The suffering was already severe, but it reached a point of horror at the end when Jesus cried out, *"Eli, Eli, lema sabacthani?'* which means, 'My God, my God, why have you forsaken me?'" (Matt. 27:46). At this point, Jesus experienced the effects of the covenant curse "under the sun" in a way that the Teacher had only remotely tasted.

And why? Jesus experienced the curse in order to free us from the curse (Gal. 3:13). He died in order to free us from the ultimate fear of death. His death opens up the way for our experience of the "glorious freedom" that Paul spoke of in Romans 8.

Jesus' death leads to resurrection. The second half of the hymn cited by Paul in Philippians 2 spells this out: "Because of this, God raised him up to the heights of heaven and gave him a name that is above every other name" (Phil. 2:9).

And the New Testament tells us that we follow in Jesus footsteps. We will suffer; we will decay; we will die. Because of Jesus, we can add, "But we will also rise!" (See 1 Cor. 15:20-28.) In the apostle Paul's great chapter on death, he concludes by quoting Hosea in celebrating the defeat of death: "Death is swallowed up in victory. O death, where is your victory? O death, where is your sting?" (1 Cor. 15:54-55).

Does this mean we do not feel the pain of death today? Look at Jesus in the Garden as he contemplated the Cross. He looked death in the face, and he trembled, even though he is the Son of God. Yes, we fear death; it is a horror. But we also affirm that it is not the end of the story. We live on—because of Jesus.

Finding Life in the Shadow of Death

In 1 Corinthians 15, Paul counters those who worship Christ without believing that he has won a victory over death. He says it is foolish to do so. If Jesus did not conquer death on the cross, then those who follow him are pursuing something "useless" (1 Cor. 15:14). In words reminiscent of the Teacher's, Paul recommends that such people rather adopt the pleasure-seeking philosophy "Let's feast and get drunk, for tomorrow we die!"

But those who follow Christ know better. Glory follows suffering. Life follows death. Resurrection follows crucifixion. We have a certain hope.

What, then, does it mean for people of hope to live in the light of death?

Enjoy the Moment

We have seen that the Teacher urged the enjoyment of momentary pleasures because he felt that what we experience here in this life is all there is. His advice was grab whatever gusto you can get out of this miserable life. We have since observed that the Teacher wrongly restricted his views to "under the sun" and did not embrace the truth that death is not the end of the story. Nonetheless, even those of us who, in Christ, see that death is not the conclusion can appreciate the fact that we should live life to the fullest in the light of death.

God does give us glimpses of joy in the midst of present trouble, and it would be wrong to deny them. Indeed, it is not wrong for us to seek blessings in the present. And as Christians who know that death is not the end, our honest affirmation—"Yes, we will die"—can serve to intensify whatever joy God grants us in the present.

The Teacher even gives us some proverbs that encourage living life in the light of death: "The day you die is better than the day you are born. It is better to spend your time at funerals than at festivals. For you are going to die, and you should think about it while there is still time. . . . A wise person thinks much about death, while the fool thinks only about having a good time now" (Eccles. 7:1-4).

Since death is not the end, thinking about it does not destroy us. And, indeed, when we have a wonderful moment, the remembrance of growing old and dying intensifies the pleasure.

Perhaps you know someone who has had a brush with death and lived to tell the story. Often after they recover, they have a new level of appreciation of the small pleasures of life.

We don't need to have a hospitalization to live in this life-affirming way. We only have to take the Teacher's advice in chapter 7 to spend time meditating on our death, envisioning the moment when our participation in our everyday activities will be no more. Perhaps then we will find an increased sense of happiness not only in the special moments but even in everyday routines like washing dishes or taking out the garbage.

Appreciating the Stages of Life

Once the sting of death is removed by Christ's act of dying and rising, we don't have to fear the process that leads to that end. We have already commented on the fact that our culture desperately affirms youth and vitality and shuns the aging process. Those of us who, in Christ, don't fear death can find a new appreciation in the different stages of life. We don't have to think that once we pass the age of thirty, we are "over the hill." We don't have to look with envy on those who are younger than we are.

The truth is that every stage has its inevitable burdens and its potential joys. The burdens are always there since the human condition has never been problem free since the Fall. The joys are there, but they are only potential since they are less frequent and easily missed.

Teenagers struggle with insecurities of their sexuality and independence, among other things. But they also are on the threshold of adulthood with their future still flexible and exciting. They have more time on their hands than their parents do to explore new relationships and experiences.

Those of us in midlife struggle with being the "sandwich" generation, with worries about our children, often teenagers, as well as our aging parents. This position often brings intense financial responsibilities as we must consider helping others with college and/or nursing homes. But there are potential joys in midlife as well. We are more settled, perhaps a little more worldly wise, and possibly more financially secure than we were when we were younger.

People in their seventies can look back over a lifetime of memories, both good and bad. Memories, in other words, can be a source of both trouble and joy in their lives. People in their later years may be plagued with physical ills, or they, like my own parents, may wake up and play four hours of tennis to start the day. Though seventy-year-olds could live another twenty years, they also know that the end might be around the corner. For those who know God and live in the light of the end, this can be a moment of great enjoyment because deep down they have affirmed with Paul, that "living is for Christ, and dying is even better" (Phil. 1:21).

Dying Is Even Better

And with this, we come full circle. The Teacher said that life is meaningless in the light of death. Paul, on the contrary, asserts that life is meaningful only in the light of death. The difference is Jesus Christ.

Because of Christ, we know that death is not the end but the final birth. Death is not the final chapter but the first chapter of a never-ending sequel to our life story. Death leads from a life of struggle, trouble, hurt, and pain to an existence where God will wipe away every tear. We do not know the details of our heavenly existence; we know only that it will be wonderful. We know that injustice will be righted and that bliss will follow pain.

Jesus Christ has won the victory over death, and that turns us into followers who are life-affirming, deeply joyful in the midst of suffering. That victory transforms our lives.

Life: Above the Sun

Under the sun, life has a definite and inglorious end. Fear of death propels all our other fears and renders control, relationships, pleasure, wisdom, or spirituality meaningless. Why bother if it all ends in the blackness of the grave?

Our above-the-sun perspective bursts the chains of death. Death is a defeated enemy. Christ has led the way. While the process of dying is a sign of the Fall and is not to be embraced as a friend, we know it is not the end but rather a new beginning, a beginning of a far better story. Death is the path not to oblivion and forgetfulness, but rather to the bliss of life with God.

Above the sun we do not fear death. We rejoice in the victory Christ has over it. Above the sun our life matters for eternity. "Living is for Christ!" (Phil. 1:21). This is because we know that "dying is even better" (Phil. 1:21). God has given us a glimpse of the bliss to come (Rev. 21–22).

An under-the-sun perspective fueled the Teacher's resignation to a life of meaninglessness in which

- Control *will always slip out of our grasp.*
- Relationships *will always disappoint.*
- Work *will leave us frustrated.*
- Pleasure *is always fleeting.*
- Wisdom *is never an adequate guide.*
- Spirituality *usually gives in to legalism.*
- Life *ends in decay and death.*

BUT the above-the-sun perspective charges all aspects of our earthly life with new and everlasting significance, so that

- Control *leads to surrender to God's will.*
- Relationships *lead to trust in God's love.*
- Work *leads to laboring for God's kingdom.*
- Pleasure *leads to a hunger for God's coming.*
- Wisdom *leads to a humble curiosity to know God.*
- Spirituality *leads to embracing God's wild heart.*
- Life *leads to a joyous celebration of death and resurrection.*

THE LESSON of Ecclesiastes is that Christ makes the difference. Christ infuses our lives with meaning.

27

The Beginning of Life

NOAH'S RETURN to Chicago felt like a homecoming for a long-lost sailor who had been presumed dead. Except that no one knew he had been lost or that his return had embarked him on a different course of life.

While Noah was eager to tell Joan about his time with Jakob and Rosie, he had difficulty finding the words to express his new insights and direction. Joan listened to the stories, awed that her husband was talking to her at all, let alone talking about things that had touched the core of his soul. She knew without being told that Noah had come home awakened even more than he had been after the last New York trip.

Noah spent much time that week preparing for the Bible study. He had called Jack and asked if he could take some time to talk about his most recent trip to New York. "Sure, Noah. But what happened this time?" Jack replied.

"Jack, more than the last major trip, for sure. I don't know if I should head back there anytime soon. I don't know what God is up to, but honestly, I have never felt more aware of the agony of life and the utter wonder and joy of living for God. I shared my life and my faith with Jakob and Rosie. I don't know what they thought, but I walked away from them more human and more aware of God's strange, wonderful, wild ways than ever before. I can't wait to share the whole story with the group." Jack later told Marcia that he had never heard Noah sound so calm, strong, and alive.

Joan learned later that week that Jack and Noah had gone over to Jessie's house after work to talk with her about her job situation. At first Joan thought it was strange that Noah had said nothing, but when Jessie excitedly told her that Jack and Noah had arranged for her to work in Noah's firm on the condition that she would go back to school to get an accounting degree, Joan understood that Noah was likely awkward with this new level of involvement with others.

Jessie remarked, "I don't know what's gotten into him, Joan. He was warm, gracious, and, frankly, downright insistent that he would not help me if I was unwilling to go back to school. He was so different, but he was so Noah. He had the school schedule and had already figured out beforehand the financial aid the firm would provide and what I would need to save per month to pay for school over the next three years. I could have cracked a rib. He said, 'Now, Jessica, you know that as one of your employers I will be twice as hard on you as I would be on someone who did not know Jesus. So, I expect great things from you.' I'm telling you, Joan, when he gets real fatherly, he looks like he ought to put on a gray sweater vest and smoke a pipe. But he was so dear. What has happened, Joan? What's up with this man?"

Joan replied, "I just don't really know. I don't. God is acting in his life; that's obvious. I know I *love* him. I have always loved him, but now I know why I married him. He is different. I can't explain it, but I tell you, Jessie, I like him. I *like* him too."

That night Joan asked Noah what had transpired with Jessie. Noah reddened and said it was no big deal. A job had opened up in the firm, and he thought Jessie would be excellent at the entry-level job. "Come on, Noah. Admit it. You went to bat for her. You stuck your neck out, and you came through for her."

"No, I didn't. I was just trying to fit a good person to a basic and not-too-demanding job," he defensively replied.

"Oh, yeah. Well, then, why did you insist on her pursuing a degree and figure out beforehand what she needed to save to get through school? Noah Adamson, you are a dog. You are loving people better than you ever have, and I, for one, am not willing to let you ignore that reality no matter how uncomfortable it makes you feel."

Noah blushed. His eyes turned from her, but she could tell that he was thrilled that she was not rebuffed by his evasiveness.

THE DAYS hung like stars in a constellation that brightened the sky with a new pattern of glory. Joan watched as Noah spent hours wasting time with his boys. The old Noah would never have constructed a model airplane with them without carefully assembling it, precisely putting on the decals, and worrying over it until the boys became bored and turned the project over to him. The new Noah hastily built a P-57 Mustang with his sons, and when Joan wasn't looking, they took the plane outside and blew it up with some M-80s Noah had gotten somewhere. He looked mischievous, and the boys were tickled out of their minds. They actually had fun with their dad. So did Joan.

No one could quite explain or comprehend what had happened to Noah. Those closest to him did not need explanation. He was awake, and he made no apparent movement to escape to numbing sleep. And those who did not know him well simply suspected he was finally taking Prozac.

By the time the Bible study came on Thursday night, everyone in the study had heard that Noah's relationship with the Lord had grown so deeply that it was as if he had only now become a Christian. They drove to the study at Mimi's apartment with keen anticipation.

Bible Study

Mimi was angry. She looked at her threadbare, brown couch and felt that it mirrored her dark heart. She hated her poverty and the years of wasted, riotous living. She had found the couch beside a Dumpster, and for a few beers and a few laughs with some boys at work, she had convinced them to help her get it into her apartment. The couch was ugly, but it was better than an empty third-story apartment. She had also inherited her sister's beanbag chairs when her sister had to move to flee the man she was living with.

Mimi felt sick. She hated that she had stayed in the Bible study. No one was like her, and no one liked her. She knew the conversations with Marcia were true and good, but everyone else seemed either in such a different class or so familiar with this Christian stuff that she couldn't quite fit in. Not that she wanted to, but she couldn't go back to drugs and sex. It had almost killed her. Although she didn't fit with the Bible study, she felt more at home with them than with her friends who were speeding their life away on Ecstasy and dropping back into gravity with Quaaludes.

Mimi had heard from Marcia that Noah was going to share. She had heard words about his "coming alive," "having an awakening," and "being anointed." She just wanted to see if he looked like a middle-aged prune that had been left in the sun and had stiffened to a rock-hard consistency. She liked bugging Noah. He seemed so proper and prudish. She loved saying one or two flagrantly naughty words in his presence to see him tighten his lips and walk away with self-righteous condescension.

She got out some paper cups for the soft drinks and put the stale pretzels in a pale green plastic bowl. She grimaced when she realized she did not have any ice, but she did not have time to run out or call anyone. As she slammed the refrigerator shut, she heard someone knocking on her apartment door. She thought to herself, *I hope it's not Noah and Joan. Lord, let it be anyone but them.*

She opened the door, and Noah said, "Hi, Mimi. It's great to finally be at your place."

Joan brushed by Noah and put her arm around Mimi, "Anything I can do to help?"

Mimi did not know whether to yell at them to get out of her place or smile and endure another one of God's jokes of giving her exactly what she had just prayed for him not to do.

"Well, honestly, I forgot to make ice. If you stay here, I'll run out and get some at the convenience store down the block."

Noah turned and said, "You two chat. I'll get the ice. Anything else you need?"

Mimi's smile turned slightly sinister. "Yeah, Noah, why don't you look for a black kid, about fourteen, with a red Oklahoma Sooners cap. He'll be loitering near the phone. Ask him if he's got any 'dust.' I may need it to get through this night." She expected Noah to pale slightly and then chide her or turn away in disgust.

Noah's smile was penetrating without being sardonic. He said, "Sure will, Mimi. I'll ask him to come to the study tonight so you can share with him what Jesus has done to rescue your lovely heart."

Mimi blanched when he said *lovely*.

Joan laughed, "Mimi, you are lovely. I agree with Noah. You work too hard to appear tough. What do you really want us to think of you?" Joan bustled about the kitchen as if she had forgotten that she had asked a question. She cleaned up a few dishes and picked up the papers littered near the brown couch. Mimi, whose face had turned slightly red, stood at the sink without words or irritation.

Over a half hour later everyone except Mark and Suzi had arrived. Mark had the flu, and Suzi did not want to drive to that area of town without him. The others gathered like children before being sent off on an Easter-egg hunt.

Mimi was the one to say, "Well, welcome to my digs. It's not much, but it's home. Let's get this show on the road. You ready, Noah? I hear you've got religion now." Noah laughed the hardest and longest.

He really did find himself liking Mimi. Her brusque and rude exterior could not hide her playful, kind heart. They gathered on the brown couch and the beanbag chairs. Joan picked up a metal chair from the wobbly kitchen table and perched herself near Noah, who seemed to go straight for the chartreuse beanbag chair. He settled himself in the enveloping presence of the chair like a dog padding down its bed.

Noah burrowed into the chair, shifted, sank deeper into the bag, and then began the process all over again. Every eye watched his look of intense consternation and his Elvis-like wiggles. In a sudden burst of incredulity, the room exploded in laughter. Noah looked up, and his serious, intent face joined immediately in the frivolity. His warmth and the companionship only heightened the pleasure, and they laughed for five minutes. Jessie, who was not one to cut loose, wept. Marcia put her arms around Joan, and they shook together like two bowls of Jell-O.

Jack's eyes caught Noah's, and they stopped laughing. Jack spoke first. "Noah, thank you. Whatever you have to share with us, something about joining us in laughing with you—and at you—is just more than I thought possible when we began this study a few months ago."

"Me too, Jack." Noah spoke quietly as tears welled up in his eyes. "I feel sort of crazy. I would like to keep laughing for the rest of our time, but I also feel like weeping."

The room quieted. The laughter did not so much die as slowly evolve into a holy stillness. Noah leaned forward, at first speaking slowly and then his pace quickened: "I don't quite know how to tell you what I have been through again in New York. The last time I came home from New York, I felt overwhelmed by the love you showed me. I was really out of control, I know. This time I feel more out of control and yet more here and at rest than I have felt my whole life. But it is not a rest that feels peaceful and serene. Maybe it's supposed to be that, but in fact, I feel crazy. I feel more disturbed than I ever have before. I feel more hungry for something I can't name. I know all of this is leading me to God, to his purpose for me. Does this make sense?"

Everyone looked at Noah; not a mouth opened to respond. He nodded. It was clear no one really understood, and yet it seemed in some way that everyone knew what he was saying. Jessie eventually asked, "Noah, first tell us what happened in New York."

Noah looked out of the window and said, "You recall what happened the last time." Noah told the story again of what had happened during his first trip and what had happened after the deposition. He recounted his first visit to the hospital and the contact with Sam Andrajian. But when he came to telling the story of Rosie's hunger for a family after being torn from her mother, he put his face in his hands and shook. He eventually looked up and said, "I know this is crazy, just crazy, but I realized the Holocaust really, really did occur. I knew it did, but I felt as if Rosie gave me a survivor's view of death and evil, and it was unlike anything I have ever seen in my life."

He slowly told the story. Every person wept. Mimi left the room. She came back soon with a couple rolls of toilet paper. No one even gave a second thought as they passed the rolls to each other. Mimi thought to herself, *This is wild. The last time a group was here, we passed joints. What has happened to me?"*

Noah finished telling about Rosie's joy in being part of his rescue and her prizing of him as a son. The story seemed nearly over, but Noah spoke in almost a whisper. "They have more love for each other than I have ever allowed for Joan, and they love life with more depth, fight, and awe than I see when I look at most of the people I know. I shared with them my faith in Christ. They were quiet and respectful, but it was clear by my story and life that I had little to offer them beyond my gratitude and the fact that Jesus had died for Gentiles and Jews alike."

Jessie jumped in. "Well, what did they say when you talked about Jesus?"

Noah said, "Not much. An hour after I shared with them what they had done to draw me back to Joan and to Jesus, Jakob left the room and Rosie looked at me and whispered, 'I didn't know a Gentile could be so kind or open to learning from us old Jews. You make me proud to be your mother, but this Jesus, well, I will think about him differently now that I have met you."

Jessie jumped back in and said with even greater intensity, "But did you tell her that she would go to hell if she did not trust Jesus?"

Noah sat forward quickly, but his face was tender and wistful. "No, Jessie. I told them he was the Paschal Lamb and that his blood covered my doorpost so that I would never face the coming scourge, but I also had to ask their forgiveness as one man to one man and one woman for the centuries of cruelty and shameless brutality their people have suffered. It was a gracious moment. Jakob's eyes were full of wild fury and a strange kindness that he could not vocalize. He could say nothing. He needed to say nothing."

Marcia's eyes were filled with warmth. "Noah, Jessie, really all of us, thank you. I can't tell you what this evening means to me. When Jack said he wanted to do a study on Ecclesiastes, I thought he was nuts. Not that I haven't loved this book for many years. It was simply that I knew it would change him. I knew it would either ruin our marriage or make it. It would ruin Jack or further redeem him in a frightening new way. But I knew God would touch Jack. I really did. But Noah, I can tell you that I did not feel the same about you. I'm sorry. I really need to—no, I want to—ask you to forgive me. I doubted God could get your heart, as insulated and self-righteous as you have been, especially to Joan. What has happened to you, Noah? It is really important to me to know what has happened to you."

Noah looked into Marcia's face. Joan's hand was on his shoulder. He recalled how he had previously looked into Marcia's eyes with lust and shame. But he realized that those feelings were gone. He lowered his head and shrugged. "I don't know. I really don't know. I guess if I did, I would have some sense of what happened and how to then make it occur again. I don't know. I guess it would help to read the section at the end of Ecclesiastes first. Let me read it. It says: "'Meaningless! Meaningless!' says the Teacher. 'Everything is meaningless!' Not only was the Teacher wise, but also he imparted knowledge to the people. He pondered and searched out and set in order many proverbs. The Teacher searched to find just the right words, and what he wrote was upright and true. The words of the wise are like goads, their collected sayings like firmly embedded nails—given by one Shepherd. Be warned, my son, of anything in addition to them. Of making many books there is no end, and much study wearies the body. Now all has been heard; here is the conclusion of the matter: Fear God and keep his commandments, for this is the whole duty of man. For God will bring every deed into judgment, including every hidden thing, whether it is good or evil.'"

Noah turned and said to the group, "Do you mind if I tell you what I have learned from this book?"

Marcia spoke first and obviously spoke for the group. "Go ahead, Noah."

Noah looked at Joan and said to her, "Joan is the one who needs to teach. She is the one who has won me, suffered for me, and prayed for me like no one else on the face of the earth. I will share a few thoughts, but it is my wife—my beautiful wife—whom I look to when I say that the surprising work of God has changed my heart. No human being has loved me more than my wife has."

Joan glowed. Her tears were gone, and her smile burst like a rainbow that emerges with a splendor that makes people stop to gaze in wonder. "Tell them, Noah, what you've told me this week."

Noah started, "I have seen two things from this passage. First, the teacher chose the right words, and his message was upright and true. We can't dismiss him by saying he was merely a cynic or a depressed man. The message is simple: Nothing works. And nothing is *meant* to work. I know that more now than I did two months ago. In many ways my career and family and marriage are doing better than ever. Yet life hurts more than ever before. I think I see eternity clearer, and as a result I feel less in control, less normal, as I look at myself in comparison to how most people live. I am happier than I have been for a long time, and yet I am more frustrated and feel an ache inside in a way I never did before. Life doesn't work. My job, marriage, health, the pursuit of wisdom and God—nothing works to take away the daily sting of the Fall. But somehow in submitting myself to that reality, I'm happy. And that has to do with the bottom-line point of the book."

Mimi was irritated but intrigued. She said, "Noah, I don't understand what you are saying. How does knowing that nothing works make you happy? I mean, it ticks me off. It's a rip-off. Like buying a stereo that you put hard money into and knowing full well it's not going to work, or maybe it will work for an hour or a day, but it's, like, going to frizz out on you and drive you crazier than if you didn't buy it. So why buy the thing if you know it's not going to work but only frustrate you?"

Jack finally spoke. "That's the cosmic joke. You want something. God gives you a taste of it, then yanks it away. Or, even worse, maybe he lets you enjoy it, but then you realize it's not what you really want."

Joan's head was bobbing slightly as Jack spoke, and she added, "I agree. But is it a joke? Is it a mean trick? Or is it a gift, wrapped up in newspaper that looks cheap but really is the second greatest of God's gifts?"

"Joan, I think you're right," Noah inserted. "What feels like a joke is really God's gift to wake us up. Somehow, once I admitted I was really asleep, or blind, then I could see that God was lovingly trying to wake me up rather than let me sleep to death. I have finally come to see frustration, futility—even loneliness—as an incredible gift. That gift may feel that God is being mean, I agree. But it jumps out of the blue and snags you, drags you out of the path of danger in order to offer true life.

"Well, you asked, but that is only the second-most important thing I learned from Ecclesiastes. The first is to *fear* and to fear what really is the only thing in the universe to fear—God."

The people in the group sighed. They knew Noah was right. They were more alert and alive in their battles than they would be if the matters of their lives were truly working. But each person wanted to hear what Noah had to say about the joy he so obviously had begun to enjoy. "So get to it, man," Mimi quipped.

"All right, but this is the hardest part. I don't even know how to say it, but this part requires eyes that are more than simply facing what's true; it means seeing what can be seen only by the vision given from the Spirit."

As Noah shifted in his beanbag chair, he looked almost like a little kid perched on his green nap mat in kindergarten. "To me, fear is not like terror but is more like the time I went up in a private plane and I knew at some point the pilot was going to turn the stick over to me. I wanted that moment and dreaded it at the same time. I guess fear is both a hunger for a glimpse of mystery and a terror of what comes with it."

Mimi interrupted, "Get to it, Noah. First you say it's not terror, and then you say it's terror. Is this just more Bible gobbledygook?"

"Sort of, I guess," said Noah, "but not really. You see, I knew I couldn't fly the plane alone, but the pilot was there, and he was going to do all that was necessary to get us back down alive. But I was definitely going to fly the plane, and our direction was in my hands. I felt the terror, or maybe the better word is *thrill*. Fear to me is the thrill of knowing that God has orchestrated my life to know him, and today or tonight or tomorrow I'm going to turn a corner, and he may be there. Or he might not. Any moment might be so infused with his presence that I would have to be totally blind not to see God. On the other hand, most moments are ordinary, expected. I never know when I turn the corner whether it will be a moment infused with God or one in which it is harder to see anything other than what is plain and visible.

"I started to cross a street in a stupor, and not only was I rescued, but I was also saved. I don't know when that moment is going to occur again, but in a way that is very new for me. I live with a new sense of reality: not that life is bad and is going to get worse but that it *is* bad and is *certainly* going to get worse. But somewhere in that moment, I will be saved again. God will save me and meet me.

"And so I'm to fear God and be obedient. But even my obedience will one day be seen for what it really is, either my effort to avoid pain or someone's judgment, or my desire to join God in his work. You see, life doesn't work, but God does. He works not to make life work but to surprise us and invite us to be in relationship with him. He is really good, in spite of. I suppose that's the phrase that stands out most to me: *in spite of*. In spite of the fact that the world seems hopeless, God is wildly extravagant. He gives life. He gives glorious moments that have opened my heart to what I know I will one day hear and what I live more and more to hear, 'Welcome home.'"

Mimi was still. She gazed out the window. Marcia noticed that her face had softened, though she seemed less comfortable and more lonely than when she appeared hard and cocky. Mimi finally spoke, but it was to no one in particular, or at least to no one in the room, "Is it true? Could it all really be true?"

Her face softened into a smile. "I hate you, Noah. I really, really do. You make me think it just all might be true."

> ➤ *How Do We Chase after Life?*
>   1. Do you fear death or growing old? Is it wrong to fear death?
>   2. Is it vain to care about your physical beauty?
>   3. Is it legitimate to use the fear of death to jar people into considering the claims of Christ?
>   4. What stage of life are you in? What do you like about that stage of life? What bothers you?
>   5. Do you enjoy the present?
>   6. What gives your life meaning?
>   7. Do you look to the future with hope? Why?
>   8. What Scripture passages describe the meaning that a relationship to Christ offers us?

Chapter 5: Restoring Power through Surrender
1. Bernie Siegel, M.D., *Peace, Love, and Healing* (New York: Harper & Row, 1989), 191.

Chapter 14: "Pleasure Ought to Satisfy Me"
1. Patricia Meyer Spacks, *Boredom: The Literary History of a State of Mind* (Chicago: University of Chicago Press, 1995), 130.

Chapter 15: Restoring Pleasure through Joy in Suffering
1. Patricia Meyer Spacks, *Boredom: The Literary History of a State of Mind* (Chicago: University of Chicago Press, 1995), 250.

Chapter 17: "Wisdom Ought to Put Me on Top"
1. Daniel Goleman, *Emotional Intelligence* (New York: Bantam, 1995), 34–6.
2. Ibid., xii.
3. Ibid., 34.

Chapter 19: Restoring Wisdom through Relationship
1. C. S. Lewis, *Till We Have Faces* (Grand Rapids: Eerdmans, 1966), 308.

Chapter 26: Restoring Life through Death
1. January 13, 1997.

About the Authors

DAN B. ALLENDER received an M.Div. from Westminster Theological Seminary and a Ph.D. in Counseling Psychology from Michigan State University. He teaches and counsels at Western Seminary in Seattle, Washington, and presents workshops about sexual-abuse recovery and counselor training. He is also a founding director of the Mars Hill Forum and senior editor of the *Mars Hill Review*, a journal that seeks to reveal Christ in culture. He is the author of *The Wounded Heart*, coauthor, with Larry Crabb, of *Encouragement: The Key to Caring* and *Hope When You're Hurting*, and coauthor, with Tremper Longman III, of *Bold Love; Cry of the Soul;* and *Intimate Allies*. Dr. Allender and his wife, Rebecca, live in Seattle, Washington, with their three children, Anna, Amanda, and Andrew.

TREMPER LONGMAN III is married to Alice and has three children, all sons. Tremper IV is keeping the family first name alive and is presently a student at Clemson University. Timothy is a senior at Chestnut Hill Academy in Philadelphia, and Andrew just enrolled at that school in the eighth grade. They keep Alice and Tremper happy (at least some of the time) and always busy.

Tremper has an M.Div. from Westminster Theological Seminary, where he served for many years as professor and chair of the Old Testament Department. He is currently professor of Old Testament at Westmont College. Longman earned a Ph.D. in ancient Near Eastern languages and literature at Yale University. Tremper is the author and editor of a number of books. Besides the books coauthored with Dan Allender, mentioned above, he has also written commentaries (*Ecclesiastes* [Eerdmans]), reference and textbooks (*An Introduction to the Old Testament* [with R. B. Dillard; Zondervan]), academic monographs (*Literary Approaches to Biblical Interpretation* [Zondervan]), and other books for the general market (*Reading the Bible with Heart and Mind* [NavPress]).